THE NEW CHINA

THE NEW CHINA

Comparative Economic Development in Mainland China, Taiwan, and Hong Kong

Alvin Rabushka

Routledge
Taylor & Francis Group

LONDON AND NEW YORK

First published 1987 by Westview Press

Published 2019 by Routledge
52 Vanderbilt Avenue, New York, NY 10017
2 Park Square, Milton Park, Abingdon, Oxon OX14 4RN

Routledge is an imprint of the Taylor & Francis Group, an informa business

Library of Congress Cataloging in Publication Data
Rabushka, Alvin.
    The new China.
    "Published in cooperation with the Pacific
Research Institute for Public Policy."
    Bibliography: p.
    Includes index.
1. China—Economic policy—1976-. 2. Taiwan—
Economic policy—1975-. 3. Hong Kong—Economic
policy. I. Pacific Research Institute for Public
Policy. II. Title.
HC427.92.R33   1987   338.951   87-10574

ISBN 13: 978-0-367-29431-1 (hbk)
ISBN 13: 978-0-367-30977-0 (pbk)

CONTENTS

LIST OF TABLES

PREFACE

On March 1, 1963, I boarded my first trans-Pacific flight for Hong Kong. I spent ten months as a Chinese language student at Hong Kong University, during which I became impressed with the colony's relatively poor but extremely hard-working Chinese population. Since 1964, I returned almost annually to Asia, extending my territorial ambit to encompass Singapore, Malaysia, Taiwan, Korea, and mainland China. During these years of travel, I watched these East and Southeast Asian countries transform themselves from what are commonly termed less-developed countries (LDCs) into a wholly new category, recently popularized as newly industrializing countries (NICs). The exception to this trend in East Asia was mainland China, which lagged sorely behind in per capita levels of output and consumption. But in 1978, mainland China shifted course. After Deng Xiaoping consolidated power, he implemented a series of rural and urban economic reforms that increased the mainland's economic vitality.

This book is rooted in nearly a quarter-century of personal observation of economic change among largely Chinese-populated communities in East and Southeast Asia. The idea for a book comparing the postwar economic development of mainland China, Taiwan, and Hong Kong—three different political economies populated almost entirely by Chinese—grew from several conversations I had with David J. Theroux in the early 1980s, then president of the Pacific Research Institute for Public Policy, and Charles W. Baird, then Senior Economist with the Institute. The Institute obtained a grant from the Asia Foundation, which financed several research trips to East Asia. The World Media Association made it possible for me to visit Beijing and Taipei in 1986, during which I had lengthy discussions with academics and government officials in both countries on aspects of economic policy and development. In organizing the book, I received helpful suggestions from Greg Christainsen, Senior Economist with the Institute and member of the economics department at California State University, Hayward.

Several people read portions or all of previous drafts of the manuscript. For their helpful comments and bibliographical suggestions I want to thank Robert Dernberger of the University of Michigan, Don Lavoie of George Mason University, Stanley Spector of Washington University, Ramon Myers of the Hoover Institution (Stanford University), Leland Yeager of Auburn University, Zheng Shiping of Fudan University (Shanghai), Teng Maotung of Anhui University (Hefei), Y.C. Jao and George Hicks of Hong Kong University, John G. Greenwood of G.T. Management (Asia) Ltd. in Hong Kong, and Gregory Christainsen and Shyam Kamath of California State University, Hayward.

Pamela Riley, director of public affairs at the Pacific Research Institute, was instrumental in shepherding the manuscript through the publication process. I appreciate the enthusiastic support for this project from William H. Mellor III, president of the Institute. I also want to thank the Hoover Institution for providing an exciting environment in which to tackle research topics of all shapes and sizes. An important part of that environment is a set of interesting colleagues who provide intellectual stimulation and constructive criticism.

I gratefully acknowledge the help I received from all the above sources, who are, of course, not responsible for any errors, shortcomings, or conclusions in my book.

Alvin Rabushka

1

INTRODUCTION

Since the end of World War II, more than one hundred new nations scattered throughout Asia, Africa, Latin America, and the Caribbean faced the task of transforming their poor, traditional societies into modern economies. The majority followed a strategy for economic development that emphasized government intervention in economic matters and, in some instances, state ownership of key industrial sectors. A few attempted comprehensive central planning for the entire economy. The specifics of these policies varied among countries, but often included government-directed capital formation, foreign-exchange controls, limitations on overseas investment or ownership, high tariffs to encourage domestic industry to develop substitutes for imports, high marginal rates of direct taxation for the purpose of redistributing income, and other regulations on economic activity. Most sought, received, and remained dependent on foreign aid.

Basic indicators of economic development published in the World Bank's annual *World Development Report*[1] reveal that the most successful examples of post–World War II economic development in the world are located in the Pacific Area Basin. Hong Kong, Singapore, Taiwan, Malaysia, and Korea grew so rapidly that they graduated from the ranks of the developing world.

Why did these Asian countries prosper? Was it because they chose the correct economic policies? Or, rather, because their Oriental populations were diligent, thrifty, and ambitious? It would be a mistake to dismiss these personal traits out of hand. Oriental people inherited an old Confucian tradition, which emphasized love of learning; personal advancement through hard work and self-sacrifice to gain "face" for one's family, community, and country; respect for elders and authority; and moral virtue. Chinese people flourished almost everywhere they settled. Southeast Asia is replete with stories of penniless Chinese

1

immigrants who went from rags to riches. Indeed, Chinese helped promote major economic progress in such countries as Thailand, Indonesia, the Philippines, and Malaysia, all of which enjoyed higher growth than most African and Latin American nations.[2]

The view that development depends on cultural traits lends little hope to millions living in famine-starved Africa and in other stagnant or slow-growing economies. No analyst of development seriously advocates importing millions of Chinese to invigorate other poor economies. To the extent that culture explains development, the design and implementation of economic policies becomes less important. Development is simply a matter of good luck!

The Chinese-culture thesis of development may itself be subject to inquiry. The presence of Chinese people cannot account for sharply higher growth rates in Taiwan and Hong Kong than in mainland China during the past three decades or for the fact that per capita income in Hong Kong in 1985 was thirty times more than that in mainland China.[3] In fact, mainland China enjoyed a greater abundance of natural resources than Taiwan or Hong Kong, which suggests that other factors such as political stability, economic institutions, secure property rights, the rule of law, and individual incentives play a role.

MAINLAND CHINA, TAIWAN, AND HONG KONG: A PREVIEW OF COMPARATIVE DEVELOPMENT

In 1949, Mao Zedong[4] established Communist rule over the Chinese mainland. His defeated adversary, Chiang Kai-shek, retreated to the island of Taiwan, where his Nationalist government imposed authority over an economy decimated by war. Meanwhile, on the Southeast coast of China, the British restored administrative rule over their Crown Colony of Hong Kong, which the Japanese had sundered during World War II.

Between 1949 and 1985, these three territories, populated by people of Chinese descent (save a minuscule foreign community in British-run Hong Kong), pursued economic policies that ranged from attempts at comprehensive central planning to almost complete laissez-faire. In mainland China, Mao Zedong implemented a program of Soviet-style emphasis on heavy industry coupled with his own radical version of rural collectivization. Government planners controlled all factories, farms, and enterprises, set prices for all goods and services, assigned production inputs and specified output targets, allocated labor, rationed goods in short supply, determined individual incomes, and chose the mix between consumption and investment.

Since 1978, Deng Xiaoping, China's liberal economic reformist leader, had deemphasized Soviet-style central planning in favor of greater reliance on market forces. He instituted far-reaching rural reforms that placed primary responsibility for agricultural production in the hands of individuals and households and moved gradually in the mid-1980s to establish labor and capital markets in the urban, industrial sector.

In Taiwan, Chiang Kai-shek's government initially undertook policies of land reform and import-substitution-based industrial development, which entailed substantial government participation in the economy. In the 1960s, following the withdrawal of U.S. economic assistance, his government switched directions to a private-enterprise-based, export-oriented strategy of industrialization. To this day, however, the government has continued to undertake major industrial development projects. In short, Taiwan has combined some state ownership of heavy industry, the banking system, and provision of infrastructure with a largely free-enterprise, export-oriented economy.

Finally, Hong Kong maintained its historically based free-market, free-trade, low-tax policies. The British territory remained the industrial world's closest approximation to the model of perfect competition found in economics textbooks. Although many of its political, social, and economic characteristics were unique, it nonetheless illustrated the workings of a largely private-enterprise, market-disciplined economy.

In September 1982, China announced that it would recover sovereignty over Hong Kong on July 1, 1997, when Britain's 99-year lease over Hong Kong's New Territories expires. The prospect that China intended to replace British rule sent the colony's financial, stock, and property markets into a sharp tailspin, which reflected an initial loss of confidence in Hong Kong's future. Confidence was temporarily restored after Britain and China signed a Joint Declaration on December 19, 1984. Britain agreed to restore sovereignty over Hong Kong to China; in return, China agreed to allow Hong Kong to maintain its capitalistic economic system for 50 years after 1997.

None of the three was a Western-style democracy. A Communist totalitarian regime maintained a firm grip on the mainland; an authoritarian Nationalist government ruled Taiwan; and a benign, slightly antiquated British colonial regime, struggling to localize and democratize, administered Hong Kong. In general, decision makers in all three regimes were able to impose long-term economic policies of their choosing, relatively free from the public pressures and voting interests that influence politicians in genuine democratic systems.

The three societies experienced different growth patterns in the postwar era. In Hong Kong, per capita income grew from about $180 in 1949 to surpass $6,000 during 1985. In Taiwan, per capita income rose from $70 to exceed $3,000 over the same period. In each case, annual real growth in gross national product (GNP) averaged between 8 and 9 percent for more than 30 years. At annual growth rates of 9 percent, economic output doubles in 7 to 8 years, quadruples in 15 to 16 years, grows eightfold in 23 years, and multiplies sixteenfold in 31 years. Sustained 9 percent annual growth over one generation increases national output sixteen times.

On the mainland, in comparison, per capita income grew from $50 in 1952 to about $180 by 1985, reflecting slower growth.[5] Sustained growth of 5 percent, China's postwar experience, doubles national income in 14 years and quadruples it in 28.[6] Five percent was fast compared with many African countries, some of which lost ground in the past 20 years, but it lagged far behind rates of 8–10 percent. The gap meant that the gulf in living standards separating mainlanders from Chinese in Taiwan and Hong Kong during the postwar era increased in both absolute and relative terms. Moreover, much of mainland China's postwar investment went into heavy industry, with little emphasis placed on the production of consumer goods.

More than three decades have passed against which to evaluate the performance of these three different economic systems. The comparison is especially significant for the Chinese-culture thesis of development inasmuch as the population in each is of the same genetic stock and each is situated in the same part of the world.

Admittedly, not all Chinese are alike. Hong Kong and Taiwan are disproportionately populated by coastal (Shanghai and Fujian) and Southern Chinese, who are renowned as hard-working, ingenious, competitive, and entrepreneurial peoples. These two lands have few of the more conservative, less venturesome people who inhabit Northern China and the vast hinterland. (Foreign travelers in the nineteenth century noted the laziness of the average inland Chinese, who seized every excuse to sit, drink tea, gossip, and consume hours chewing melon seeds.) Hong Kong, in particular, is home to several million refugees from mainland China, who displayed considerable effort, talent, desire, and courage to cross a dangerous border and start over again from scratch.

But these hard-working coastal and Southern Chinese made little economic progress in their own homeland in the late nineteenth and early twentieth centuries, when South China was being torn by civil war and rampaging warlords. Many fled for the relatively greater political security and economic opportunity afforded in the Dutch, French, and British colonies of Southeast Asia. The colonial powers maintained law and order, established well-defined systems of property rights, and, in keeping with prevailing Western beliefs of the time, left the creation and distribution of wealth largely to the private sector. This simple comparison illustrates the observation that differences in economic performance between mainland China and Taiwan or Hong Kong cannot be explained solely by reference to regional characteristics of the Chinese population.

Many factors bear upon productivity. These include availability and productivity of land, climate and weather, floods and drought, natural resources, size and scale of the economy, location, internal distances, the presence and magnitude of a rural hinterland, technology, national-defense requirements, sophistication of the economy, continuity in economic policies, individual incentives, property rights, opportunities for social mobility, immigration patterns, the development of human capital, the quality of political leadership, legal systems and practices, tax structures, subsidies, budgetary practices, orientation toward trade, and monetary policies.

To anticipate but one example: Three years of bad weather, coupled with the policies of the Great Leap Forward that destroyed individual incentives, produced famine in parts of China during 1959–1961. Three years of good weather combined with incentive-enhancing rural reforms introduced in 1978 enabled the same Chinese population to produce three successive record harvests during 1982–1984. Both good weather and the higher prices farmers received for their produce stimulated higher output.

COMPARING ECONOMIC POLICIES

Many factors influence economic growth. As mentioned before, culture, resources, economic system and policies, weather, the introduction of new technology and physical capital, and the development of human capital—as well as the interactions among these factors—affect economic activity. A single historical comparative study of three economies cannot prove beyond any doubt a proposition about the relative virtues of different economic policies and systems and the relative importance of different economic factors that impinge upon economic growth. But it can highlight differences in economic performance among people of common cultural extraction.

This book seeks to explain why Taiwan and Hong Kong grew much faster than mainland China. Two critical factors in explaining these different rates of growth are the structure of institutions and the effects of different degrees of government intervention in the three economic systems. Growth depends on more than injections of technology and capital. It also depends on the underlying incentives that motivate and reward individual behavior. These incentives are determined by political and economic institutions, which supply rules and mechanisms for enforcing those rules. The key rules include the definition and enforcement of property rights, which encourage improved productivity and the expectation that individuals will be able to reap the rewards of their own work or investments. Political institutions bear critically on the enhancement or destruction of individual incentives.

In addition to the structure of institutions and the presence of incentives, the degree to which free competition exists affects levels of output in each system. For example, economic planners in centrally directed economies may attempt to run an entire economy, but many day-to-day decisions are still made by local decision makers. The planners interfere with, distort, and slow down market forces, but never fully destroy them. They distort, but never wholly eliminate, price information.[7] In short, interference with market forces and erosion of incentives retard economic efficiency and growth.

The degree of free competition varies widely from one economic system to another. This book compares different degrees of government intervention and free competition in economic markets in three Chinese-populated societies. It compares the extent to which markets were regulated and how differences in public policies and practices affected output in these markets.

Markets exist in all economies, regardless of the degree of government regulation that is exercised. A market is a place or device enabling people to negotiate exchanges. In a market, individuals or firms buy or sell whatever goods and services may be available. Buyers and sellers conclude their exchanges after settling on a price, which is typically expressed in the units of some currency, unless goods are rationed by coupons or allocated by some other nonprice mechanism that might include instructions from state planning officials. Prices signal to both producers and consumers the relative worth of any given item compared with any other item. When the price of any item goes up, producers tend to supply more of that item and consumers tend to demand less. When the price declines, the reverse happens. Sometimes prices are set by the state and are not free to move in response to changing demand and supply conditions, which often produce surpluses or shortages.

Markets not only allow individuals to exchange the goods and services they produce for those they want; they also allocate resources for the society as a whole. People interacting in markets determine what products and services are provided within a society and how much of each is produced, although the government often dominates these decisions in centrally planned economies.

The objective of any economic system is to produce the largest possible supply of goods and services from an existing stock of natural and human resources: This is the notion of maximizing economic efficiency. Another objective of any economic system is to increase output from one year to the next, thus raising living standards: This is the notion of growth. Thus it makes sense to adopt policies that increase efficiency and yield high growth. However, some governments emphasize egalitarian or other nonmaterial values and are willing to trade off some efficiency and settle for slower growth in exchange for greater equality in the distribution of income or other social goals.

The notion of a free-market economy is a simplified model employed by economists, a point that is helpful in understanding the concept of economic efficiency. In a free-market economy, the government does not interfere with the prices established by market forces—the supply and demand conditions resulting from millions of individual decisions to buy and sell—nor does it protect existing firms from the pressure of competitors. New producers are allowed to compete with existing ones, and existing producers are allowed to go out of business if they wish. In a free market, prices reflect true scarcities, thus enhancing the efficient use of scarce resources. However, only in exceptional cases are markets completely free of all government regulation. Still, there is considerable variation in the degree of competition and the degree to which relative prices reflect relative scarcities, and thus efficiency, in different economies.

Of course, markets do not exist in a vacuum. Somebody has to define property rights, enforce contracts, and protect people from fraud. The responsibility for these tasks falls upon government. Government comprises the legally based institutions of a society that make legally binding decisions. With a legal monopoly on coercion, government officials have the power to tax and regulate economic activity to attain a variety of national objectives. These may include preventing monopolies, cleaning up pollution, provisioning a standing army, negotiating international treaties, redistributing income, and constructing public works such as dams, bridges, roads, harbors, and airports. Social or political objectives might include advancing education, imposing religious values, or preventing abortion. When government officials make these choices, they, not consumers, exercise sovereignty.

In the real world, economic activity always takes place in some political, institutional setting, where government officials make a wide variety of economic decisions and allocate large amounts of resources. Regardless of the form of government, whether it be democracy based on universal suffrage or the absolute dictatorship of one man, political decisions on how to tax, spend, regulate, print money, manufacture, distribute, export, and import all have the potential to enhance or harm efficiency and economic growth. How property rights are defined determines which goods and services will be privately produced and exchanged, and which the state will control, and whether individuals are willing to undertake the long-term investments that increase rates of growth. How taxes are levied can affect the performance of different industries. And so on.

This book systematically examines the structure and resources of three Chinese-populated economies and the effects of different political and economic institutions and economic policies on economic performance between 1949 and 1985. In Parts I, II, and III, the three cases of mainland China, Taiwan, and Hong Kong are reviewed. Each part first describes the demographic, economic, political, and social setting, covering such topics as physical setting and population, natural resources, pre-1949 economic history, the constitution, the official ideology, the political system, the structure of economic institutions, national security considerations, the overall strategy for economic development, the general administration of economic policy, and the mechanisms of public finance, money, and banking. Subsequent chapters examine the details of economic policy, identifying periods of continuity and change, and the effects of specific policies on economic performance and living standards.

In Part I, Chinese economic history is divided into pre- and post-1978 periods. Before 1978, Chinese planners attempted, with varying degrees of intensity, a method of central planning to develop heavy industry; after 1978, Chinese leaders adopted policies that stressed light industry and placed greater reliance on market forces to uplift living standards. In Part II, Taiwan's experience is discussed in terms of its transition from an import-substitution phase of industrial development to the post-1959 switch in favor of export-oriented development. In Part III, Hong Kong's generally constant economic policy during 1949–1985 is described, followed by an explanation of how the colony adjusted to the economic shocks caused by China's 1982 announcement that it would take over Hong Kong in 1997. In Part IV, conclusions from these three cases are drawn and the future prospects for economic development are briefly assessed.

NOTES

1. *World Development Report 1985* (New York: Oxford University Press, 1985). Each annual report contains an annex of "World Development Indicators" covering measures of production, consumption, investment, agriculture, industry, energy, trade, the composition of imports and exports, balance of payments, borrowing, fiscal reserves and debts, population, labor force participation rates, life expectancy, health indicators, education, and defense spending for more than 120 countries; it also includes a set of basic indicators for another 30-plus small countries with populations of less than 1 million.

2. Yuan-li Wu and Chun-hsi Wu, *Economic Development in Southeast Asia: The Chinese Dimension* (Stanford, Calif.: Hoover Institution Press, 1980).

3. Throughout this book, I shall use the terms *Taiwan, Hong Kong,* and *mainland China* as shorthand for their full names—the Republic of China, the British Crown Colony of Hong Kong, and the People's Republic of China, respectively.

4. The pinyin system of romanization is used throughout, except for such widely recognized Chinese names as Chiang Kai-shek and English names as Canton, the Yellow River, and so forth.

5. In January 1984, the Central Bank of China officially pegged the nation's currency, the Renminbi yuan, to the dollar at an official exchange rate of US$1 = 2.02 yuan. (Between 1955 and 1971 the rate was fixed at US$1 = 2.46 yuan. The devaluation of the U.S. dollar in the 1970s brought an appreciation of the yuan up through 1983.) During 1984, the Central Bank gradually devalued the yuan to US$1 = 2.80 yuan, where it stood until August 1985. Between August and November 1985, it further devalued the Renminbi to a rate of US$1 = 3.19 yuan, where the rate remained until July 5, 1986. On that date, the Central Bank abruptly devalued its currency by 13.9 percent, setting the rate at US$1 = 3.69 yuan. Between January 1985 and July 1986, the cumulative devaluation against the U.S. dollar was 24.5 percent; compared with January 1984, the cumulative devaluation came to 83 percent.

China's economy turned in a much stronger performance during 1978–1985 as compared with 1949–1977. In U.S. dollar terms, however, per capita income fell from a peak of $246 in 1980 to $196 in 1984. If we apply to these numbers the exchange rate in force after July 1986, per capita income in China fell further in 1985 and 1986 despite sharp gains in output. Thus the figure of $300, which appears in World Bank and other reports, is much too high. The devaluation of China's currency also means that the value of China's economic output was overstated in U.S. dollar terms throughout the 1970s and early 1980s. Most economists in China believe that the Renminbi is still overvalued and that a correct rate for 1986 would be in the neighborhood of US$1 = 5.2 yuan. See *Far Eastern Economic Review* (July 17, 1986), pp. 50–51.

6. The 5 percent figure is probably too high in light of revelations documented by Chinese economists after 1978 to the effect that much of China's industrial output was of substandard quality or completely unusable. (See Chapters 3 and 4 of this volume.)

7. Paul Craig Roberts, *Alienation and the Soviet Economy* (Albuquerque: University of New Mexico Press, 1971).

PART I

MAINLAND CHINA

2

PEOPLE, RESOURCES, AND POLITICS

When Mao Zedong officially proclaimed the People's Republic of China on October 1, 1949, the Chinese Communist Party controlled the world's oldest, continuously recorded civilization. Unlike ancient Mesopotamia or Egypt, whose cultures disappeared, China sustained the continuity of its history and civilization despite incursions from northern tribes, Mongols, and Manchus. Its people, some 94 percent of whom are classified as Han Chinese, shared a common written language, culture, and traditions for several thousand years.

Chinese civilization developed along the middle course of the Yellow River. The earliest known capital in China was Anyang, seat of the Shang Dynasty, which held sway during the second millennium before Christ. Its successor, the Zhou Dynasty of Confucian fame, moved to Changan, which is directly adjacent to the present city of Xi'an. During the second century B.C., Qin Shihuang Di, the first emperor credited with unifying China, moved his capital to Xianyang, which is upriver from Changan. Qin's repressive regime lasted less than two decades, replaced by the Confucian-based Han Dynasty, which survived for about four centuries. The Western early Han returned to the traditional capital of Changan, while the Eastern late Han, which ruled during the first two centuries of the Christian era, resettled in nearby Loyang. A succession of dynasties marked the next seventeen centuries as the Han peoples expanded northward and southward, gradually unifying the territory that today encompasses the national borders of China.

The Chinese word for China, *Zhongguo*, means middle kingdom. The Chinese word for foreign country, *waiguo*, literally means outside country, but figuratively speaking symbolizes uncivilized nations. The idiomatic translation of the word *foreigner*, from a Chinese perspective, is barbarian. The *Confucian Analects,* the official ruling political philosophy for 2,000 years, warns that "the study of strange doctrines is injurious indeeed."[1] Confucianism justified centuries of autocratic imperial rule so long as the ruler practiced moral virtue. It also placed mercantile or business activity on the lowest rung of the social ladder. Moral leadership was paramount in the Confucian political scheme; nonetheless, for Confucius, "the rude tribes of the east and north have their princes, and are not like the States of our great land which are without them."[2] China in anarchy, which was anathema in the Confucian doctrine, was preferred to foreigners with all their leaders.

When Western Europe was in the throes of the dark ages, China made great strides in art, literature, science, and technology.[3] China is renowned for inventing the art of printing and converting gunpowder from use in fireworks to true explosives. China developed stable administration, an integrated transportation network of inland waterways, and a monetized economy; it also experimented with early industrial techniques before the thirteenth century. Inculcated in the upbringing of the Chinese is the belief that China was the world's most literate and advanced material society centuries before the emergence of modern Western Europe.

The industrial revolution that transformed Western Europe left China in a comparative state of economic backwardness. Compared with Great Britain in the early nineteenth century, China was an industrial pygmy and a pitiful military Goliath. A handful of British warships deploying several thousand well-armed troops easily defeated the world's largest country.[4] The Opium War (1840–1842) marked the beginning of a century-long decline in China's social cohesion and political independence. Growing Western influence in China accelerated the internal decay of the Qing Dynasty, which shattered centuries of peace, internal stability, and a national sense of cultural superiority. Barbarians brought the world's most civilized nation to its knees. Chinese intellectuals and leaders found it difficult to cast off traditional ways of thinking as they struggled to modernize and restore national integrity. China's cultural unity, its long history of technological advancement over all foreigners, its disdain of commercial enterprise, and its isolated geography created an inward-looking society and economy that was slow to accommodate foreign ideas or institutions.

The dynastic system of government could not remain intact against the pressures of Western intrusion and social change.[5] Under the leadership of Sun Yat-sen, who tried to graft the Western values of democracy and equality as well as modern economic concepts onto Chinese culture in his great work, *The Three Principles of the People,* patriotic Chinese overthrew the remnants of the Manchu Qing Dynasty, which had ruled since 1644. They proclaimed the formation of a new Republic of China on October 10, 1911, and imported an American legal scholar to help draft its first constitution. But old practices died slowly.

Sun Yat-sen was elected president of the provisional government but resigned on April 1, 1912, in favor of General Yuan Shikai, who was considered the most likely person to work out an early abdication of the Qing monarch. Yuan Shikai took advantage of the presidency to enlarge his sphere of influence. Precursor to China's warlords, he purged his government of members of Sun Yat-sen's Kuomintang Party, ruthlessly crushing all opposition. He subsequently dissolved the legislature, hand-picked his own law-making body, and promulgated a new constitution that gave himself despotic powers comparable to those of former emperors. In the spring of 1915, he began the process of trying to change the republic back to a monarchical government with himself installed as monarch. He proclaimed 1916 the first year of a new dynastic cycle. But Yuan died in misery and disgrace in June 1916, as fate had dictated, and China lapsed into deeper internal turmoil as warlords vied with each other for control.

Generalissimo Chiang Kai-shek restored partial unity in 1927, when his forces occupied the major areas surrounding the Yangtze River Valley, seat of China's newly developing industry, stretching upriver from the vibrant port of foreign-dominated Shanghai. But Chiang never really governed the whole of China. Portions remained under the control of regional warlords, and a newly emerging Communist Party movement led by Mao Zedong continually threatened Chiang's rule. Still, portions of China made major economic strides during the late 1920s and most of the 1930s. The tallest buildings in the world outside New York were found in Shanghai.[6]

Japan's invasion of China in 1937 forced Chiang Kai-shek's Nationalist government to retreat inland to Chongqing, interrupting national economic development. The burgeoning industries of the Yangtze Valley had to be disassembled and carried piece-by-piece inland for reassembly. Nor did Japan's defeat in 1945 end China's turmoil: Nationalists and Communists waged a bloody civil war that brought Mao Zedong to power and exiled Chiang Kai-shek's Nationalist government to the island of Taiwan. Mao's proclamation of the People's Republic of China on October 1, 1949, ended more than a century of internal division, social upheaval, and Western influence.

PHYSICAL SETTING AND POPULATION

China is the third largest country in the world, with a land area of 3.7 million square miles (excluding the island of Taiwan) and a 1984 population estimated at 1,034,750,000.[7] It consists of a large portion of continental Asia and a number of offshore islands. It measures approximately 3,100 miles from east to west, and stretches 3,400 miles from north to south. Most of the country lies in the temperate zone, but the climate varies from severe winter cold in the north to tropical typhoons in the south.

Land use reflects the different climatic conditions and topography. More than half of China's land consists of largely desolate plateau, steppe country, and desert, which is sparsely populated, chiefly by minority nationalities whose language and culture differ from the Han majority. About 90 percent of the people live in the eastern half of the nation, crowded around three major river systems—the Yellow River, the Yangtze, and the Pearl River Delta—and their tributaries, as well as some two dozen major cities.[8]

Four-fifths of all Chinese are peasants, earning their living from agriculture and sideline rural pursuits. Of the total land area, mountains comprise 33 percent, and plateaus, basins, plains, and hills respectively comprise 26, 19, 12, and 10 percent.[9] Land under cultivation runs to 247 million acres, about 11 percent of the total land area, and amounts to about one-quarter acre per person. Wheat, grown in the north, and rice, cultivated south of the Yangtze, are the two main crops, supplemented by twenty lesser staples such as corn and sweet potatoes. Most of the raw materials used in such light industries as textiles, oil processing, sugar refining, tobacco, and food processing are grown in China.

Annual rainfall was about 25 inches in 1984 but is unevenly distributed throughout China. More than 80 percent falls during the summer monsoon season between May and October. As a result, floods and drought have been a painful legacy of Chinese history. For example, three years of severe drought during 1959–1961 were disastrous. Scholars have estimated that reduced food availability during 1958–1962 caused about 30 million premature deaths in China; at the same time, declining fertility caused 33 million lost or postponed births. This period was the largest recorded famine in human history.[10]

The Yellow River, aptly named for its heavy silt content, earned the reputation of "China's sorrow." Silt deposits have raised the river bed so high that over the last 500 miles of its course to the sea, the river flows at or above the surface level of the surrounding plain, necessitating an extensive system of dikes. The heavy silt content also minimizes the potential for irrigation.

The population of China tripled in less than two centuries. It numbered 362 million in the early nineteenth century. Despite 150 years of chronic war and social upheaval, fecundity increased. By 1946, China's population numbered 450 million. Mao's takeover of the mainland accelerated population growth on two counts. First, peace and stability fostered reproduction and lowered the death rate. Second, Mao insisted that a rapidly growing labor force would speed up economic development.

Mao's government conducted its first comprehensive census in 1953 and its second in 1964; its third such census was completed with technical assistance from the United Nations in 1982.[11] The natural growth rate, the difference in birth and death rates, has ranged from

2 percent in 1952, 2.3 percent in 1957, and 2.8 percent in 1965, falling to 1.08 percent in 1984.[12]

Rapid population growth since 1949 means that the Chinese are disproportionately young. The fact that more than 350 million people are under age fifteen has created a major task of providing education, housing, and employment.

One billion people exert great pressure on Chinese agriculture. By the nineteenth century, virtually all arable land was being farmed. Falling farm sizes forced intensive farming practices, including terracing, irrigation, drainage, multiple cropping, and careful use of human and animal manure. Some economists believe that the high ratio of population to land will handicap China's development.[13] They note the rising population's increased demand for food and other necessities at the same time that total cultivated acreage has fallen more than 10 percent since 1950 due to the encroachment of irrigation, urban development, road construction, and industrial development.

RESOURCES

China is relatively rich in mineral and other natural resources.[14] It has significant deposits of iron ore, coal, molybdenum, asbestos, tin, tungsten, antimony, mercury, and other metals and minerals.[15] Since 1949, widespread oil deposits have been confirmed, prompting large-scale oil prospecting. Estimates of recoverable oil run in the neighborhood of 40 billion barrels. Natural gas reserves have been estimated at 1.1 trillion cubic yards.

China has vast coal reserves with estimates ranging as high as 1.5 trillion tons, which are sufficient to sustain current annual usage for more than 1,000 years. Reserves of coking coal are adequate for steel production and other metallurgical processes. Known deposits of iron ore are put at 44 billion tons, a total that meets projected development requirements into the twenty-first century. China exports tungsten but imports copper, lead, and zinc.

Forests supply materials for the construction, paper, textile, furniture, utensil, and tool industries. Timber trees are numerous in variety and high in quality, including many special and rare species. Since 1950, however, China has experienced significant deforestation. Mao's blind pursuit of grain cultivation at the expense of everything else caused significant ecological damage.[16] Land terracing, hill leveling, and grassland management were handled in a nonprofessional way.

The major river systems, mentioned before, not only provide irrigation and limited navigation but also offer the potential for hydroelectric power. Water supplies are unevenly distributed. Government officials have discussed the possibility of diverting the Yangtze River north to irrigate the drier Northern China plain. Underground water resources complement the interwoven network of major and minor river systems, but cities have experienced shortages of drinking water.

China's 18,000-mile coastline touches the Yellow Sea, the East China Sea, and the South China Sea. Its ports are conveniently situated for coastal shipping and international trade. The surrounding seas and ocean support marine products industries, and sea salt supplies the chemical industry and is converted into consumer table salt.

Although no country in the world is self-sufficient in all mineral and natural resources, China possesses a large stock of proven resources required for industrialization. It is free to plan to use the resource inputs of industrial development with little dependence on imports. Internal self-sufficiency does not guarantee, however, that such resources will be used efficiently.

THE ECONOMY BEFORE 1949

China has always been a rural country. Throughout the first half of the twentieth century, about three-quarters of the population lived in the countryside and produced about two-thirds of the economy's net output of goods and services in the form of primary products and local handicrafts. Land tenure was highly uneven: The 12 percent of the population classified as absentee landlords and rich farmers owned half the total cultivated acreage, while 60 percent owned only one-quarter, with an average farm size of about one acre.[17] Floods and drought perpetually threatened large numbers of peasants with starvation. Warlords, bullies, ruffians, and government officials exacted oppressive taxes, which in some instances were paid more than twenty years in advance. Small wonder that peasants found the "land to the tillers" doctrine of Mao Zedong so appealing.

Industry contributed less than one-fifth of the national output and was concentrated in a few geographical areas. Apart from the prewar Japanese investment in steel and heavy industry in Manchuria, industrial development was confined to the treaty ports, most notably those of Shanghai and the adjoining Yangtze River Valley area. Economic links between urban manufacturing areas and the vast Chinese hinterland were thin. By all measures, including industrial output per capita of coal, pig iron, crude steel, electric power, cotton spindles, and cement, China was primitive, lagging behind even India.

China's chronic instability during the first half of the twentieth century was not conducive to rapid economic growth. Modernizing Chinese revolutionaries spent the first decade struggling to overthrow a decaying Manchu regime. To the victors went few spoils. Sun Yat-sen's fleeting victory dissipated into thirteen years of warfare between warlords and ideologically hostile political factions. The one brief stretch of relative calm between 1927 and 1937 was broken by the war of resistance against Japan between 1937 and 1945. Peace finally came to China when the Red Army drove Chiang Kai-shek's Nationalist forces to Taiwan in 1949.

But a half-century of turmoil had taken its toll. The modern sector of the economy lay in virtual ruins. Heavy industrial output was 30 percent of peak mid-1930s levels, and agricultural output had declined 30 percent. To make matters worse, victorious Soviet troops physically dismantled and carried off heavy industrial installations from northeastern China. Inflation totally destroyed Chinese paper money and credit. The government of the newly proclaimed People's Republic faced such necessities as stabilizing the economy, rebuilding industry, restoring output and distribution, and controlling inflation—a tall order.

SHANGHAI INTERLUDE

Shanghai occupies a unique place in modern Chinese history.[18] A small mud village along the Huangpu River in 1800, it became the major dynamo for the Chinese economy in the mid-nineteenth century, a role it never relinquished. Shanghai dominated both heavy and light industry. It was the center of trade, finance, and education in China. It gave birth to the Chinese Communist Party in 1921 and, more recently, to the notorious "Gang of Four," who tried to impose radical leftist policies on China's economy after Mao Zedong unleashed the Cultural Revolution. In 1950, the city produced a fifth of all of China's industrial output and provided through taxes and profits the funds to finance 64 percent of all basic industrial construction during the first five year plan of 1953–1957. It achieved a 14 percent growth in industrial output despite its receipt of only 1–2 percent of national investment funds.[19]

Shanghai's rise to economic prominence was directly traceable to the period of "foreign exploitation," when Shanghai enjoyed the privileges of extraterritoriality (extrality, for short) and international rule. Prewar Shanghai was the liveliest and most dynamic commercial and intellectual center in China. The entrepreneurial and commercial experience of that period remained alive in the post-1949 period, even though much of the city's indigenous capital and its most talented people fled to Hong Kong in 1948–1949.

Shanghai was an oasis of calm in tumultuous China—a city governed by its own municipal council, with its own police force, its own customs authorities, and its own volunteer force to protect the traders. It was the most prosperous city in Asia, with over 400 million pounds sterling in British investments. Between 1870 and 1930, Shanghai's place in the value of China's total foreign trade ranged from 45 to 62 percent.[20] During 1925–1935, for example, Shanghai processed 55 percent of the foreign trade and 38 percent of the domestic trade passing through Chinese ports.[21] In the mid-1930s, Shanghai accounted for about half of China's large-scale, Western-type industrial production. The city housed 1,200 of China's 2,435 modern factories of all types: 64 of its 136 modern cotton mills, 46 of its 60 modern tobacco factories, and 41 of its 83 modern flour mills. Forty-three percent of China's industrial workers in modern manufacturing were employed in Shanghai.[22] The development of credit and modern Chinese banking took place in Shanghai, although foreign banks monopolized the financing of foreign commerce and controlled the flows of precious metals and foreign currency. Paper currency may have been worthless elsewhere in China, but money was relatively stable and convertible in the International Settlements.

The population of Shanghai grew from virtually nothing to 4 million by 1936, making it the fifth most populous city in the world. Shanghai's population was more than double that of Beijing or Tientsin. The foreign population peaked at about 60,000, of whom 20,000 were Japanese, 15,000 Russians (predominantly White refugees), 9,000 British, 5,000 Germans and Austrians, 4,000 Americans, and 2,500 French. It was basically a Chinese city politically dominated by a handful of foreigners, but foreign domination provided the political and economic institutions within which Shanghainese of all races could prosper.[23]

The foreign settlement of Shanghai was defined by nineteenth-century treaties and diplomatic procedures that granted all treaty ports extraterritorial rights. Shanghai was open to foreign trade on November 17, 1843, following ratification of the Treaty of Nanking.[24] It provided that, within the treaty ports, British subjects with their families and establishments would have the right of residence for carrying on their mercantile pursuits. Following the British action, the United States and France signed similar treaties in 1844, thereby acquiring the right of trade by their nationals in the treaty ports.

The French Settlement was created on April 6, 1849, when the French Consul reached an agreement with Chinese authorities that defined 164 acres of a specific district that would be under the direct rule of the French government in Paris through the French Consul. The initial British Foreign Settlement, encompassing 138 acres, merged in 1863 with the American Settlement, which was founded in 1843, to form the International Settlement; by contrast, France maintained separate jurisdiction of its special district.

Shanghai owed much of its commercial success to its geographical position near the estuary of the Yangtze River, which was a natural artery of trade for the shipment of raw materials and finished goods.[25] The Yangtze watershed encompassed half of China proper, with Shanghai standing at the apex of China's most fertile and populous area. The Yangtze possessed an all-year ship channel into such interior cities as Hankow and Chongqing, supplemented by a network of 30,000 miles of inland waterways that linked nearly 200 million people. Shanghai's orientation to the sea was equally favorable, lying less than a hundred miles east of the great circle route followed by shipping between North America, Japan, China, and Southeast Asia. It was also a terminus for the coasting trade—the natural division point for the carrying trade of junks from northern and southern ports.

But Shanghai's predominance owed much more to the political security that its foreign-dominated Municipal Council offered the merchant, whether foreign or Chinese.[26] Shanghai was a tiny island of relative security during an extended period of civil disorder in China, where the presence of foreign consuls and the quasi-independent status of the foreign settlements both attracted and protected large numbers of Chinese within its borders. This was demonstrated time and time again, during the Taiping Rebellion (1850–1864), the war between France and China (1884–1885), the Sino-Japanese War of 1894 (from which Shanghai was excluded as a theater of operations), the Boxer Uprising (1899–1900), the Chinese Revolution of 1911, World War I and Japanese intervention (1915–1918), factional fighting among warlords and political parties in the 1920s, and the Nationalist advance northward during 1926–1927.[27]

Noel Barber's graphic description of Shanghai's magnetism to the Chinese included references to "its own police force, its Western code of justice, its independent courts, [which] offered them a last despairing sanctuary in a country where half the people died before they reached the age of thirty." These favorable conditions contrasted with conditions elsewhere in China of "hunger, brutality, indignity, torture, humiliation, inflicted by corrupt authorities or venal landlords."[28]

Altogether, the elected Municipal Council in the International Settlement and the appointed French Consul in the French Settlement controlled a total land area of 12.66 square miles (out of the greater city government under Chinese direction encompassing 320 square miles). Executive direction of the International Settlement was vested in the Shanghai Municipal Council, two-thirds of whose members were foreigners, chiefly British and Americans. One-third were locally prominent Chinese, limited to five members. The foreign members were elected by expatriate taxpayers, and the Chinese members were chosen by Chinese residing in the international borders.[29]

The foundation or constitution of civil government was embodied in the "Land Regulations," which defined the boundaries of the settlement, provided for the acquisition and lease of lands from China, defined electoral qualifications (voters must own land and pay taxes), and provided for administrative government. The registered foreign electorate never exceeded 2,000 voters. Apart from annually electing city councillors, the taxpayers met yearly to approve or criticize the city report and to pass the budget for the coming year. Congestion forced some foreigners to take up residence along 48 miles of roads outside the settlement, which the Municipal Council constructed under its acquisition powers in the Land Regulations. Municipal departments provided basic public works, police and fire protection, and other services.

The French Settlement was also under the management of a Municipal Council, but the resident French consul general exercised supreme local authority with the power to veto the council's actions. He was accountable to the French minister to China and to the French government in Paris. By the 1930s, the consul had hand-picked all members of the municipal government, of which about two-thirds were French and the remaining third was Chinese.

A distinguishing feature of Shanghai was the privilege of extraterritoriality, a treaty arrangement whereby a nation acquired exclusive jurisdiction in civil and criminal matters over its recognized citizens residing in a foreign country.[30] Thus a Chinese individual who wished to sue an American in Shanghai had to apply to an American court. Chinese courts in the international zones functioned only for Chinese and foreigners without extrality rights.

The commercial implications of this arrangement meant that Western commercial law governed contracts in the International Settlement. Typical Chinese practices of bribery, graft, and corruption were less prevalent under foreign administration.

In the two settlements, foreigners designed their own parks, built their own churches, schools, colleges, hospitals, and brought in their own missions, clubs, charities, bars, cafes, and hotels. They developed a special postal service and published more than a dozen daily and weekly newspapers. Contracting companies provided electricity for light and power (their plant was the most powerful in China and its prices were among the lowest in the world), gas, water service, electric trains, and an urban telephone network. The Park Hotel on Bubbling Well Road, with its 205 luxuriously furnished rooms, apartments, and unfurnished flats, was proudly advertised as the tallest building in the Far East.[31]

Shanghai became the business center of China. It was home to such large British, German, and Japanese trading firms as Jardine, Matheson and Company, and the head office of twenty foreign banks.

Taxation in Shanghai was extremely favorable to business. No Chinese taxes could be collected within the foreign settlements except a modest customs charge (administered by a foreign-staffed organ of the Chinese government) and a small land tax, given that Shanghai's land technically remained Chinese property. The Shanghai Municipal Council was free to impose types and rates of tax on residents of the International Settlement, but such taxation first required annual budget approval from the small commmunity of less than 2,000 taxpaying voters.[32] Indeed, the representation of Chinese taxpayers in the Municipal Council of the International Settlement was a consequence both of Chinese protestations of "no taxation without representation" and of the periodic refusals of Chinese residents to pay municipal taxes.

The decline of Confucian ideology in the twentieth century in Western-dominated greater Shanghai loosened the hold of the bureaucracy over Chinese entrepreneurs. Industry boomed. Reinvested profits—annual dividends of Chinese enterprises often surpassed 30 percent—brought rapid economic expansion. Between 1914 and 1927, the number of looms in cotton mills quadrupled. Accompanying industrialization was the development of a working class. In 1921, Shanghai accounted for about one-quarter of the entire Chinese labor force employed in modern factories and related transport, postal service, and dock activities. These 300,000 to 400,000 laborers sought employment and opportunity in Shanghai's burgeoning economy in an attempt to escape rural squalor and political instability.

Shanghai became the intellectual center of China.[33] Intellectuals were driven from Beijing, home of China's intellectual renaissance between 1915 and 1919, by the chaotic and brutal regime of the warlords. They found sanctuary in Shanghai, which was also the center of the foreign press (26 newspapers and magazines in 1921) and Chinese press (more than 80 publications).

Shanghai demonstrated what Chinese people could achieve under a system of private property and the rule of law. "The exceptional rise of Shanghai in the 1920s was born of the coincidence between the retreat of bureaucratic restrictions which freed the energies, and the existence of an island of relative security and order—'the refuge of the Settlements'—which preserved them."[34] In short, the municipal government of the International Settlement defined and protected property rights, maintained law and order and external defense, minimized business regulations, kept taxes low, limited public spending to essential public services, and permitted free external trade. Due process of law provided protection against seizure of property, extortion, excessive taxation, and other illegal practices common in China. The period of 1919–1927 was truly the "golden age of a colonial-style Shanghai," when "Shanghai reached the height of its time-honored destiny."[35]

Sour came with the sweet. Shanghai was reputed to be one of the wickedest cities in the world. It led the world's cities in prostitution and brothels as a speciality. Opium dens flourished publicly. Kidnapping constantly threatened Chinese merchants. Organized gambling was big business, perhaps on the largest scale of any city in the world. Law enforcement treated foreigners with exceptional lenience. The city gave rise to the practice of "Shanghaiing" innocents to serve on ships. Police expenses, which consumed 40 to 50 percent of the Municipal Council's budget, were insufficient to eliminate crime or achieve morality.[36]

Of course, the Chinese were outraged over foreign occupation of sacred Chinese soil and sought to eliminate foreign influence in Shanghai. From 1927 on, Chiang Kai-shek gradually gained control over the activities of Chinese residents in the settlements.[37] The Kuomintang regime was generally hostile toward a free-market economy and private enterprise, and took steps to supersede the local Chinese middle and upper classes in their economic functions while excluding them from local administration. To accomplish these ends, the children of rich merchants were kidnapped and ransomed, and merchants themselves were arrested or forced to flee. The bourgeoisie in Shanghai, which had funded Chiang with millions of dollars, was transformed from a dynamic economic force for development to a source of funds for Kuomintang coffers.

The restoration of customs and excise autonomy to Chinese authorities, so long demanded by various Chinese Chambers of Commerce as a matter of patriotic right, brought high import taxes on raw materials and industrial equipment that drove many Chinese factories situated outside the International Settlements out of business. The financial power and independence of the indigenous Shanghai Chinese banking group fell under the direct control of the government when it took over the Bank of China and the Communications Bank. The Kuomintang imposed a policy of bureaucratic capitalism.

Meanwhile, dislike of the bourgeoisie was accompanied by distrust of the working-class movement. The Kuomintang waged a bloody struggle of arrest and executions to eliminate all Communist influence in the city—a struggle that succeeded in the short run but in the long run met its demise when the Communists regrouped in Yenan following the famous long march.

The city remained China's economic heart under Chiang's Nanjing regime. "But the progressive paralysis of the national bourgeoisie and the government's persistent lack of interest in commercial and industrial problems, left this [economic] growth to the vagaries of foreign stimulation and to the initiative of foreigners who at that time concentrated 46.4 percent of their total direct investment in China in Shanghai."[38] The privileges of foreigners within the international zone remained intact during the restoration of bureaucratic control over the Chinese population. But Japanese aggression in 1937 achieved in Shanghai what Chinese nationalism failed to accomplish during the previous decade. Shanghai was no longer in control of its own destiny. "The loss of its international status after 1937 was to be the direct cause of its decline."[39]

The Japanese seized direct control of the International Settlement the day after the attack on Pearl Harbor. Japan declared its intention to turn the administration of the settlement over to the puppet government of Wang Zhingwei, thus prompting the Western powers to renounce their treaty rights in January 1943. Chiang Kai-shek's government assumed control after Japan's withdrawal. Disappearance of the political independence of the settlements destroyed the institutional underpinnings of Shanghai's development. Gone were monetary stability, property rights, law and order, the sanctity of contracts, low taxes, and sound civic administration. As the Kuomintang printed money to pay its military expenses, the resultant inflation favored the political bureaucracy and destroyed the middle class. Corruption, incompetence, and despotism became the hallmarks of civic administration. In May 1949, the advancing Red Army occupied Shanghai, placing the city firmly under Communist rule.

In short, Shanghai was a sweet and sour prize. Its port, banks, factories, skilled manpower, technicians, administrators, and schools potentially played a key role in national economic reconstruction. Yet Shanghai typified the evils that communism opposed: a shameful past of colonial development dominated by the hated foreigner, consumer indulgence, reliance on imports, and urban arrogance out of touch with the Communist Party's peasant base.

THE POLITICAL SYSTEM OF CHINA

Economic activities do not take place in a vacuum. Their efficiency is conditioned by the presence or absence of political stability, law and order, honest government, and the provision of adequate infrastructure and other public services. The activities of government, in turn, are typically constrained by a country's constitution, which sets forth the basic laws against which all other political, economic, and social activities occur. The literal applicability of the content of constitutions varies among countries. Among Western industrial democracies, constitutions tend to be strictly interpreted and applied. In many African countries, democratic constitutions survived only one election. In the case of mainland China, the constitution was frequently changed and often meant little in terms of actual political behavior or the way in which China was ruled. Nonetheless, the concrete provisions of China's constitution inform our understanding of the ideological and political background against which China's leaders attempted to plan and implement economic development.[40]

The most recent constitution of mainland China was adopted at the fifth session of the National People's Congress on December 4, 1982.[41] The preamble proclaimed the central role of the Communist Party of China in the political and economic life of the nation. It chronicled the step-by-step transformation of what it termed "the semi-colonial and semi-feudal country of China" after 1840 into a socialist society. The government, officially the "people's democratic dictatorship" led by the working class in alliance with the peasants, abolished private ownership of the means of production and established a comprehensive system of state-owned industry.

Recognizing both successes and failures, this fifth revision of China's basic law stressed the new task of "socialist modernization." (See Chapter 4 for a description of socialist modernization since 1978 as a sequence of liberal economic reforms that enhanced individual incentives to produce and invest.) Let us review the main features of the present constitution, with special emphasis on economic relationships.

Article 1 declared China a socialist state under the people's democratic dictatorship. "Sabotage of the socialist system by any organization or individual is prohibited." Thus the state sector was assigned paramount economic status.

Article 2 assigned all power to the people, and that power is exercised through the National People's Congress and local people's congresses at different levels. (In practice, with the recent exception of the drafting of the fifth constitution by government, rather than by party personnel, decisions were typically made by members of the Central Committee of the Communist Party of China, which met periodically, and then presented to the National People's Congress for official unanimous ratification. Thus the Central Committee of the Communist Party, which controlled political power in China, determined policy, which in turn was transmitted to the government through the State Council and legislature.)

Article 3 proclaimed the principle of democratic centralism, which assigns administrative leadership to the central authorities.

Article 6 set forth the basis of the socialist economic system. Subsequent articles defined state or commune ownership of industry, rural enterprise, natural resources, and land. The 1982 revision of the constitution allowed some "individual" economy as a complement to the public sector, but the state exercised administrative control to guide and supervise the individual economy. Article 13, unlike previous versions of the constitution in 1954, 1975, and 1978, gave citizens the right to own houses and other lawful property along with the right to inherit private property. Article 15 provided for central economic planning but assigned a supplementary role to regulation by the market.

Beginning with Article 19, the constitution assigned to the state responsibility for education, scientific research, medical and health services, development of art and literature, control of the media, family planning, protection of the environment, public order, and the suppression of treason and "counter-revolution." The state remained pervasive in the social, economic, and cultural life of mainland China.

Articles 30 and 31 established the administrative structure of China, which was broken down into provinces, autonomous regions, municipalities, prefectures, counties, and towns.

Chapter Two of the constitution stipulated the fundamental rights and duties of citizens. These included the right to vote and stand for election, freedom of speech, press and assembly, freedom of religion, protection from arbitrary seizure and search, privacy of correspondence, the right to criticize any state organ or functionary, the right as well as the duty to work, guaranteed retirement and welfare benefits for the ill and disabled, free education, academic freedom for research, women's equality, and the duty to practice family planning. Notably absent is the right to strike or sue the government. It has been a basic tenet of Communist ideology that socialist transformation of the economy eliminated the exploitation of workers by capitalists, thus obviating the need to strike. Nor can individuals sue the official representatives of "the people."

The enumeration of these rights may surprise those who view China as a totalitarian society that did not respect human rights. On the other hand, it should be noted that China never signed the International Human Rights convention. Analysts of China generally agree that human rights in China existed only on paper, not in practice.[42] This paradox is resolved in Article 51, which stated that "the exercise by citizens of the People's Republic of China of their freedoms and rights may not infringe upon the interests of the state, of society and of the collective." Article 54 further precluded the commission of acts detrimental to the "security, honor and interests of the motherland." Inasmuch as the state is defined as a people's democratic dictatorship under the leadership of the Communist Party of China, party or state officials can suppress individual rights by recourse to Article 51.

The exercise of individual economic, political, and civil rights is a distinguishing characteristic of Western market economies. The general absence of such rights in mainland China greatly weakened the economic opportunities and behavior of its citizens compared with those enjoyed in Western nations. An especially critical difference for economic efficiency was virtual state preemption of private property in mainland China since 1949.

Chapter Three of the constitution outlined the state structure of China. It specified the duties and powers of the National People's Congress and its related committees, the offices of president and vice-president, the State Council (the highest executive organ of state administration), the Central Military Commission, local units of government, and the courts. The State Council, in particular, was assigned responsibility for drafting national economic plans and budgets and for guiding economic development.

As previously noted, the government was the executive arm of the Communist Party, which, in turn, was controlled by the Central Committee and its Political Bureau, an inner core of powerful political leaders.[43] The party exercised power partly by placing its members in key positions in the government. Every state-owned enterprise had an internal political organization—a party committee that tied together labor unions, the party office, and youth league members—that paralleled its business organization. Or, party officials told government or state officials what they wanted them to do.[44]

For our purposes, the structure and workings of the Communist Party were important as the elements of the policy-making body of China, but our focus is on the substance of economic policy and how it was implemented through the mechanism of government.

ORGANIZATION AND ADMINISTRATION OF ECONOMIC PLANNING

Described in this section are the machinery of central planning that was in place through 1977; the conduct of public finances, monetary policies, and banking practices; and the ownership of economic assets.

The Chinese government, through the State Council and its associated commissions, ministries, and bureaus, attempted to practice comprehensive central economic planning.[45] It tried to control what was produced, by whom, and the uses to which it was put. Government intervention in the economy was so pervasive that nearly four-fifths of all central government agencies dealt solely with economic affairs.

Under the jurisdiction of the State Council, the State Planning Commission drafted five-year and medium-term plans, while the Economics Commission reviewed the fulfillment of the annual economic plans and instituted economic reforms. More than two dozen separate ministries dealt with different segments of the economy, including agriculture and fisheries, forestry, coal, petroleum, railroads, labor, finance, trade, and banking. In addition, such separate bureaus as the Bank of China, the Civil Aviation Administration, the State Statistics Bureau, and the Administration Bureau for Commodity Prices, to name just four, were involved in the management of economic affairs. By contrast, there were fewer than a dozen remaining ministries of the State Council to cover foreign affairs, defense, culture, civil affairs, justice, education, and so forth.

A relative handful of central economic planners tried to make as many decisions as possible concerning consumption, production of outputs, employment of inputs, distribution of income, and investment. In principle, the planning authorities controlled all physical productive resources, including land, buildings, machinery, and other capital goods. They directly or indirectly controlled all enterprises, farms, and factories. They assigned a production target to each farm and factory, and told it how much of each good to produce. They controlled all sources of supply of inputs, including raw materials and machinery for both agriculture and industry. They assigned labor by directing workers to different factories or assigning individuals to specific farms. In short, the planners tried to control both the allocation of inputs and the production of goods and services.[46]

Planners attempted to control the consumption of final goods and services. Either they set the price of goods sold through public retail outlets, letting the consumer decide what and how much to buy, or they rationed goods through ration coupons that fixed the amount of specific commodities that consumers acquired each month. (The reason that such essential commodities as grain, vegetable oil, meat, sugar, and cotton cloth were rationed in mainland China is that planning authorities set prices at artificially low levels, thereby creating excess demand. If consumers bought as much of these staples as they wished at these fixed low prices, stocks would quickly deplete, leaving those last in line holding empty bags.)

Planners also attempted to determine individual incomes. They set factory wage rates (which remained unchanged in China between 1957 and 1977) but also usually prevented dismissal or reassignment, thus guaranteeing job security. Farmers shared in the overall income of the farm through a system of work points, in which the final allocation of output and farm income was divided up on the basis of each person's share of total points. Farmers divided up what was left after paying the costs of production and selling a portion of their output to the government. The planners varied farm income by changing the purchase quotas and prices of farm products. (For years, the government paid below-market prices for grain, thus effectively taxing agriculture to support industrialization.)[47] Finally, the planners tried to determine the mix between consumption and investment. They decided the amounts of each consumer good and capital good to be produced.

Flows of economic information were vertical. Production units submitted statistics on past economic activities to the central planners, who in turn issued commands expressed in physical planning targets and state-set prices. Transactions among firms were regulated by the planners, as payments between them were made through book entries and transfers in the state bank. Planned profits were remitted to the state budget at regular intervals. The planners allocated fixed capital to state firms as budgetary grants; interest was not charged for the use of capital. Nor were the rental costs of land included in the planners' economic calculations. The government centralized property, which was overwhelmingly socialized. (Private property was limited to small family plots and artisan-type production.)[48]

The actual annual planning document relied on a system of "material balances" whereby the inputs were assigned to firms in light of what was available (regardless of the true price or scarcity value of the item) and output targets for production were written in terms of physical units (such as tons, yards, bushels, and barrels). The planning bureau in each province and county prepared a similar local plan. The system was integrated in that county plans were coordinated with provincial planners, whose documents were coordinated by the State Planning Commission.[49]

It is useful to compare the information requirements of a relatively free-market economy with that of a centrally planned economy. In the free market, individuals make decisions to consume and produce. Given one's income and the prices of different products, each consumer decides what to buy. When the price of any given good goes up, the consumer buys less; when it goes down, he or she buys more. In turn, given the prices of inputs and the selling prices of their goods, producers decide how much to supply. In the end, prices will adjust such that the quantities produced will equal the quantities demanded by consumers. In a market economy, each firm needs to know only its own economic circumstances and the prices of its inputs and products. On the basis of its own individual knowledge, each firm will respond efficiently to consumer demand (or go out of business).

Under central planning, the state assigned production quotas and inputs to millions of productive units. To allocate resources efficiently, it had to know the economic conditions (method of production or technology, the productivity of its workers, the capacity of its capital equipment, the kinds of inputs required, managerial skills) of all these units. The lack of appropriate statistical data often resulted in errors and misallocations. Central planners required large staffs to collect information and supervise all these units.[50]

Compilation of the annual plan entailed monumental paperwork. Beneath the general planning umbrella, responsibility for specific commodities was divided among different agencies. The Food Ministry dealt with food, the Commerce Ministry with nonstaple foods and other consumer goods, the State Material Supply Bureau with industrial goods, and individual ministries with specialized items. Each agency had subordinate or counterpart units at provincial and county levels, with similar division of responsibility among the various levels of government. About 1,000 important goods were initially allocated among provinces and centrally controlled organizations, which in turn were allocated to counties and provincially controlled organizations and finally subdivided among rural communes and county-controlled organizations.

For each good and at each level of government, the allocation procedure was broadly similar. Communes, county-controlled enterprises, construction units, and departments submitted requisitions for the coming year to the relevant county agency, which prepared a draft allocation based on preliminary information on the availability of goods from provincial and local sources. Following discussion with local users and producers, the document was discussed at a provincial conference, which ultimately culminated in a national conference of user and producer representatives. Then, following vigorous negotiations, the documents were revised and lower-level allocation plans were finalized.

Subsequent distribution of goods was channeled through producer or retail state outlets. Foreign trade was centralized through foreign trade companies under the Ministry of Foreign Trade.[51]

Problems with Central Planning

The chief political, economic, and social goals of central planning included (1) high growth of producer goods, (2) economic independence from foreign suppliers, (3) stability of prices and employment, and (4) elimination of opposition to Communist rule.[52] During Mao's political preeminence, they also included the placement of equity above growth as a social priority.[53]

China's central planners faced a number of institutional deficiencies and structural defects in pursuing these goals. Institutional deficiencies included the assault by Mao and his accomplices on China's state planning apparatus, which often made it impossible for the planners to do their jobs. Structural defects included (1) the inability of consumers to signal their demands, which often produced surpluses of unwanted goods and shortages of highly desired goods, (2) difficulties in collecting and coordinating required information, (3) the absence of labor markets,

(4) low incentives, (5) lack of entrepreneurship, (6) misallocation of resources, and (7) political interference in economic tasks.[54]

Central administrative command planning, carried to its extreme, eliminates market relations. In markets, prices signal the opportunity cost of the resources used in the production of goods and services, and are determined by supply and demand conditions under competition. Under planning, bureaucrats issue memoranda in hierarchical order. The golden rule of bureaucratic planning is to maintain a climate conducive to routine and to avoid disruptions of the administrative process. This rule was grossly violated in China in the form of such mass mobilization movements as the Great Leap Forward (1958–1960) and the Cultural Revolution (1966–1976), both of which purged the planning fraternity. As one scholar has noted, "The history of five-year plans in China is a history of still-born, unfinished, unfinishable, and discarded wrecks."[55]

During these two periods of mass movements, the theory and techniques of central planning were neglected. The statistical apparatus so critical to accurate information flows was dismantled (see Appendix). Planning concepts could not be discussed in public or private. The result was "a low level of theoretical and practical competence in economic planning and management."[56] "Indeed, viewing the last three decades in China, the overall impression is more one of an economy that is improvised than planned, if planning implies systematic coordination and keeping to a program."[57] Thus China's planners were handicapped by conditions that made it virtually impossible to implement a regime of central planning, even if such a regime was practicable.

Planning is far more difficult in practice than appears in principle. China's efforts at central planning encountered several structural defects. The first was the inability of consumers to signal their wants to the planners, except for the small peasant markets and some negotiated contracts in which prices were free to move to adjust to supply and demand. The operation of the market in China was hobbled by the planners' unwillingness to free prices. Market forces were allowed to assert themselves only through an extremely limited private economy. The inevitable consequence was chronic shortages of desired goods and surpluses of substandard or unusable products (see Chapter 3).

In order to reflect the opportunity cost of the resources used in the production of goods and services and to permit resources to be shifted to more highly valued uses, prices must be free to move. In China's planned economy, the central authority set prices.[58] Each year, the central Price Bureau published a price catalog for all commodities, ranging from grain and cooking oil to shoelaces and socks, and stipulated which level of government had control. Although prices affected consumption by discouraging demand, they did not encourage production because state-owned enterprises did not operate to make profits; rather, they turned over all their revenue to the government, including any profits that remained after production costs.

In setting prices, central planners tried to reproduce the workings of the price mechanism in the market, which automatically balances production with consumption. State-owned enterprises were denied the independent ability to determine their own activities given that the state sets input and output prices. The state tried to match the costs of production in each enterprise with the selling price of its output. If revenue exceeded production costs, the state appropriated the surplus; if costs exceeded revenue, it provided a subsidy.

Domestic prices were insulated from world prices.[59] No attempt was made to use the exchange rate to bring domestic costs and prices in line with world costs and prices to ensure an internationally competitive position for Chinese exports. Foreign trade companies sold imported goods, regardless of their real cost, to local enterprises at state-set prices equivalent to the prices of locally produced goods. Similarly, trading companies bought from domestic suppliers at local prices but sold abroad at world prices.

An overvalued exchange rate retards efficiency inasmuch as producers acquire inputs on an artificially cheap basis (a practice that often results in wasteful usage), and exporters are either priced out of world markets or forced to sell at substantial losses because the foreign exchange they earn is worth less at the official exchange rate than the costs of production. This condition held for certain sectors of Chinese industry, whose costs exceeded world prices at the official exchange rate, thus causing exporters of manufactured goods to suffer substantial losses. Conversely, as China's prices of heavily subsidized agricultural and mining products are below world prices, state-owned trading companies profited handsomely from these exports. Of course, all profits were remitted to the central government, and all losses required subsidies.

Information requirements in a planned economy are daunting. The production, collection, analysis, and transmission of economic statistics were accompanied by a huge statistical, ministerial, and planning apparatus. Millions of prices had to be set and adjusted. Often the adjustments were late, infrequent, or unrelated to the realities of production. Individuals faced incentives to misreport statistics to claim above-target production, thus causing planners to set even higher targets in subsequent plans.

Central planners often lacked expertise in the productive use of farmland. Some land was better suited for growing wheat, other for cotton, and so forth. But planners often disregarded soil condition and quality by insisting that land be used for grain, when it would have been put to more productive use growing cash crops.

Perhaps the key structural defect in the Chinese system of central planning was the lack of material incentives given to peasants, factory managers, and workers. Egalitarianism, the absence of competition, and an emphasis on income redistribution adversely affected incentives.[60] Rural production-team members generally received income on a straight per capita basis, thereby weakening the applicability of peasant workpoint incentive systems; urban industrial productivity was rarely reflected in wage differentials or earned bonuses; and nonmaterial, normative incentives, such as building socialism or awarding red flags and stars to successful work teams were stressed in place of material rewards.

Let us look at each sector in turn. In the rural commune, where the means of production were collectively owned and output was collectively distributed, any farmer who worked harder got to keep very little of the additional output because it was shared by all members of the work team, regardless of their work effort. In economic terms, individual farmers were not paid according to the marginal products of their labor.

The industrial sector also suffered from a lack of incentives. The state assigned workers to enterprises, regardlesss of whether they desired the post or had suitable skills. More desirable jobs were often assigned as compensation for favors or as a form of bribery or corruption. Once assigned, a worker could not be discharged for incompetence and received the same pay as other workers no matter how hard he or she worked. The general level of wages remained unchanged for twenty years, and morale was damaged. Under the impact of radical leftist philosophy, wage differentials were compressed; workers with specialized training received few additional benefits. Bonuses, overtime work, and piecework were curtailed or abolished.

Factory managers faced a plethora of disincentives. Some were reluctant to practice serious accounting lest they be accused of putting material production before politics, or of becoming soiled in quest of profits. Sound business practices—such as labor discipline, prevention of absenteeism, attention to quality, and industrial safety—were rejected as "elitist." Managers and key technical personnel were reeducated in ideology schools and through manual labor to ensure correct class consciousness. Managerial effort was not rewarded with substantially higher salaries. All enterprise receipts were surrendered to the state, thus limiting managerial choice.

As factory managers could not fire their workers, they faced difficulties in getting them to work harder. In addition, because managers were trying not to maximize profits but, rather, to meet production targets, they lacked the incentive to exceed those targets lest future targets be increased and subect them to criticism for failing to meet those higher targets. Given the process of formulating the annual plan, factory managers faced incentives to supply low estimates of potential factory output, which would be easier to meet. Even more important, factory managers had no incentive to economize on the use of inputs or capital because planners provided both on a cost-free basis. Indeed, it made sense to request more inputs and capital than could be utilized efficiently as insurance in the event that fewer inputs were provided than requested. Such an arrangement was conducive to both large-scale waste and the accumulation of large inventories. In 1980, for example, stockpiles of steel products totaled nearly 20 million tons—well over half the annual production, of which much had only scrap value.[61]

Plan and production targets were capriciously changed. And as there was no solid legal basis to the economy, personal factors, bureaucratic infighting, and changing political coalitions often produced new regulations and directives.[62] Planners often succumbed to misguided zeal, setting targets that disregarded economic constraints. The Great Leap Forward, motivated by Mao Zedong's objective of modernizing China overnight, produced major economic dislocations, three years of severe recession during 1959–1961, and famine conditions in which up to 30 million people perished. The state banks failed to exercise supervisory authority, especially during periods of political tension. Many projects were declared on-again, off-again, thus wasting scarce capital.[63]

Routine and risk aversion, the politically safe forms of factory management, replaced spontaneity, competition, diversity, and autonomy. Potential entrepreneurial functions of increasing the production of goods and services that enhance consumer satisfaction, or of seizing cost-reducing opportunities, were suppressed in favor of administrative command.

Even if the authorities were able to work out on paper a balance between the production and use of each product, bottlenecks owing to shortages of certain materials arose in actual production while other inputs were in excess supply. Planning provided neither an incentive nor a mechanism for shifting resources from one enterprise to another to eliminate shortages and surpluses.

Public Finance

The central government reinforced its control over the economy through the state budget.[64] Although provincial and county governments since the late 1950s had collected more than two-thirds of all revenue and spent about half, county and provincial budgets were consolidated within the central state budget. Beijing specified tax rates and policies as well as the level and composition of local expenditures. The precise degree of control varied from year to year, reflecting the constant tension between the desire for central control and the need to enhance incentives through decentralization. Central control was used to dictate patterns of investment and to redistribute tax revenues from rich to poor provinces. Periodic decentralization, allowing local governments discretion over some portions of their budget, was used to encourage local governments to improve revenue collection and economize on expenditure. The Chinese Communists were great believers in balanced budgets to prevent inflationary issue of bank notes to cover deficits, and they usually achieved a balance or slight surplus in their budgets.[65]

The sources of receipts bore no resemblance to those of the Western industrial democracies. Income taxes applied to a bare handful of upper-income Chinese and resident foreign businessmen. In contrast, enterprise profits supplied nearly half of all revenue throughout the postwar period. Until the advent of industrial reforms in the 1980s, state-owned enterprises remitted virtually all their profits to the state. Remember, the state set prices of industrial inputs and outputs, thereby determining "profitability." Three-quarters of industrial net output constituted not wages but profits and taxes.

The share of government revenue derived from the profits of state-owned enterprises rose from 31.2 percent in 1952 to a maximum of 63.9 percent in 1960, and remained above 40 percent every year until 1981.[66] In 1957, for example, the wage share of Chinese workers as a percentage of costs in industry was 28.6 percent (compared with 52.5 percent in India). A lower wage-cost ratio resulted in a higher profit-wage ratio, which meant that the relative share of income between workers and the government was very much in favor of the government. Inasmuch as wages remained unchanged during 1957–1977, this policy shifted enormous economic resources to the government for its disposal, thus leaving workers with meager incomes.[67]

State sales of agricultural inputs illustrated this form of implicit taxation through conscious pricing policy. The state sold machinery and other farm inputs to peasants at prices well above those prevailing in world markets—prices that showed up as enterprise profits and, ultimately, as taxes. Nicholas Lardy estimated that the relative price of Chinese-produced tractors was at least twice the world level.[68] The major chemical fertilizers of nitrogen and ammonium sulfate were also priced at twice international levels. In all, the implicit tax burden from overpricing nitrogenous fertilizer relative to the world price was triple explicit agricultural taxes.

The second leading source of revenue, nearly equal to enterprise profits, was a mix of industrial and commercial taxes that included salt, customs duties, and direct tax on agriculture. Foreign borrowing and other miscellaneous revenue made up the balance (about 5–6 percent).

About 30 percent of national income flowed through the state budget. Half took the form of grants for fixed and working capital formation to finance industry, commerce, and infrastructure. The balance went largely for defense and consumer subsidies.

Money and Banking[69]

Monetary policy focused on three objectives: controlling inflation, promoting savings to finance investment, and maintaining effective control over enterprise budgets.

Party leaders believed that hyperinflation brought the demise of Chiang Kai-shek's government in the late 1940s. In the waning days of Nationalist control over Shanghai, price increases averaged 33.7 percent a month during 1945–1948.[70] Setting the price level at 100 for 1931 as the base year, we find that inflation pushed wholesale prices in just the one month of October 1947 from 74,367 to 108,350. Chiang's government literally printed $40 billion a day in new Chinese paper currency. In all, from May 1946 to May 1949, wholesale prices rose seven and one-half million times. Hyperinflation brought financial panic, destroyed the middle class, and undermined any remaining support for the Nationalist government. Once in power, China's new leaders set out to control inflation.

China's planners immediately established systems of cash control and credit planning to stabilize prices.[71] Every effort was made to minimize currency circulation to prevent holders of cash from bidding up prices or creating excess demand for goods in short supply. In early 1950, the government compelled all state enterprises and cooperatives to deposit all currency notes in the People's Bank of China (PBOC), and limited petty cash holdings to no more than three days' requirements. The government also introduced indexed bonds and savings deposits to combat hyperinflation. Starting in 1951, all transactions between socialist enterprises were conducted by bank transfers, mutual credit or deferred payments between state enterprises were banned, and all proceeds of cash were deposited with the PBOC.

Apart from cash payments to households in the form of wages and agricultural sales in free markets, as well as those transactions reflecting consumer purchases (which required ration coupons for certain items), all financial transactions were made through book transfers at the PBOC. In 1979, for example, 95 percent of total PBOC transactions were noncash. Although individuals had savings accounts, they could not hold current checking accounts.

Credit controls were equally severe. All enterprise and cooperative cash was deposited into the banking system. By law, enterprises could not extend credit to each other. Thus the central government controlled and allocated all credit in the form of direct state appropriations, grants, and loans. Cash withdrawals were permitted only for wage payments. Banks were permitted to make short-term credit loans only after receiving official approval for repayment schedules.

The government met its objectives of curtailing inflation and maintaining stable prices. Inflation was checked almost overnight. Setting 1950 equal to 100 as the base year, we find that the general retail price index rose less than 40 percent during 1950–1979,[72] although much of China's inflation was repressed in the form of rationing and shortages. (For purposes of comparison, the price level in the United States tripled during 1967–1984.)

Outlets for private savings consisted of bonds and savings accounts in the PBOC or the Agricultural Bank. To stimulate savings, deposits could be transferred to heirs and were free of tax. From time to time, the government raised interest rates to attract new deposits. High rates of savings were attributed to the absence of alternatives for the use of money, inasmuch as consumer goods were limited and private investment outlets were largely banned until the late 1970s.

China's currency, the Renminbi (people's money) yuan (dollar), was not freely convertible into other currencies. The government generally overvalued the official yuan exchange rate, and until it joined the International Monetary Fund in 1980, it failed to disclose financial reserves and balance-of-payments figures.[73]

China strictly enforced exchange controls. All foreign exchange holdings were deposited with the Bank of China (BOC). It was illegal for individuals, enterprises, or state agencies to use or deposit abroad any foreign exchange except by or through the BOC, although enforcement was imperfect. A license was required from the General Administration of Exchange Control to trade or hold foreign exchange.

STRUCTURE OF THE ECONOMY

Chapters 3 and 4 examine the wildly shifting mosaic of rural and industrial economic policies and their effects on economic output and living standards. Set forth here is the basic structure of mainland China's economy as it existed up through the mid-1970s.

Ownership of economic assets fell into the categories of state owned, collectively owned, and private.[74] Assets under state ownership belonged to the central government or its agencies. Those under collective ownership belonged to rural communes. Private ownership is self-explanatory.

The government set out to practice socialism through central planning. Socialization of the economy proceeded to the extent that by 1975 the state controlled 97 percent of industrial fixed assets, employed 63 percent of all employees, and contributed 86 percent of gross industrial output. Communes, representing the "collective sector" of the economy, owned 3 percent of fixed assets in the form of small-scale rural enterprises, employed 36.2 percent of the industrial work force, and generated 14 percent of industrial output. The private sector consisted solely of 0.8 percent of the nonagricultural labor force, which largely provided services.

State control over commerce paralleled industry. By 1975 state-owned retail outlets accounted for 92.5 percent of retail sales; collectives delivered 7.3 percent, with a negligible 0.2 percent in private hands. Between 1950 and 1975, China virtually destroyed the entire private industrial and urban retail sector.

A network of state and party posts controlled industry. State ministries or agencies, paralleled by central and provincial party revolutionary committees, oversaw the operation of each state-owned enterprise. A coal mine, for example, had an enterprise director and his deputies, as well as several chief engineers and departments responsible for accounting, production, quality control, marketing and transport, labor and wages, welfare, utilities, and so on. The post of party secretary on the firm's organization chart was equivalent to director, with the party office equivalent to a department. Within each workshop, extending all the way down to subsections and teams, small party groups involved themselves in day-to-day affairs of the enterprise, both in production and propaganda work. The party was omnipresent in industry.

About 80 percent of all Chinese lived in the countryside. Apart from a handful of state-owned farms under army control and a small percentage of land classified as "private plots," communes collectively owned about 90 percent of cultivated land and irrigation equipment. A typical people's commune consisted of 15,000 people broken into 13–15 brigades; each brigade, in turn, was subdivided into 7–8 production teams of about 1,100 members total. Each production team numbered about 150, comprising some 30 to 40 families.

From the top down, the commune operated secondary schools, clinics, and small-scale industries and provided marketing services and civil administration. Each production brigade ran its own primary schools, health facilities, and small-scale industries. The production team itself directed agricultural production and distributed grain and other forms of income based on the proportions of total work points earned by each family. Finally, the family, the smallest social unit of production, exercised direct control over its own private plot.

Although it did not legally own this plot—the constitution prohibited private ownership of land—the household retained the rights to all that it produced on the designated private parcels. Families were allowed to own the homes they built on commune land. Because farmers got to keep what they produced on their private plots, they put as much labor and fertilizer as they could into this minuscule "private sector." The output of these private plots represented between 30 and 50 percent of all vegetables, fruit, pigs, and poultry produced in China. The World Bank estimated that family activities on private plots, along with a wide range of sideline activities (hat making, basket weaving, knitting, tailoring, and pottery) generated about 30 percent of total agricultural income and the great bulk of cash income.[75] Private plots supplied the bulk of peasant consumption of meat and vegetables.

State control over the "collective" rural economy took two forms. First, it prohibited labor migration from communes into the urban areas, or even from one region to another. Unless the government recruited a rural subject for a specific task elsewhere, that subject could not change his or her residence. Any Chinese person, whether rural or urban, needed a pass or travel authorization from a party official to move even temporarily or on holiday, let alone migrate. Although these movement restrictions allowed for orderly urban planning, they also caused several million Chinese couples to live apart from each other and imposed costs in economic efficiency due to reduced labor mobility. Workers could not move to where the value of their marginal product was highest. Indeed, from time to time, the government conducted campaigns to send urban residents back to the countryside to increase rural output, receive class-based ideological training, relieve the pressures on limited urban amenities, and prevent the emergence of urban unemployment. These migration restrictions and forced relocations took a heavy toll in morale.

A second form of control was established through the supply and marketing systems. Apart from products consumed locally, the government acquired most of the remaining agricultural output according to a system of fixed quotas and prices. Free-market sales paled against the quantities collected directly by the government's procurement machinery for distribution to cities, the military, and the food-short regions of China. Similarly, the government supplied commune residents with virtually all of its nonagricultural products, including agricultural inputs and consumer goods. The state-owned Agricultural Bank handled rural credit.

In both the industrial and rural sectors, political control was pervasive. Party cadres exercised direct administrative responsibilities in factories and on the communes to ensure rigid compliance with state directives. They were especially active in such social areas as family planning and political education.

NOTES

1. James Legge, *Confucius: Confucian Analects, The Great Learning and The Doctrine of the Mean* (New York: Dover Publications, Inc., 1971), p. 150.
2. Ibid., p. 156.
3. In late 1980, an economic mission from the World Bank comprising several teams of economic and statistical specialists visited China. They prepared a three-volume country study entitled *China: Socialist Economic Development* (Washington, D.C.: World Bank, 1983). Volume I contained the main report on the economy, an annex on the statistical system, and an annex of basic statistical tables. Volumes II and III contained detailed analyses of various economic and social sectors. All citations and quotations used in this book refer to Volume I. For an overview of China's historical development, see pp. 36–38.

Members of another economic mission visited China twice in 1984, for four weeks in February/March, and for five weeks in April/May. They prepared a report entitled *China: Long-Term Issues and Options* (Baltimore and London: Johns Hopkins Press for The World Bank, 1985), which examines China's prospects for economic growth over the next twenty years. The report, published in late 1985, encompasses a Main Report and six annexes on education, agriculture, energy, an explanation of a twenty-sector model of the Chinese economy with three alternative growth projections, China's economic structure in international perspective, and transport. All of the citations and quotations from the second mission that appear in this book were taken from the Main Report.

4. Maurice Collis, *Foreign Mud: The Opium Imbroglio at Canton in the 1830s and the Anglo-Chinese War* (New York: W.W. Norton and Company, 1968).

5. Two thorough accounts of modern Chinese history are Immanuel C.Y. Hsu, *The Rise of Modern China* (New York: Oxford University Press, 1970); and Li Chien-nung, *The Political History of China 1840–1928* (Princeton, N.J.: D. Van Nostrand Company, Inc., 1956).

6. *All About Shanghai: A Standard Guidebook with an Introduction by H.J. Lethbridge* (Hong Kong: Oxford University Press, 1983), p. 38. The 1983 version is a reissue of the original 1934–1935 edition (Shanghai: University Press, 1934).

7. A good summary of physical setting and population appears in Chu-yuan Cheng, *China's Economic Development: Growth and Structural Change* (Boulder, Colo.: Westview Press, 1982), pp. 1–5. A summary of demographic and natural-resource statistics is presented in *Statistical Yearbook of China 1985*, compiled by the State Statistical Bureau, PRC (Hong Kong: Economic Information and Agency, 1985), pp. 3–5.

8. The Chinese words for law (*fa*) and politics (*zhi*) contain a symbol (i.e., a radical) that means water. The etymology of the Chinese language implies that law making and the exercise of political power were synonymous with the administrative ability to control China's rivers.

9. *Statistical Yearbook of China 1985*, p. 3.

10. Basil Ashton, Kenneth Hill, Alan Piazza, and Robin Zeitz, "Famine in China, 1958–61," *Population and Development Review* 10, no. 4 (December 1984), pp. 613–645.

11. *China: Socialist Economic Development*, p. 231.

12. *Statistical Yearbook of China 1985*, p. 186.

13. The prospect of a Malthusian trap ensnaring China is expressed in Thomas G. Rawski, *Economic Growth and Employment in China* (New York: Oxford University Press for the World Bank, 1979), p. 122.

14. See Chu-yuan Cheng, *China's Economic Development*, pp. 6–17. See also *Statistical Yearbook of China 1985*, p. 3.

15. See *China: Socialist Economic Development*, Volume II (Washington, D.C.: World Bank, 1983), pp. 180–270 for a comprehensive analysis of China's energy sector. See also Annex C, "Energy," of the World Bank's 1985 report entitled *China: Long-Term Issues and Options*.

16. Jan S. Prybyla, "Key Issues in the Chinese Economy," *Asian Survey* 21, no. 9 (September 1981), pp. 945–946.

17. The next few paragraphs draw from *China: Socialist Economic Development*, pp. 41–44.

18. In addition to *All About Shanghai*, a valuable collection of essays on Shanghai's past and present contributions to China's development appears in Christopher Howe, ed., *Shanghai: Revolution and Development in an Asian Metropolis* (Cambridge: Cambridge University Press, 1981). See also Rhoads Murphey, *Shanghai: Key to Modern China* (Cambridge: Harvard University Press, 1953); and Noel Barber, *The Fall of Shanghai* (New York: Coward, McCann & Geoghegan, 1979).

19. Lucian W. Pye, "Foreword," in Christopher Howe, ed., *Shanghai*, pp. xii–xiii.

20. Rhoads Murphey, *Shanghai*, pp. 65, 116–132.

21. Ibid., p. 121.

22. Ibid., pp. 166–170.
23. Ibid., pp. 19–24.
24. *All About Shanghai*, p. 13; and Rhoads Murphey, *Shanghai*, pp. 15–19.
25. Rhoads Murphey, *Shanghai*, pp. 45–56.
26. *All About China*, pp. 4–12.
27. Rhoads Murphey, *Shanghai*, p. 11–12.
28. Noel Barber, *The Fall of Shanghai*, pp. 25–26.
29. *All About Shanghai*, pp. 14–21.
30. Ibid., pp. 21–26. See also Marie-Claire Bergère, "The Other China: Shanghai from 1919 to 1949," in Christopher Howe, ed., *Shanghai*, pp. 6–7.
31. *All About Shanghai*, p. 38.
32. Marie-Claire Bergère, "The Other China," p. 7; and Rhoads Murphey, *Shanghai*, p. 16.
33. Marie Claire-Bergère, "The Other China," p. 12.
34. Ibid., p. 14.
35. Ibid., p. 3.
36. Rhoads Murphey, *Shanghai*, pp. 7–9.
37. See Marie Claire-Bergère, "The Other China," pp. 16–20. See also Park M. Coble, *The Shanghai Capitalists and the Nationalist Government, 1927–1937* (Cambridge: Harvard University Press, 1980). Coble argues that the common generalization that Chiang Kai-shek's regime was closely allied with the capitalists in Shanghai during 1927–1937 is incorrect; rather, the Nationalists sought to control the capitalists politically and economically.
38. Marie Claire-Bergère, "The Other China," pp. 21–22.
39. Ibid.
40. Constitutions in mainland China were designed to outline political goals as well as to establish a state structure. Thus there was a need to adopt a new constitution after major political upheavals. Each new state constitution since 1954 was preceded by a new party charter: Party charters in 1969, 1973, 1977, and September 1982 preceded new constitutions in the National People's Congress (NPC) in 1970, 1975, 1978, and December 1982. The 1982 constitution represented significant progress in the legal development of China, restoring numerous provisions from 1954 that had been suspended in the intervening years. In it, Deng Xiaoping strengthened the role of the National People's Congress vis-à-vis the Communist Party in matters of law making. Indeed, the fifth draft was prepared by the NPC, not by the Communist Party. See Constance A. Johnson, "The 1982 Constitution of the PRC: One Small Step for Legal Development," *Journal of Chinese Studies* 2, no. 1 (April 1985), pp. 87–93.
   In "Some Key Aspects of the 1982 Draft Constitution of the People's Republic of China," *The China Quarterly*, no. 91 (September 1982), pp. 492–506, Byron Weng argues that the fifth constitution more directly bound the Communist Party to abide by the basic law; that it embraced economic revisionism, thus protecting the lawful rights and interests of the "individual" economy, with clear references to market regulation as a balance to the collective economy; and, that it strengthened the state machinery of government, by stressing the rule of law. Retrenchment included repealing from earlier constitutions the freedom to strike and speak out freely. Only time will tell whether the government honors the letter and spirit of the fifth constitution more faithfully than those of earlier renditions.

41. *The Constitution of the People's Republic of China* (promulgated for implementation on December 4, 1982) (Beijing: Foreign Languages Press, 1983). China's constitution can be amended by a simple majority vote of the National People's Congress.

42. See, for example, Fox Butterfield, *China: Alive in the Bitter Sea* (New York: Times Books, 1982); Steven W. Mosher, *Broken Earth: The Rural Chinese* (New York: Free Press, 1983); and Amnesty International's 1978 report on "Political Imprisonment in the People's Republic of China."

43. Christopher Howe, *China's Economy: A Basic Guide* (New York: Basic Books, Inc., 1978); p. 32 and Gregory C. Chow, *The Chinese Economy* (New York: Harper & Row, 1985), p. 69.

44. When Deng Xiaoping assumed power, greater emphasis was placed on developing state institutions. Because economic development was his top priority, state institutions were entrusted with greater responsibility in economic affairs. The National People's Congress met more frequently, its standing committee met virtually without recess, the State Council called numerous national conferences, the old network of auxiliary national organizations was revitalized, and veteran cadres in both party and government were coaxed into retirement. The role of the party in economic policy was played down. See Lowell Dittmer, "Ideology and Organization in Post-Mao China," *Asian Survey*, 24, no. 3 (March 1984), pp. 349–369.

To improve efficiency in the performance of the state's economic activities, Deng Xiaoping bought out large numbers of high level bureaucrats. He planned to merge twelve ministries and commissions into six, and to reduce the number of ministers, vice-ministers, directors, and deputy directors by more than half. He also proposed to remove 200,000 cadres from central-level posts in the party, government, and military—a one-third reduction. See Hong-yung Lee, "Deng Xiaoping's Reform of the Chinese Bureaucracy," *Journal of Northeast Asian Studies* 1, no. 2 (June 1982), pp. 21–35.

45. Christopher Howe, *China's Economy*, pp. 32–38.

46. For a model of how a centrally planned economy is supposed to work, see Gregory Chow, *The Chinese Economy*, p. 41–52. Throughout his analysis, Chow shows that China's attempts at central planning imposed inefficiencies on the economy as compared with the way in which a free-market economy would work.

Jan S. Prybyla has written a series of articles in which he analyzes some of the structural problems the Chinese encountered in their attempts to implement central planning. See "Changes in the Chinese Economy: An Interpretation," *Asian Survey* 19, no. 5 (May 1979), pp. 409–435; "Key Issues in the Chinese Economy," *Asian Survey* 21, no. 9 (September 1981), pp. 925–946; "Where Is China's Economy Headed? A Systems Analysis," *Journal of Northeast Asian Studies* 1, no. 4 (December 1982), pp. 3–24; and "Economic Problems of Communism: A Case Study of China," *Asian Survey* 22, no. 12 (December 1982), pp. 1206–1237. Another account of the weaknesses in planning is found in Audrey Donnithorne, "The Chinese Economy Today," *Journal of Northeast Asian Studies* 2, no. 3 (September 1983), pp. 3–21.

47. Nicholas R. Lardy, *Agricultural Prices in China,* World Bank staff working papers, no. 606 (Washington, D.C.: World Bank, 1983); and Robert C. Hsu, "Agricultural Financial Policies in China, 1949–80," *Asian Survey* 22, no. 7 (July 1982), pp. 638–658.

48. See Jan S. Prybyla, "Economic Problems of Communism," pp. 1218–1219.

49. *China: Socialist Economic Development,* pp. 48–49.
50. Gregory C. Chow, *The Chinese Economy,* p. 44.
51. *China: Socialist Economic Development,* p. 49.
52. Jan S. Prybyla, "Economic Problems of Communism," pp. 1219–1220.
53. Jan S. Prybyla, "Changes in the Chinese Economy," pp. 411–413.
54. Jan S. Prybyla, "Where Is China's Economy Headed?" pp. 8–11.
55. Jan S. Prybyla, "Key Issues in the Chinese Economy," p. 932.
56. Ibid., pp. 932–933.
57. Audrey Donnithorne, "The Chinese Economy Today," p. 4.
58. *China: Socialist Economic Development,* p. 53.
59. Ibid., p. 54.
60. Jan S. Prybyla, "Key Issues in the Chinese Economy," pp. 935–938.
61. *China: Socialist Economic Development,* p. 148.
62. Some political analysts have claimed that factionalism is at the heart of Chinese politics. A review of both pre- and post-Mao Zedong politics reveals ongoing policy disputes and abrupt shifts in the balance of influence among groups at the top. See Carol Lee Hamrin, "Competing 'Policy Packages' in Post-Mao China," *Asian Survey* 24, no. 5 (May 1984), pp. 487–518. For a detailed exposition of the influence of different factions in the formulation of economic policy during 1978–1981, see Dorothy J. Solinger, "The Fifth National People's Congress and the Process of Policy Making: Reform, Readjustment, and the Opposition," *Asian Survey* 22, no. 12 (December 1982), pp. 1238–1275.
63. Hsin Chang documents three instances of capital overinvestment crises since 1949—namely, the Great Leap Forward, the 1970 crash program, and the rush to invest in the immediate aftermath of the Cultural Revolution. The three crises had in common the causes of excessive ambition and irrational planning. See "The 1982–83 Overinvestment Crisis in China," *Asian Survey* 24, no. 12 (December 1984), pp. 1284–1285.
64. *China: Socialist Economic Development,* pp. 50–53.
65. Audrey Donnithorne, "The Chinese Economy Today," p. 14.
66. *Statistical Yearbook of China 1985,* p. 524.
67. Jung-Chao Liu, "Wages and Profits of Selected Industries in China," *Economic Development and Cultural Change* 26, no. 4 (July 1978), pp. 747–761.
68. Nicholas Lardy, *Agricultural Prices in China,* pp. 64–66.
69. For a general review of money and banking, see Katharine H.Y. Hsiao, *Money and Banking in the Chinese Mainland,* Mainland China Economic Series No. 1 (Taipei: Chung-Hua Institution for Economic Research, 1984).
70. Marie-Claire Bergère, "The Other China," p. 27.
71. Paul D. Reynolds, *China's International Banking and Financial System* (New York: Praeger Publishers, 1982), pp. 6–13.
72. *Statistical Yearbook of China 1985,* p. 530.
73. The definition of a correctly valued exchange rate is one that would prevail under conditions of free trade, which excludes restrictions of any sort on imports or exports. A correctly valued exchange rate equates domestic and world prices by allowing buyers and sellers to conduct their exchanges on a least-cost basis in both domestic and international markets so that each country exploits its comparative advantage in any good or service.

Evidence that the yuan was overvalued is found both in the introduction of a special scrip for foreigners to act as a foreign-currency certificate and in the existence of currency black markets, in which the yuan was sometimes valued at only one-third to one-fourth the official rate. Between the end of

1983 and late-1986, the Central Bank of China took a series of measures to correct the gross overvaluation of the yuan. It devalued China's currency from a rate of US$1 = 2.02 yuan to US$ = 3.71 yuan. The fact that the black market rate in Hong Kong in mid-1986 exceeded US$1 = 5 yuan suggests that the yuan was still overvalued against its free-trade exchange rate.

74. The figures that follow appear in Christopher Howe, *China's Economy*, p. 31. The annual edition of the *Statistical Yearbook of China* presents dozens of tables on agriculture and industry, including the composition of gross industrial and agricultural output value by type of ownership.

75. *China: Socialist Economic Development*, p. 56.

3

POLITICS TAKES COMMAND

Economic and political stability foster a healthy business climate. Continuity in economic policies allows investors, producers, and workers to make long-term calculations about acceptable levels of risk and profitable lines of work and business activity. On the other hand, frequent changes in the economic rules of the game create uncertainty. Political decisions that alter economic policies change rates of return on different investments, raise or lower cost/price calculations for producers of different commodities, and enhance or diminish incentives for people to work. For example, higher taxes may discourage investment and work; subsidies may lure investment to otherwise unprofitable endeavors; regulations may raise production costs, thus dampening output; printing money to cover budget deficits may stoke inflationary fires, driving up interest rates and borrowing costs in the process; and restrictions on international trade may force producers to substitute higher-cost domestic inputs.

When policies change in a market economy, prices adjust to revalue assets and to balance supply and demand. But the adjustment mechanism in a planned economy is not so simple or straightforward. Planners must redo millions of input-output calculations depending on the extent of change. The history of post-1952 mainland economic policy is replete with constant shifts in emphasis and direction. Sometimes political leaders carefully thought out changes in policy and announced them well in advance. At other times, they adopted new policies in midstream, giving planners no time to adjust the calculations that went into preparing the annual or five-year plans.

To take but one example, Mao Zedong tried to condense fifteen years of planned rural collectivization into one year when he declared the Great Leap Forward in 1958. As a result, massive short-run dislocations in output were largely responsible for the economic depression

45

of 1959–1961. It took the planners three years to rebuild the economy and put growth on an upward path.

Oscillation has characterized economic policy ever since the Chinese Communist Party came to power.[1] In China's centrally controlled economy, political leaders determined economic policy. They set general guidelines that informed party and state workers, who exercised day-to-day authority over individual workshops and production teams.

Economic policy shifts in China were frequent. No less than nine major developmental strategies have been installed since 1949.[2] In sequential order, they were (1) period of recovery, 1949–1952, (2) first five-year plan, emphasizing heavy industry following the Stalinist model, 1953–1957, (3) the Great Leap Forward following the extreme Maoist model, 1958–1960, (4) period of readjustment and retrenchment from Mao's policy of communization, 1961–1965, (5) the Cultural Revolution following the Maoist model, 1966–1970, (6) period of readjustment, 1971–1975, (7) the "Gang of Four" ultra-leftist model, 1975–1976, (8) the new great leap forward, 1977–1978, and (9) period of readjustment as well as the "Four Modernizations" and the "Open Door Policy," which introduced liberal reforms, 1978–1985.

At least three camps pursued different overall objectives: The "radicals" sought to achieve the Communist ideal of absolute equality; the "bureaucrats" emphasized state control and central planning; and the "marketeers" pushed a complementary role for markets and prices in a general system of state ownership.[3] These camps differed on questions concerning the speed and scope of economic nationalization, on whether "reds" or "experts" should be in charge of economic decisions, on the role of the market (e.g., private plots, free fairs, incentives in the form of wage bonuses), on the role autarky in heavy industry, on the extent of central dominance or the flexibility of commune management of its own goods, on the proper degree of central budget control or provincial autonomy, on the role of foreign trade, and on how to resolve crises, among many topics. Different factions prevailed at different times, thus causing major swings in overall policy. Party officials sometimes reversed course in the midst of a five-year plan.

This chapter examines the evolution and culmination of the "leftist" model of central planning, which fell from favor after 1976. Chapter 4 describes the systematic efforts made since 1978 to liberalize the rural, urban, industrial, and trading sectors of the economy after the defeat of the ultra-leftist "Gang of Four."

EVOLUTION OF DEVELOPMENT STRATEGIES

Twelve years of continuous warfare between 1937 and 1949 left China's economy in tatters. Industrial production was 70 percent beneath peak 1930s' levels, and agricultural output was off 30 percent. The infrastructure sustained severe war damage. Therefore, the urgent tasks confronting China's new Communist masters were to stabilize the economy, control inflation, and restore both production and distribution.[4] As described in Chapter 2, the party took control over the monetary and fiscal systems, quickly bringing inflation under control. It also fulfilled its revolutionary promise of land to the tillers by implementing a comprehensive land reform, which distributed land and other agricultural assets to the rural population, simultaneously eliminating the political and economic power of landlords. The resumption of peace brought agricultural output up to peak pre-1949 levels in three short years.

The party did not immediately socialize industry, which, along with retail shops and the service sector, remained in private hands. By 1952, the industrial sector had largely recovered from wartime damage.

Rehabilitation of the national economy was completed in late 1952, thus freeing party planners to ponder how best to attain a large-scale industrialization plan. Of greatest appeal to Mao and his colleagues was the Soviet model of forced industrialization under Stalin's rule. The Soviets, ideological kinsmen of the Chinese Communists, were also a likely source of aid and technical assistance. Lacking any other experience in hands-on economic management, and engaged in the Korean War against the United States and its allies, China gravitated toward the Soviet model.

The basic outline of the Soviet model included high rates of capital formation, priority for heavy industry, concentrated investments in large plants, and the squeezing of agriculture through procurement of crops at below-market prices to support industry. The first five-year plan, 1953–1957 (which was not officially published until 1955), followed this model. The planners raised the proportion of national income allocated to investment, which they financed by taxing agriculture and state-owned enterprises. They collectivized agriculture and gradually placed industry and commerce under state control. They instituted compulsory purchases of grain and cotton and rationing of certain consumer goods. The initial five-year plan turned in a solid economic performance. The combined gross output value of agriculture and industry rose 68 percent. Agricultural output increased 25 percent. Reflecting the plan's emphasis on industrial development, industrial output rose 128 percent, with heavy industry up 210 percent. Capital formation quadrupled, and foreign trade grew two-thirds.[5]

Buoyed by favorable results, Mao Zedong launched the most extraordinary economic adventure the world has ever seen—the Great Leap Forward of 1958. He combined agricultural cooperatives into communes, which mobilized surplus labor for collective work on irrigation, flood control, and small-scale rural industrial production to complement the capital-intensive industrial sector. The government confiscated private plots, abolished rural free markets, and distributed grain on an egalitarian basis. To Mao's dismay, grain output fell 20 percent in 1960 from 1957 levels, causing widespread famine and an estimated 30 million unnecessary deaths during 1958–1962. Industrial production suffered similar disruption. In contrast with an 18 percent annual increase in gross industrial output value during 1953–1957, increases averaged a meager 3.8 percent during 1958–1962. Both light and heavy industrial output fell in real terms during 1961 and 1962.[6]

Mao temporarily conceded the formation of economic policy to his opponents. The fourth stage (1961–1965) was a period of economic readjustment, featuring the reintroduction of private plots, the withdrawal of all Soviet technicians, and an emphasis on agricultural growth and consumer goods over capital-goods heavy industry. Industrial investment shifted to support farming in such areas as chemical fertilizers and agricultural machinery. "Self-reliance" replaced dependence on foreign assistance, and population control received priority. Material incentives were reemphasized, and workers and employees received a pay increase.

Incessant change is the watchword of Chinese economic policy. Taking revenge against his opponents, Mao launched an even more aggressive assault on "capitalist road" tendencies in 1966. He urged millions of Red Guards to assault the Chinese economic and administrative system to transfer power from the pragmatic economic planners to the radical elements of the Communist Party. The Great Proletarian Cultural Revolution (1966–1976), a longer replay of the Great Leap Forward, subverted material incentives in production, replaced skilled personnel with ideologues, and forcibly resettled 16 million urban dwellers in rural and border areas.

Within the decade of the Cultural Revolution, economic policy oscillated. Between 1966 and 1970, the government abolished workers' bonuses, curtailed peasants' private plots, and restricted the range of commodities that could be offered for sale in rural free markets. Revolutionary committees replaced technical managerial personnel in industry. To counteract declining output, readjustments were implemented between 1971 and 1975 that restored experienced administrators to factories, and the country was reopened to foreign trade. In early 1976, the ultra-leftist radicals, led by four Shanghainese known as the Gang of Four (which included Mao's wife, Jiang Qing), again gained the upper hand. They capped incomes, minimized wage differentials, and reduced imports in a new great leap. Prices and wages remained frozen throughout this decade of economic madness.

The demise of Mao in September 1976 brought down the ultra-leftists. The arrest of the Gang of Four in October 1976 terminated a quarter-century of erratic twists and turns in development, in which periods of radical experimentation alternated with periods of retreat and adjustment. Under Deng Xiaoping's direction, China in 1978 announced its "Four Modernizations" campaign, which brought forth a variety of liberal rural and industrial reforms.

AGRICULTURE

The broad outlines of institutional change in agriculture have already been set forth. Party leaders implemented land reform between 1949 and 1952, collectivized agriculture during the next five years, and boldly leapt into rural communism in April 1958. Decentralization restored primacy first to the production brigade in 1960 and then to smaller production teams in 1961. Private plots and rural fairs waxed and waned. Farmers rarely knew from one year to the next how their livelihood would be affected by changing policies.[7]

Against this backdrop of institutional change, several features of Chinese agriculture remained constant.[8] Government and party officials restricted labor mobility, assigned labor and material inputs, set quotas and procurement prices for agricultural products below those that would prevail at free-market levels, kept economic decisions in the hands of production teams or other units higher than farm households, and handled all trade and distribution in the countryside. Production units had no conception of, nor were they required to pay for, the costs of some of their inputs. No matter how hard individual farmers worked, additional efforts did not necessarily translate into additional personal rewards. The costs of inputs and the benefits of hard work applied only to the limited existence of private plots and rural markets, when these were allowed to flourish.

Returning to the details of agricultural policy, Mao decided to speed up rural collectivization in 1955. He consolidated the mutual-aid teams (collections of households) that were formed in 1951 into elementary cooperatives (larger units of agricultural organization) by 1955. He transformed these into advanced cooperatives (larger units still) in 1956, and abolished private ownership of land. By early 1958, he had formed 26,000 rural communes, the highest and most populous form of rural collectivization, which contained 98.2 percent of all peasant households.

Mao hoped the communes would destroy traditional family organization. Communes operated their own economic and social enterprises, distributed income according to earned work points, forced everyone to eat together in public mess halls, and organized labor into 3 million production teams. The commune administration, in its most advanced phase, confiscated all private property, including private plots, private consumer goods, houses, bank deposits, and domestic animals. It literally tried to exterminate rural private markets and replaced material incentives with ideological norms to increase production. It ordered women into the rural labor force. Some regions of China escaped the full brunt of Mao's communization program, but the aggregate economic effects of his strategy were devastating.

The rural economy contracted sharply. Grain output declined by one-quarter in two years, from 220 million tons in 1958 to about 158 million tons in 1960, causing widespread famine. Grain production did not recover to 1958 levels until 1966. Rice production plummeted by one-third.[9] Thomas Rawski summarized the consequences of Mao's efforts at rural communization: "The disastrous harvests of 1959–61 . . . stemmed from unrealistic ambitions, inexperienced management, and the erosion of incentives associated with egalitarian distribution of income at the commune level."[10]

Agriculture Procurement and Pricing

The central characteristic of Chinese agriculture before 1978 was the virtual regulation of all prices.[11] The government exercised strict control over agricultural prices to accomplish the objectives of stable prices for urban consumers and to transfer resources from agriculture to finance industrial expansion through the implicit tax of compulsory, below-market-price state procurement.

The government procured grain by two methods. The first was a direct agricultural tax, which was a specified share of "normal" output. This category was termed "public grain" or "requisition grain." It took between 11 and 14 percent of farm output during the 1950s but settled at 6 percent or less after 1960.[12] The government often exempted poor collectives and households from this tax.

The second, and by far the more important, method of procurement, by which more than 80 percent of grain procurement took place, was the system of "unified purchases"—that is, centralized planning and state monopoly at state-set prices. Between 1952 and 1978, the government procured no less than 20 percent of all grain output; the percentage hovered at 30 and above in the late 1950s and early 1960s.[13] (Most grain was consumed locally in the countryside.)

For purposes of pricing and market distribution, the government officially classified agricultural products into three categories according to their importance. "First-category products" included major crops such as grains, cotton, soybeans, rapeseed, and peanuts. These products were subjected to a system of unified planned purchase, under which the State Planning Commission set annual compulsory delivery quotas by product for each province, which in turn were disaggregated into quotas for each production team. The State Council set the procurement prices. First-category products were rationed to consumers at state-set retail prices.

"Second-category products" encompassed more than 100 items, including pork, dairy products, sugar, hides, wool, marine products, and fruit. The state commercial departments purchased these under the system of "unified purchase" at state-set prices. However, collectives were permitted to sell above-quota products on the open market at market prices. Second-category products were generally not rationed to consumers.

"Third-category products" included minor local products and sideline products such as medicinal herbs, poultry, and animal by-products. They were not procured within the quota system but, rather, were sold on rural free markets. When free markets were suspended during periods of ideological fervor, peasants sold third-category products to state-run supply and marketing cooperatives at "negotiated prices."

Government procurement of agricultural products subject to unified purchase was based on a scheme of ascending prices—quota purchases, above-quota purchases, and negotiated purchases. The government listed an initial low purchase price for a fixed quota of cereals and other products. The price was so low relative to the prices of other agricultural products and prices that would prevail in free rural markets that peasants made little money in selling quota grain to the state. Peasants facetiously termed the quota purchases "patriotic grain."

Once peasants fulfilled the quota requirement, they sold additional grain to the state at a higher, above-quota purchase price. The government set targets for above-quota purchases but imposed no penalties for failure to meet these targets. Although above-quota prices often ranged 30–50 percent higher than initial quota prices, they, too, were invariably below market prices.

Grain sales beyond the above-quota amounts were sold at even higher "negotiated prices," but this category of state grain purchases was relatively unimportant until the 1980s. It constituted only 3.6 percent of state-purchased grain as late as 1978.

For first-category products in excess of "negotiated" sales, for above-quota second-category products, and for all third-category products, the applicable price was that which prevailed in rural or urban markets—the free-market highest price.

Varying the size of the quotas and the purchase prices determined both the level of implicit taxes and rural incomes. The larger the initial fixed quota, the greater the tax imposed on peasants, inasmuch as the initial purchase prices were invariably well below levels that prevailed in private markets. Some products, such as cotton, could not be legally sold in rural markets.

The state approximately doubled procurement prices between 1950 and 1976, but the upward revisions occurred in just two installments. Reflecting market forces, it increased prices by one-third between 1950 and 1953, when unified purchase of first-category commodities began. Thereafter, the government modestly raised prices by 13 percent during the first five-year plan. It granted the bulk of the remaining increase, a 20–30 percent upward revision, to stimulate production after the collapse of the Great Leap Forward. Between 1966 and 1978, wheat, rice, and corn prices remained unchanged.

Free markets allow people to bid freely for the use of resources in production, and this process of bidding determines their correct price or opportunity cost. Since China generally lacked free agricultural markets, it is hard to know the true cost of labor and capital inputs. Nicholas Lardy estimated that procurement prices fell below production costs.[14] Producing below cost was accomplished by depreciating the value of a labor day, squeezing internal reinvestment, and reducing consumption. Surveys of agricultural operations disclosed that the value of a labor day declined 20 percent from 0.70 to 0.56 yuan per day between 1965 and 1978. Losses as a share of production costs ranged from 15 to 18 percent. As previously noted, the state sold chemical fertilizers and agricultural machinery to farmers at above-market prices, constituting another form of taxation.

The counterpart to below-market procurement prices was subsidies to urban consumers and state employees. The price of rationed urban grain and other commodities was generally set below procurement prices. In addition, the administration of coupon rationing for 160 million people was costly. The total value of food subsidies, directed at about one-sixth of the population, consumed as much as one-quarter of public revenue.

The government prohibited long-distance private transport of cereals and most other agricultural commodities. Marketing was confined to producers, not traders, within limited rural markets.

Declining Efficiency in Agriculture

Between 1957 and 1975, inputs in agricultural production increased sharply. The rural labor force, with a participation rate that remained relatively constant at about 45 percent, grew by more than 100 million people, with no significant addition to cultivated acreage.[15] Reclamation efforts barely kept pace with the alienation of arable land to housing, industrial construction, roads, and irrigation projects. Supplies of industrial inputs, including power, machinery, building materials, steel, petroleum products, and chemical fertilizer, increased at average annual rates of 20–25 percent. Rural electrification and farm machinery mechanized grain processing, spinning, irrigation, threshing, transport, and land preparation, thus substantially reducing human and animal labor requirements.

Much of this labor was redirected into intensified cropping practices, largely in the application of organic fertilizers to prepare land for cultivation. Collecting, preparing, and applying organic fertilizer consumed enormous quantities of labor, up to 30–40 percent of total manpower and animal power during the year. Increased farm labor also intensified the cropping cycle, raising the index of multiple cropping (growing more than one crop of any given product per year) and intercropping (simultaneous cultivation of more than one crop in a single field). Labor-intensive rural products, such as silkworm cocoons, grew more rapidly than the output of grain crops. Rice cultivation, twice as labor-intensive as wheat, spread northward. Vast manpower was also absorbed during the winter months in water-conservancy and land-improvement projects.

By 1975, rural idleness had been greatly reduced. The average number of work-days for each farm laborer stood at 272–284, up sharply from

175–190 in the late 1950s. Yet, despite the greater utilization of manpower, as many as 200 million peasants still had per capita incomes below subsistence levels, reflecting sharp regional differences in agricultural output.

How did agricultural efficiency fare during this period? The annual output of the average member of China's rural work force did not decline even though nearly 100 million members had been added to the labor force. However, when productivity is measured in output per man-day (the number of man-days rose by nearly half), the fall in output per man-day ranged between 15 and 36 percent (depending on the assumptions chosen concerning the labor-intensity of cultivation and fertilizer preparation).

Estimates of total factor productivity in agriculture—including labor, land, current inputs, and capital—revealed a decrease of one-third to one-quarter between 1957 and 1975.[16] As against 1957, each additional unit of input produced between only two-thirds to three-quarters of an additional unit of output in 1975. Low productivity in agriculture reflected politically imposed organizational deficiencies. In particular, curtailed migration and limited private plots restricted individual incentives to produce more and to make investments in the land they worked to produce still more in future years.

Rural Consumption

How did peasants fare under state-controlled agricultural activity between 1952 and 1978? What was left for individual peasants to consume after the government diverted much of their effort to industrial investment through the taxes of agricultural procurement at below-market prices and the sale of agricultural inputs at above-market prices?

Grain output grew each year from 2 to 2.5 percent between 1952 and 1975 (grain represents about four-fifths of China's total food supply).[17] However, grain growth barely exceeded annual population growth of about 2 percent. In the two six-year periods 1953–1958 and 1970–1975, the average level of grain consumption in the entire country remained virtually unchanged.

Consumption of food grain, the source of 80–90 percent of all caloric intake, declined by 3.2 percent between 1957 and 1979, from 448 pounds to 430 pounds per capita. In particular, it reflected a 5.9 percent reduction in average cereal consumption by the peasantry due to a worsening in the distribution of income.[18] Although consumption of sugar, fruit and meat modestly increased, consumption of edible vegetable oils, soybean products, and cereals declined to produce an overall per capita food intake in 1978 below the 2,000–2,100 level of 1957. After twenty years of Communist rule, peasants had little to show in the way of increased living standards.

Trends in consumption may also be judged on the basis of data on personal incomes, although care must be used in interpreting Chinese statistics to take into account changes in the price level, the inaccuracy of survey data, labor-force participation rates, and the value of state-provided subsidies. Thus, although personal income per commune member grew from 73 yuan in 1957 to 133.5 yuan in 1978 (these figures include income derived from collective sources, private sideline production by households, and transfer payments), most of the increase represented rising prices rather than rising real farm income. Moreover, the female labor-force participation rate increased sharply, reducing the number of dependents per rural worker from 2.3 to 1.06. Finally, subsidies for consumption were allocated almost exclusively to the nonagricultural population. Thus, increases in the personal income of peasants expressed in yuan were largely illusory.[19]

In a paper prepared for the Joint Economic Committee of the United States Congress, Robert Dernberger specifically focused on the rural population.[20] Between 1955 and 1977, the total annual per capita disposable income of peasants increased by 17 yuan (which was equivalent to US$10 at the then official exchange rate of US$1 = 1.7 yuan). Using data collected from four surveys conducted between the 1950s and 1970s, Chinese economist Yang Janming concluded that the per capita real income of farm families did not materially increase between 1955 and 1977.[21] Gregory Chow estimated that per capita agricultural consumption increased at a maximum of 22.2 percent during 1957–1975.[22] The World Bank claimed a 1.3 percent annual increase in national per capita consumption from 1957 to 1977, but noted that per capita personal income in urban areas grew nearly twice as fast as that for peasants.[23] Furthermore, two-fifths of the total increase in consumption during 1957–1979 occurred between 1977 and 1979, after new rural reforms had taken hold.

In 1978, two years after the death of Mao Zedong and the arrest of the Gang of Four, per capita rural income from all sources was estimated at 143 yuan (US$84). But the distribution of rural income was uneven. As many as 200 million peasants received annual incomes of less than 100 yuan, which was below the subsistence level of 120 yuan.[24] Although the average peasant income was marginally above subsistence, nearly a third of the production teams had per capita incomes below subsistence and depended on a mixture of state and family assistance. As late as 1979, more than 100 million people were consuming just over 1 pound of food per day, much in coarse grains.[25]

No matter which estimate is used, the annual percentage increase in rural consumption was negligible. The state siphoned off any surplus in agricultural output produced between the early 1950s and late 1970s to finance industrial development and subsidize urban consumers. This was, after all, the strategy underpinning industrial policy—a policy that suppressed peasant living standards.

Several Chinese economists also evaluated the effects of agricultural policy prior to 1977. Ma Hong, president of the Chinese Academy of

Social Sciences and adviser to the State Planning Commission, criticized the harmful policies of the Great Leap Forward and the Cultural Revolution.[26] He noted that a predominantly rural population failed to attain national self-sufficiency in agricultural output, thus necessitating periodic grain imports. Moreover, slow growth in the output of other agricultural products retarded light industrial production.

Shifting from production to consumption, Ma observed that many peasants had fallen into dire straits by 1978. In 20 percent of all rural households, expenditures exceeded income. About 16.5 percent of the rural population received an average yearly income of 40 yuan ($1 = 1.7 yuan), well below the subsistence level. In addition, overemphasis on capital investment in industry suppressed peasant consumption levels.

In an essay devoted solely to agriculture, economists Zhan Wu and Liu Wenpu stated that rural policies stifled grain and marine-product consumption and caused per capita consumption of cotton and oil-bearing crops to decline.[27] They estimated that the average annual gain in consumption for peasants during the twenty years encompassed in 1957–1976 was 1.1 percent, which was two-thirds less than the total gains in peasant consumption during just the first five-year plan. Chinese and Western economists alike agree that peasant living standards stagnated for more than two decades following the completion of the first five-year plan in 1957.

INDUSTRY

From 1949 until 1978, the development of heavy industry was the major aim of Chinese economic policy. An overview of statistical evidence suggests that Chinese planners largely met that goal. Between 1952 and 1978, the index of gross industrial output value rose about sixteen times, and for heavy industry almost twenty-eight times.[28] The share of industry as a proportion of the combined gross output value of agriculture and industry rose from 30 percent in 1949 to 72 percent by 1978; it achieved an all-time high of 78 percent during the Great Leap Forward in 1960.[29]

The composition of industrial output changed in favor of such heavy industries as engineering and petroleum, which replaced textiles and food processing as the largest contributors to the value of output. Heavy industry increased as a share of overall industrial output value from 26.4 percent in 1949 to 56.9 percent by 1978, thus surpassing all years except for 1959–1961.[30]

The value of fixed assets in industrial enterprises rose from 10.7 billion to 300.2 billion yuan (in current prices).[31] Total industrial employment increased from 12.5 million in 1952 to 50 million in 1978; in state-owned industrial enterprises, employment rose sixfold from 5.1 million to 30.4 million.[32] In constant (inflation-adjusted) prices, output per person in state-owned industrial enterprises nearly tripled. Using Chinese figures, Gregory Chow calculated that the ratio of capital employed per worker in state-owned enterprises rose fivefold, from 2,102 yuan per worker to 10,464. Overall, he estimated that injections of new capital contributed about three-quarters, and additional labor about one-quarter, of the growth in industrial output.[33]

In general, industrial policy was more consistent than farm policy. Shortly after seizing power, the Communist government moved to gain control over the private sector in urban areas. By 1957, the state had absorbed or eliminated the entire private sector of several million private firms and tens of millions of independent peddlers and handicraftsmen, thereby eliminating the Chinese bourgeoisie as a political force.

Socialist Transformation of Industry

Chiang Kai-shek bequeathed to the Communists in 1949 a largely private-enterprise-based industrial sector.[34] Apart from those industries previously owned by his government, termed bureaucratic capitalist enterprises, foreign and Chinese capitalists owned the assets of major industrial enterprises, with small businessmen and handicraftsmen in charge of the traditional sector. In 1949, state-owned enterprises produced only about 35 percent of industrial output, handled 24 percent of wholesale trade, and carried on 15 percent of retail trade. By 1950, the state had confiscated all enterprises owned by the Nationalist government—nearly 2,900 industrial firms employing 750,000 workers. The state instantly controlled the production of electric power, coal, pig iron, steel, cement, cotton yarn, railways, modern communications and transport, and most of the banking and foreign trade.

Just prior to the outbreak of the Korean War in 1950, China began the process of confiscating the assets of foreign-owned enterprises. Their methods included higher taxes, restrictions on production and marketing, and the requirement that all Chinese employees be retained with no reduction in wages. British firms in Shanghai spent 375,000 pounds sterling each month to stay afloat, and the value of their shares declined to almost nothing. Under these impossible conditions, some firms closed and others transferred their property to the state without compensation.[35] The departure of British firms terminated Western investments in China. The Chinese and U.S. governments froze each other's assets in December 1950.

To avoid major economic disruptions, Mao Zedong initially instructed party cadres not to confiscate private-owned enterprises. It temporarily served the regime's interests for private capitalists to believe that the private and state sectors could coexist under Communist rule. During 1949–1952, the government placed orders with private firms to rehabilitate the economy and supply its Korean War effort. Indeed, the value of private industrial products rose 70 percent between 1949 and 1952, a period that also witnessed the return of those capitalists who had withdrawn their capital from China and moved to Hong Kong.

The Chinese Communist Party Central Committee originally accepted a moderate program for socialist transformation of the economy over a fifteen-year timetable. In early 1952, the government shifted course, launching a fierce attack on domestic capitalists: It accused them of tax evasion, bribery, theft of state property, cheating on government contracts, and stealing state information for private speculation. Under Mao Zedong's harsh criticisms of "rightist" tendencies, the process of socialist transformation was completed in five years. By the end of 1952, the state had nationalized private financial institutions, thus virtually eliminating the creation of private credit. It also eliminated goldsmiths, pawnshops, and firms dealing with overseas Chinese remittances, and closed the Shanghai stock exchange.

Between 1952 and 1953, the regime stepped up its restrictions. The "five anti-capitalists" campaign drove many businessmen to suicide.[36] Large fines exacted on the pretense of Korean War profiteering deprived private firms of their working capital. To replace the private sector, state corporations and stores expanded to complement the development of rural supply and marketing cooperatives. By the end of 1952, the state controlled 64 percent of wholesale trade, as against 24 percent in 1950, and the share of state control over retail trade had tripled to 43 percent. The state also monopolized foreign trade.

Private management of state-capitalist enterprises was converted to direct state management; interest payments to prior owners were reduced and completely eliminated in 1966. State commercial enterprises took over wholesale and retail distribution from private firms, and the government terminated the payments of annual profits to prior owners. As the climate for private business eroded, firms lost interest in improving or expanding their operations. The remaining private businessmen, resigned to fate, almost voluntarily changed over from private establishments to joint state-private operation, thus converting themselves from proprietors to state employees. Apart from the small interest payment they received, which averaged $44 per person each year, former capitalists lost all rights to the use of their property.

By 1956, the private sector had disappeared; the state directly produced 68 percent of output, and joint enterprises accounted for the balance. Private commerce declined from 85 percent of retail sales in 1950 to less than 3 percent by 1957. Handicraft cooperatives embraced 92 percent of the nation's 6 million handicraftsmen by 1956. Similarly, peddlers were absorbed into the supply and marketing cooperatives.

The elimination of foreign influence (apart from the Soviet Union) and the nationalization of the economy provided the regime with a basis for attempting the policy of central planning. It controlled the purchase and sale of all major commodities, having acquired industrial assets at well below cost.

Initially, China focused its planning efforts on such heavy industries as iron and steel, chemicals, metal processing, and machine-building capital goods, which they seized from the Nationalists. They accorded the defense industry high priority.

The planners regarded Soviet aid as a key to large-scale heavy industrial development and readily accepted Soviet offers of economic assistance. In any event, the Chinese were at war in Korea with the Western industrial democracies. By 1955, 156 Soviet-assisted major projects had become the backbone of modern Chinese industry. Together with 143 ancillary projects, these heavy industrial projects absorbed over half of all industrial development during the first five-year plan. The Soviets supplied between 50 and 70 percent of all equipment in these projects.

In 1960, the Soviets suspended technical aid due to irreconcilable ideological differences. China repaid all Soviet debts by 1964, well ahead of schedule. For the next decade, China pursued a go-it-alone approach, focusing on the renovation of older plants and the construction of new plants. The brief stress laid on rural industry during the Great Leap Forward disappeared on its collapse. During the relatively quiescent period of 1972 to 1974, China purchased more than 100 plants from Japan and Western Europe, concentrating on petroleum and chemical fertilizers. Apart from this brief outward-looking interlude, until Mao Zedong's death in 1976 and Deng Xiaoping's assumption of leadership on economic policy in 1978, China generally stressed autarky in heavy industry as the foundation of the economy.

The party and government met their objectives of socializing industry. In 1949, state-owned firms produced only 26.2 percent of gross industrial output value, compared with private firms, which produced 48.7 percent, and individually owned businesses, which accounted for 23 percent. Joint state-private firms supplied a negligible 1.6 percent. By 1957, the state had eliminated private firms and individual businesses, which jointly produced less than 1 percent of industrial output. In 1978, state-owned enterprises produced 81 percent of gross industrial output value, with rural collectives supplying the balance. Other economic forms of ownership largely ceased to exist.[37]

Industrial Efficiency

The regime met its first objective of a high investment rate. Investment as a share of national income ranged from a low of 10.4 percent in 1962 (the year after the severe depression of 1959–1961), to a high of 36.5 percent in 1978, although it exceeded 20 percent in every year but three.[38]

Given that virtually all investment went into industry, the composition of national income tilted toward industry. In 1952, agriculture contributed 57.7 percent of national income with industry at 19.5 percent, a ratio of three to one. By 1957, the comparative figures were 46.8 and 28.3 percent. At the end of the second five-year plan in 1962, the percentages were 48 and 32.8. Both agriculture and industry gained at the expense of the service sector, which was virtually eliminated during the socialist transformation of the economy. By 1978, industry had displaced agriculture as the leading source of national income, contributing 46.8 percent against 35.4 percent.[39] Throughout this period, construction and transportation retained their relative shares.

Within industry, emphasis was placed on heavy industry. Between 1949 and 1978, heavy industry grew from 26 percent to 57 percent of total gross output value of all industry; light industry correspondingly declined from 73 percent to 43 percent.[40] The five most rapidly growing branches of industry were petroleum, metallurgy, chemicals, machine building, and power. Consumer goods were short-changed in the process of industrialization. It was necessary to ration cloth, sewing machines, bicycles, watches, and other staples because supply could not accommodate demand at state-set prices, and the government was not prepared to risk open inflation by freeing prices to eliminate excess demand.

Earlier we noted Gregory Chow's calculation that additions of capital contributed three-quarters and labor one-quarter of the growth in industrial output. Given the relative abundance of labor to capital, which was disproportionately exacted by taxing several hundred million peasants, was scarce capital utilized efficiently?

Returns to invested capital declined during 1952–1979. In constant prices (adjusted for inflation), the ratio of capital to labor (i.e., the amount of yuan invested in state-owned industrial enterprises per worker) increased fivefold, from 2,102 yuan to 10,464. But the output per person in the same enterprises increased only 2.8 times, from 4,167 yuan to 11,790 yuan. Rising productivity was attributable to the increased amount of capital available to each worker. However, over this period, every 1 percent increase in the ratio of capital to labor increased productivity per worker by only 0.6 percent.[41]

Probing deeper, we discover the true damage of the Cultural Revolution. During 1966–1976, output per worker in state-owned industrial enterprises rose from 8,943 yuan to only 9,994 yuan (in constant 1970 prices), an 11 percent increase in a decade. Compare these ten years of dismal performance with the relatively successful growth in productivity during 1962–1965, when output per worker grew from 4,797 yuan to 8,943 yuan, a rise of 87 percent in just three years.[42] Political turmoil is clearly not conducive to economic efficiency.

Lack of economic efficiency entails, in part, the wasteful use of resources once they are allocated. Wasted potential in the Chinese economy took the form of low, stagnant, or declining factor productivity, high energy consumption, and financial mismanagement that resulted in losses and subsidies.

Total factor productivity—the returns to additional units of land, labor, and capital—rose during the first five-year plan (1953–1957). Thereafter, it declined during the 1960s and 1970s. Although labor productivity rose a modest 15 percent during 1957–1978, the productivity of capital fell to levels of one-third to one-half of those during 1953–1957.[43] At the end of the 1970s, every 100 yuan invested in capital construction yielded only 11 yuan in state revenues compared with 22 yuan during the first five-year plan. The state wasted large amounts of energy. During 1953–1957, 62,000 tons of coal were required to generate 100 million yuan of output; by 1979, the quantity had risen to 95,000 tons. Finally, declining industrial profitability reduced state receipts. In 1980, the average profit made by industrial enterprises from every 100 yuan of output was one-third lower than in 1957.[44]

Not only did state-owned enterprises remit fewer receipts per invested yuan, but the state increasingly subsidized firms with losses. The causes of rising subsidies, according to Prybyla, included the insulation of domestic producers from domestic users and foreign producers, the absence of competition among firms, guaranteed lifelong employment, the stress on quantity of output at the expense of costs, faulty computation of production costs, incorrect industrial wholesale prices, distorted relative prices, bottlenecks caused by imperfect central coordination of input-output decisions, and the importance attached to price stability.[45]

Robert Dernberger quantified the decline in total factor productivity in industry at an average annual rate of 2.75 percent between the early 1950s and 1979.[46] He blamed these inefficiencies on China's obsession with heavy industry. The planners developed excess capacity in industry, disregarded energy supplies, neglected infrastructure, and ignored the demand for its products.

World Bank figures show the link between internal stability and rates of economic growth.[47] Holding prices constant, the Bank reported high average annual growth in national income of 19.3 percent during the 1949–1952 rehabilitation period. The two distinguishing features of this first phase of Communist rule were the reestablishment of law and order and the government's heavy reliance on the private sector in both industry and agriculture.

Annual growth slowed to 8.9 percent during the first five-year plan period (1953–1957), but these rates gave hope that China could successfully modernize within a generation or two. The second five-year plan (1958–1962) destroyed these hopes: National income declined 3.1 percent on average each year due to the policy mistakes of the Great Leap Forward. Normalcy returned during the 1963–1965 adjustment period, and annual growth skyrocketed to 14.7 percent. During the next two five-year plans, average annual growth rates were 8.3 percent and 5.6 percent, respectively. But growth did not reflect rising efficiency in production; rather, it was the result of sharp increases in industrial inputs, including labor and especially capital.

Assuming that gross output figures reflect full economic scarcity costs, the World Bank estimated that annual average growth was 5.4 percent for the entire period 1957–1979. This was a positive achievement compared with many other less-developed countries in Asia and Latin America, and especially in Africa.

However, official Chinese and Western estimates of gross output value of industry must be accepted with reservation. The reason is that China lacked markets that would assign correct scarcity values for the output of each enterprise. In China, buyers and sellers could not bid against one another to determine the true value of economic resources. Gross output value was simply computed by multiplying quantities produced times official state-set prices. These calculations generated somewhat arbitrary numbers that failed to distinguish between useful and useless output.[48]

The World Bank reported, for example, that the prices of labor, energy, and many raw materials were divorced from true economic costs.[49] Machinery stood idle much of the time.[50] Large numbers of workers had little to do. It cited evidence of huge inventories, mismatches between supply and demand, inability to guarantee supplies, wasteful use of capital, and failure to properly maintain and use the limited amount of equipment available.[51] The bank assigned disproportionate blame to bureaucratic control of industry, in which economic decisions on the use of inputs were made without adequate consideration of cost, especially the failure of prices to reflect either cost or supply and demand conditions.[52]

Misallocation of resources is a hallmark of inefficiency. Steel output in 1979, for example, was 34.5 million tons, but 20 million tons of unmarketable steel lay in warehouses. The glut of steel reflected poor production decisions: Either it was the wrong assortment or quality; it could not be shipped due to lack of transportation capacity; or it could not be used because complementary building materials were missing. In general, industrial installations never fulfilled the planners' objectives. During the 1960s and 1970s, 81 large industrial installations failed, 40 were built in the wrong places, 27 never reached production capacity, 4 produced unusable products, and 9 remained unfinished.[53]

How have Chinese economists assessed the impact of central planning on industrial efficiency? The indictment of some is generally more severe than those of Western economists and institutions.[54] Ma Hong, for instance, cited declining returns to investment: During 1957–1978, the total output value produced per 100 yuan of industrial fixed assets fell 25.4 percent, whereas the profits and taxes (the single largest source of state revenue) turned over per 100 yuan of funds fell 30.3 percent. "With more input and less output, the economic results clearly declined."[55] Reasons for industrial inefficiency included overemphasis on new capital construction, neglecting improvement and modernization of existing plant and equipment, overproduction of primary and intermediate production to the detriment of consumer goods, and excessive capitalization of heavy industry.[56] Light industry remained backward.

Ma ascribed declining efficiency, in part, to hasty transformation of private to public ownership. The Chinese Communist Party, in his view, should not have rushed to eliminate the private sector. Ma cited as evidence both the decline in the number of self-employed urban laborers from 8.83 million in 1952 to 240,000 by 1975 and the collapse of commerce and the service trades.[57]

Economists Li Chengrui and Zhang Zhuoyuan supplied further details. Adjusting economic figures to eliminate what they call "political inflation," and compensating for "the inclusion of a considerable number of unsaleable and substandard products in the output value and national income," they concluded that per capita income showed no increase between 1966 and 1976.[58]

Although total national income rose during the Cultural Revolution, it was gained by greater investments of capital, manpower, and raw materials, "and not by raising economic efficiency or returns."[59] During 1966–1976, taxes and profits per 100 yuan of capital fell from 34.5 to 19.3, a drop of 44.1 percent. Taxes and profits realized from every 100 yuan of net fixed assets fell 37.8 percent, profits dropped 42.5 percent, and circulating funds rose 57 percent. The two economists inferred from the last number that the state purchased large quantities of substandard or reject products.

Two other economists, Liu Guoguang and Wang Ruisun, blamed declining industrial efficiency on "too much state control and too little power in the hands of the enterprises; unified state planning is too rigid and regulation through the market is not sufficiently used, and administrative instead of economic methods have been employed to manage the economy."[60] They documented hair-raising stories of accumulated worthless inventory, delays in delivery, shortages and bottlenecks due to the lack of a price mechanism, and the growth of barter as enterprises searched frantically for sources of inputs. They estimated that 3 million people traveled each day searching for parts and materials through personal connections, bartering, and bribery because they were unable to buy needed inputs.[61]

Industrial Wages and Urban Consumption

During the first three years of national economic rehabilitation, market forces largely determined wage rates. Once the socialist transformation was complete, state planners exercised control over wage rates. During the first five-year plan, the state permitted wage increases but immediately reduced them once the socialist transformation had been accomplished in 1957. Thereafter, as a stimulus to production following the post-Great Leap Forward depression, planners granted wage increases in 1962 and 1963; however, they took back a portion of those increases in 1964. Wages remained frozen until 1976 and did not exceed nominal 1957 levels until substantial increases were granted in 1978.

Taking living costs for staff and workers into account, Gregory Chow calculated that the real wage was actually lower in 1978 than in 1957.[62] Robert Michael Field determined that real earnings rose 30 percent during 1953–1957 but declined during 1958–1962 below 1952 levels. After a slight recovery by 1965, real earnings went into a free-fall, plummeting below the 1952 level again in 1977. But even this indicator of real earnings, which adjusts nominal wages downward to reflect rising living costs, overstated the welfare of workers and employees and state-owned enterprises, inasmuch as an increasing share of the family budget in the mid-1960s and early 1970s was spent on foodstuffs at prices higher than those in state stores. Adjusting the price level up by this additional 10–20 percent means that real earnings in 1977 were below 1957 levels.[63]

Christopher Howe wrote that freezing wages harmed worker morale. "It is no accident that some of China's weakest industrial performers are precisely those industries in which the relatively high wages of their workers have been eroded by a twenty year pay freeze and by campaigns for greater income equality."[64] Chinese planners successfully prevented the emergence of serious inequalities in income in urban areas. Wage rates varied little between industry and across regions, regardless of labor productivity: Those who worked harder or produced more did not get paid more.

Despite a freeze in industrial wages, per capita urban incomes outgrew rural incomes. The rural labor-force participation rate remained constant at 45 percent, whereas the urban rate rose nearly half from 33 to 50 percent between 1957 and 1975. Wages per worker remained constant, but the number of workers grew by half, thus increasing per capita income.[65] Urban per capita income grew at an annual average rate of 2.9 percent during 1957–1979, compared with 1.6 percent for rural dwellers.

Consumption of food, consumer durables, and quality of clothing, along with such public services as education and health facilities, was much higher in urban areas. In addition to higher real incomes, state subsidies to urban consumers (constituting one-quarter of total budget outlays) financed cheap housing, food, clothing, and other rationed goods.

Subsidies accrued almost exclusively to the urban, industrial populations. In 1978, for example, the cash value of subsidies and benefits received by each state employee was 526 yuan, or 82 percent of the average annual wage. The most important subsidies were for rationed cereals and vegetable oils, amounting to 179.6 yuan per employee. Health, retirement, maternity, disability, and similar benefits totaled 115.3 yuan per worker. Welfare benefits, such as childcare and worker recreation facilities, were worth 119.5 yuan. Housing subsidies netted 85.3 yuan; by the late 1970s, urban residential rents covered, on average, less than 25 percent of housing costs. Other subsidies included commuting, travel, and home heating and cooking coal.[66] Thus, although real earnings per worker stagnated during 1957–1978, the value of subsidies grew rapidly, increasing the gap between urban and rural living standards. In the absence of strict administrative control over labor allocation, this yawning gap ultimately stimulated large migrations of people from the countryside to the cities.[67]

The World Bank reported the results of several Chinese surveys, which revealed that the urban to rural ratio for consumption was 2.4 for meat, 1.9 for cloth, 4.7 for bicycles, 3.8 for sewing machines, and 4.3 for radios. The ratio for grain consumption stood at 1.6.[68]

The improvement in urban living standards fell short on two counts. First, as little capital was allocated to housing, per capita housing space decreased from 48 square feet in 1952 to 39 square feet in 1977. (For purposes of comparison, each Taiwanese consumed 190 square feet of housing space.) Second, the increase in urban labor-force participation came at the expense of less leisure time for children, cooking, and other private activities.

MONETARY, FISCAL, AND TRADE POLICIES

In this chapter we have examined Chinese agricultural and economic policies in the context of a centrally controlled economic system, which was characterized by the general lack of a private sector during 1957–1978. Summarizing from the World Bank report, the main features of China's state-run economy were as follows: (1) exclusive public ownership of the means of production; (2) central allocation of resources, including labor, industrial, and agricultural inputs, as well as consumer goods; (3) strictly hierarchical planning and administration by command; (4) the passive role of money and the limited role of prices (to the modest rural free market) in allocating resources; and (5) state monopoly of trade and the insulation of domestic prices from the world market price structure.[69]

In market economies, monetary and fiscal policies affect decisions to invest, produce, and consume. In a rigid, closed system of state allocations and preemptions, independent monetary and fiscal policies have little place. In economies where the means of production are largely in private hands, the domestic money supply determines the internal price level, and the exchange rate brings internal costs and prices in line with world trends. In China's closed system, a surplus or deficit in the balance of trade did not necessarily force an upward or downward revision in the exchange rate. Moreover, capital flows had no necessary effect on the exchange rate inasmuch as all capital movements in and out of China were rigidly controlled.

Money supply growth in China had less impact on explicit prices than in Western market economies. Through 1978, China could be described as a ledger-transaction society, in which state or collective enterprises transferred bookkeeping entries through the accounts of government banks. A minuscule cash economy serviced rural fairs and urban consumption. The inflationary effects of occasional excessive cash circulation were suppressed through stricter rationing requirements and longer queues, and they offered potential depositors higher interest rates. Monetary authorities faced neither the need to accommodate private demand for credit nor the effects of external trade on the exchange rate.

Widespread belief that hyperinflation caused the downfall of the Nationalist regime put a premium on price stability. Chinese leaders feared any resurgence of inflation. Prices remained remarkably stable during 1952–1978. Taking 1952 as the base year, the general index of retail prices increased only 21.6 percent by 1978.[70] In the United States, by comparison, the overall price level tripled between 1967 and 1984.

China succeeded in controlling inflation by repressing prices. Whenever prices are set without regard for supply and demand, shortages and surpluses invariably materialize. Because nearly one-third of all public outlays subsidized consumer goods, the government imposed strict rationing to cope with the excess demand that would have arisen if consumer goods had been priced well below market-clearing levels. Instead of letting prices rise to balance supply and demand, thus pushing up the price index, the government balanced supply and demand through ration coupons, forcing consumers to wait in long lines.

Success in preserving price stability came at the cost of some inefficiency. Resources were misallocated because those who placed the highest value on any commodity, and were likely to use it most efficiently, were forbidden to bid for its use by paying a higher price.

Dorothy Solinger recorded that "bribery through gift-giving was essential in commercial workers' efforts to obtain scarce, popular, or specialized goods." As one of her informants explained, "But they won't sell you the thing or produce it for you specially without a gift."

> Many of the same factors that make goods (in the form of gifts) the currency for bribery also act to reinforce the traditional reliance of Chinese people on personal connections, or *guanxi*. That is, since money and goods are scarce, prices are controlled, and rationing, both formal and informal, dictates the legal distribution of key goods and services, informal social relationships help to circumvent the restrictiveness of marketing regulations.[71]

Fiscal policy was relatively unimportant in China's system of central control, where prices bore many of the burdens that government tax and spending policies perform in most market economies. By setting all input and output prices for agriculture, industry, domestic and foreign commerce, and transport, the government determined the division of output and the distribution of income among sectors of the economy and between regions of the country. It did not have to employ tax preferences to favor one industry or region over another. It subsidized losses in unprofitable state-owned enterprises, resold food to poor outlying regions, and subsidized urban consumers and state employees. The government pursued balanced budgets in the belief that conservative fiscal policy would enhance price stability by preventing the overissue of bank notes to finance budget deficits.

Fiscal policy consisted of collecting enough money to support a defense establishment, subsidize urban consumers and state employees, and provide such related public services as police protection, parks and recreation, public education, health facilities, and general administrative overhead. As there were virtually no private firms to tax, nor did peasants and workers earn sufficient income to pay income taxes, the state relied on the profits of state-owned enterprises, receipts from customs and excises, and the implicit tax of agricultural procurement at below-market prices. From time to time, it raised deposit interest rates in state banks to attract funds. On occasion, it resorted to currency issue to balance expenditures with receipts. But so long as the government controlled all prices, owned all the means of production, and made all production decisions, thereby determining profits and subsidizing losses, fiscal policy was largely irrelevant as a tool of economic policy.

State trading agencies, which monopolized foreign trade, conducted their affairs with little regard for the true costs of imports and exports. The official exchange rate consistently overvalued the Chinese yuan. Subsidies enabled many Chinese products to compete in world markets. Moreover, any excess profits earned from sales abroad because of domestic subsidies in production were remitted to the state. State or collectively owned producers were not free either to purchase inputs or to sell their products openly on world markets.

During most of the postwar period, China earned between 30 and 40 percent of its hard-currency foreign exchange from the sales of foodstuffs, water, and consumer goods to Hong Kong. It used the acquired assets, in turn, to import wheat (when domestic production was inadequate), capital goods, and military equipment, and to accumulate foreign-exchange reserves for a rainy day.

In Chapter 4 we shall examine market-oriented policies for agriculture and industry that were adopted during 1978–1985. These policies required the state to take a more active role in using the tools of fiscal, monetary, banking, and trade policy to regulate economic activity. Such changes as replacing financial grants and appropriations with bank credit, and collecting taxes in place of full remission of all enterprise profits, required state authorities to make choices about monetary and fiscal policies. The government had to decide how to tax, what to subsidize, and how to accommodate the demand for credit without kindling inflation. As China tried to lure foreign investment and expand trade to accelerate growth, the exchange rate—the link between domestic and world prices—became more important.

NOTES

1. Between 1978 and 1985, China followed a general pattern of continuous liberal economic reforms. Despite a general trend of continuity, its leaders nonetheless completed a full swing from left to right in political and economic

thinking on whether an open-door policy to the West would foster "spiritual pollution" in China between April 1983 and April 1984. For details of this cycle, see Stuart R. Schram, " 'Economics in Command?' Ideology and Policy Since the Third Plenum, 1978–84," *The China Quarterly,* no. 99 (September 1984), pp. 417–461.

2. A detailed narrative of China's postwar developmental strategy appears in Chu-yuan Cheng, *China's Economic Development: Growth and Structural Change* (Boulder, Colo.: Westview Press, 1982), pp. 257–287.

3. Dorothy J. Solinger rejects the simple left-right distinction in Chinese politics in favor of three factions—leftist radicals, mainstream bureaucrats, and the more liberal marketeers—whose influence prevailed at different stages in the postwar period. See *Chinese Business Under Socialism: The Politics of Domestic Commerce, 1949–1980* (Berkeley and Los Angeles: University of California Press, 1984). Solinger presents a case study of policy conflict in Chinese commerce during 1949–1979 in which she identifies six distinct periods (see Chapter 2, pp. 60–123).

4. This section follows Chu-yuan Cheng, *China's Economic Development,* pp. 257–287.

5. *Statistical Yearbook of China 1985,* compiled by the State Statistical Bureau, PRC (Hong Kong: Economic Information and Agency, 1985), pp. 12–15. See the Appendix for qualifying remarks on the accuracy of Chinese economic statistics.

6. Ibid., p. 309.

7. Professor Maotung Teng of Anhui University visited the site in Anhui Province where the "rural responsibility system" was first tried in 1978. When he asked peasants about their expectations for the next few years, they replied that continuity of policy for just the next year would be a great improvement compared with the wild swings in rural policy of the past several decades (interview, August 1985, Hoover Institution, Stanford University).

8. For a rigorous economic analysis of the incentives and constraints in Chinese agriculture under central planning, see Gregory C. Chow, *The Chinese Economy* (New York: Harper and Row, 1985), pp. 77–114.

9. *Statistical Yearbook of China 1985,* p. 255.

10. Thomas G. Rawski, *Economic Growth and Employment in China* (New York: Oxford University Press for the World Bank, 1979), p. 78.

11. Nicholas R. Lardy, *Agricultural Prices in China,* World Bank staff working papers, no. 606 (Washington, D.C.: World Bank, 1983), pp. 4–12; Robert C. Hsu, "Agricultural Financial Policies in China, 1949–1980," *Asian Survey* 22, no. 7 (July 1982), pp. 639–644; and Robert C. Hsu, "Grain Procurement and Distribution in China's Rural Areas," *Asian Survey* 24, no. 12 (December 1984), pp. 1229–1233.

12. Robert C. Hsu, "Agricultural Financial Policies in China," p. 645.

13. Robert Hsu, "Grain Procurement and Distribution in China's Rural Areas," p. 1231.

14. Nicholas R. Lardy, *Agricultural Prices in China,* pp. 13–18.

15. An analysis of Chinese agricultural efficiency appears in Thomas G. Rawski, *Economic Growth and Employment in China,* pp. 71–122.

16. Ibid., p. 121. See also Robert F. Dernberger, "The Program for Agricultural Transformation in the People's Republic of China," in *Proceedings of the 7th Sino-American Conference on Mainland China: Mainland China in the Post-Mao Era* (Taipei, Taiwan: Institute of International Relations, 1978), p.

II–225, cited in Jan S. Prybyla, "Key Issues in the Chinese Economy," *Asian Survey* 21, no. 9 (September 1981), p. 933.

17. Christopher Howe, *China's Economy*, p. xxiii.

18. Nicholas R. Lardy, *Agriculture in China's Modern Economic Development* (Cambridge: Cambridge University Press, 1983), p. 158. See also Nicholas R. Lardy, "Consumption and Living Standards in China, 1978–83," *The China Quarterly*, no. 100 (December 1984), pp. 849–865.

19. Nicholas R. Lardy, "Consumption and Living Standards in China, 1978–83," pp. 850–857.

20. Robert F. Dernberger, "The Chinese Search for the Path of Self-Sustained Growth in the 1980s: An Assessment," in *China Under the Four Modernizations, Part 1*, Selected Papers Submitted to the Joint Economic Committee, Congress of the United States, August 13, 1982 (Washington, D.C.: Government Printing Office, 1982), p. 24.

21. Cited in Gregory C. Chow, *The Chinese Economy*, pp. 159–160. These surveys were used to compare the gap in consumption rates between workers and peasants.

22. Gregory C. Chow, *The Chinese Economy*, p. 160.

23. *China: Socialist Economic Development*, Volume I (Washington, D.C.: World Bank, 1983), p. 82.

24. The extreme level of poverty in the backward provinces of China is described in Steven W. Mosher, *Journey to the Forbidden China* (New York: Free Press, 1985).

25. Jan S. Prybyla, "Where Is China's Economy Headed? A Systems Analysis," *Journal of Northeast Asian Studies* 1, no. 4 (December 1982), pp. 2–3.

26. Ma Hong, *New Strategy for China's Economy* (Beijing: New World Press, 1983), p. 35.

27. Zhan Wu and Liu Wenpu, "Agriculture," in Yu Guangyuan, *China's Socialist Modernization* (Beijing: Foreign Languages Press, 1984), p. 213.

28. *Statistical Yearbook of China 1985*, p. 12.

29. Ibid., p. 29.

30. Ibid.

31. Ibid., p. 19.

32. Ibid., pp. 213, 224.

33. Gregory C. Chow, *The Chinese Economy*, p. 122.

34. This section draws from Chu-yuan Cheng, *China's Economic Development*, pp. 135–161.

35. Interview with Dean Barrett in Hong Kong, December 14, 1985. Barrett was the former director and general manager of the China Printing & Finishing Company, Ltd., textile factory in Shanghai, now known as the No. 10 Textile Factory. He remained in Shanghai as the sole expatriate manager of his firm until 1957, when he "legally" transferred ownership of the assets of his firm to the Chinese government without compensation. It took him an additional four months to gain the necessary permits to leave China for Hong Kong.

36. Dean Barrett personally witnessed about twenty suicides during his confinement in Shanghai (interview in Hong Kong, December 14, 1985).

37. *Statistical Yearbook of China 1985*, p. 308.

38. Ibid., p. 36. In the explanatory notes, the concepts used in computing the national income are explained. "National income" refers to the newly created value in a given period by workers engaged in material production sectors of the country. It is the sum of net output value of agriculture, industry,

construction, transport, and commerce, obtained by deducting material consumption of those sectors from the total product of society. It excludes nonmaterial production sectors such as the service trades, educational, scientific research, cultural, and public health departments, as well as military and government administrations, on the grounds that they are not directly involved in material production.

The national income is further broken down into consumption and accumulation. Consumption represents expenditures by individuals for personal consumption and by the public sector for government administration. Accumulation refers to funds allocated for expanded production. It can be divided into what is called productive and nonproductive uses. Productive accumulation includes newly added fixed assets (less depreciation) and the increase in circulating assets held by enterprises. Nonproductive accumulation covers newly fixed assets of nonproductive use and residential buildings (less wear and tear) and the increase in the stock of consumer goods held by enterprises. Accumulation is also defined in physical terms of fixed assets and circulating funds. Thus the accumulation rate is the conceptual equivalent of the investment rate as a share of the national income (see pp. 659–661).

39. Ibid., p. 35.

40. Ibid., p. 29.

41. Gregory C. Chow, *The Chinese Economy*, p. 126.

42. Ibid., p. 121. It should be noted that China was in the trough of a depression in 1962 and that some of the growth that occurred during 1962–1965 was recovery in nature, rather than indicative of long-term trends. Thus the comparison with the Cultural Revolution partly overstates the growth in the prior few years. Nonetheless, it is difficult to overemphasize the economic damage caused by the Cultural Revolution.

43. The relatively slow growth in labor productivity is attributed to the inefficient use of fixed capital assets. See Robert Michael Field, "Slow Growth of Labour Productivity in Chinese Industry, 1952–81," *The China Quarterly*, no. 96 (December 1983), pp. 651–652.

44. Jan S. Prybyla, "Where Is China's Economy Headed?" p. 7.

45. Jan S. Prybyla, "Economic Problems of Communism: A Case Study of China," *Asian Survey* 22, no. 12 (December 1982), p. 1224.

46. Robert F. Dernberger, "The Chinese Search for the Path of Self-Sustained Growth in the 1980s," p. 26.

47. *China: Socialist Economic Development*, p. 76.

48. Shigeru Ishikawa, "China's Economic Growth Since 1949–An Assessment," *The China Quarterly*, no. 94 (June 1983), pp. 244–246. It is necessary to separate estimates of annual output from growth rates. Chinese data may overstate annual output levels, but the growth rate of 5.4 percent reported in the World Bank study may still be correct. However, if the annual base on which the 5.4 percent growth occurred is significantly smaller than official data suggest, then real output and living standards were systematically overestimated.

49. *China: Socialist Economic Development*, p. 124.

50. Ibid., p. 123.

51. Ibid., pp. 80, 127.

52. Ibid., pp. 149–150.

53. Jan S. Prybyla, "Where Is China's Economy Headed?" p. 6.

54. This severe criticism of central planning reflects the official view of the Chinese Communist Party and government, and it must be seen as partly

political in that context. It is necessary for the government to justify its rejection of old policies and the adoption of new ones.

55. Ma Hong, *New Strategy for China's Economy*, p. 24.

56. Ibid., p. 25.

57. Ibid., pp. 26, 39.

58. Li Chengrui and Zhang Zhuoyuan, "An Outline of Economic Development (1977–1980)," in Yu Guangyuan, *China's Socialist Modernization*, p. 7.

59. Ibid., p. 13.

60. Liu Guoguang and Wang Ruisun, "Restructuring of the Economy," in Yu Guangyuan, *China's Socialist Modernization*, p. 85.

61. Ibid., p. 97.

62. Gregory C. Chow, *The Chinese Economy*, p. 143.

63. Robert Michael Field, "Slow Growth of Labour Productivity in Chinese Industry, 1952–81," pp. 652–654.

64. Christopher Howe, *China's Economy*, p. 132.

65. Thomas G. Rawski, *Economic Growth and Employment in China*, p. 35. Female labor-force participation rates grew so dramatically that the average number of dependents per worker in the state sector of the economy declined from 2.3 to 1.06. See Nicholas R. Lardy, "Consumption and Living Standards in China, 1978–83," p. 853.

66. Nicholas R. Lardy, "Consumption and Living Standards in China, 1978–83," pp. 853–857.

67. For a comparison of peasant and urban incomes see Jan S. Prybyla, "Key Issues in the Chinese Economy," *Asian Survey* 21, no. 9 (September 1981), pp. 926–929.

68. *China: Socialist Economic Development*, p. 87.

69. Ibid., p. 147.

70. *Statistical Yearbook of China 1985*, p. 530.

71. Dorothy J. Solinger, *Chinese Business Under Socialism*, pp. 57–58.

4

CHINA GOES TO MARKET

The death of Mao Zedong in September 1976 and the arrest of the ultra-leftist radicals the following month brought changes in political leadership and economic policy. During 1977–1978, the post-Mao leadership neutralized large parts of the Maoist interpretation of Marxist-Leninist ideology and removed key ideologues who had dictated the ultra-leftist policies of the Great Leap Forward and Cultural Revolution. By 1978, Deng Xiaoping had consolidated political power. Known as "pragmatic" in economic matters, Deng set in motion a series of agricultural, industrial, commercial, fiscal, financial, and other reforms that gave greater scope to market forces and began to lessen the role of the state in China's economy. In a speech published in the Chinese press on New Year's Day 1985, Deng went so far as to say, "I am afraid that some of our old colleagues have this fear: after a generation of socialism and Communism, it is unacceptable to spout some capitalism. It cannot harm us. It cannot harm us."[1]

Under Deng's direction, the Chinese Communist Party set a new economic course. A first documentary landmark was the Third Plenum of the 11th Central Committee in December 1978, which stressed the improvement of peasant living standards. Its urban and industrial counterpart was the Third Plenum of the 12th Central Committee on October 20, 1984, which released an official report on "Reform of the Economic Structure."[2]

The October 20 "Reform" emphasized individual incentives and greater reliance on market forces to stimulate economic efficiency. The landmark document repeatedly used such phrases and terms as "the individual economy," "the market," "competition," "the rule of law," and "enterprise autonomy," and it acknowledged that some people must become rich before others can improve their well-being.

71

On December 7, 1984, a front-page editorial in the party's official newspaper, *People's Daily*, proclaimed that orthodox Marxist theory was outdated and could not solve the problems faced by modern China. Although the statement was watered down the next day to read "cannot solve *all* our modern-day questions," the official newspaper stated that "socialism with Chinese characteristics" no longer required slavish adherence to the ideas of Marx, Engels, Lenin, and Stalin.[3]

Chinese economists built a solid case for the reforms contained in the sequence of reform documents. Liu Guoguang and Wang Ruisun, for example, argued that the slow pace of economic growth and living standards in China was due to excessive concentration of state power in economic decision making; complete disregard for supply and demand and for the true market price of labor, material, and capital; and political management of enterprises that stifled sound economic organization and practices. "Such a structure put the economy in a straightjacket, discouraging initiative in all quarters, causing a serious waste of manpower, materials, and capital, and greatly hampering the growth of productive forces."[4]

AGRICULTURAL REFORMS

The imbalance among agriculture, light industry, and heavy industry, as well as the excessive preoccupation with capital accumulation were detrimental to personal consumption. The first target of reform was to raise the living standards of 800 million peasants, which had stagnated for two decades. Building on free-market experiments that succeeded in Deng Xiaoping's home province of Sichuan in 1977—Jinyu Commune in Guanghan County had secretly divided the fields among its production teams, a measure that party First Secretary Zhao Ziyang[5] officially condoned in 1978—the party officially crystallized its policy on September 28, 1979.[6] The Fourth Plenary Session of the 11th Party Central Committee put forth twenty-five specific measures to develop agricultural productivity in a document entitled "Some Questions Concerning the Acceleration of Agricultural Development."[7]

Rural reform consisted of several changes. These included increased financial incentives to peasants, decentralization of planning, and, most important, changes in agricultural organization built around the agricultural (also known as "rural," "household," "individual," or "production") responsibility system.[8]

To increase financial incentives, the state reduced taxes on grain, livestock, and collectively run enterprises. An agricultural tax reduction totaling 2.6 million tons of grain, implemented in 1979, exempted from compulsory delivery rice and other grain-growing areas that suffered low peasant consumption.[9]

Of far greater importance was the raising of agricultural procurement prices. The state raised the prices of many products, including grain, cotton, oil seeds, sugar crops, pigs, cattle, and eggs. In all, it raised the "purchase price index" by 22 percent. Grain received a 21 percent increase in the basic quota procurement price, and the above-quota price was set 50 percent above that level (compared with 30 percent above the lower, basic quota price that prevailed in 1971). Negotiated prices prevailed for grain in excess of above-quota levels.[10] Further price adjustments in 1980 and 1981 increased the overall level of base prices by 3.5 percent and 2.4 percent, respectively.

Equally important to peasants, the share of grain purchased at the higher, above-quota, and negotiated prices increased from less than 1 percent in 1977 to 60 percent in 1981. Thus peasants received higher prices on a larger fraction of output.[11]

In 1985, the state announced plans to purchase 75–80 million tons of grain (about 20 percent of anticipated production), of which it would acquire 30 percent at the base price for mandatory state purchases and 70 percent at the above-quota price. The remaining 5 million tons of marketed (not locally consumed) grain would be sold at market prices and subject to market price fluctuations. In addition, the government announced that it would let the price of pork, live pigs, beef, and dairy products float in major urban markets.[12] These changes represented a first-step, partial dismantling of the system of compulsory purchases of grain, cotton, and oil seed crops.

Decentralization of planning accompanied the raising of farm procurement prices. The state reduced the number of mandatory targets sent to the provinces and shifted emphasis from targets for sown area to quantities of output.

The new responsibility system was the lynchpin of rural reform. By 1982, 70 percent of production teams embraced contracting with households. In a nutshell, under the responsibility system, the collective retained formal ownership of land, but fields were allocated to individual families. Households entered into contracts with the local brigade or commune. In return for the exclusive rights to farm designated public lands, they agreed to meet specific output quotas and payments as well as a designated portion of the investment and welfare funds disbursed by the production team. All other investment and production decisions were left to the households. Grain, cotton, and oil-bearing crops were still sold to state marketing organizations. Households retained the right to consume its excess production or to sell it at a premium over the base price. All other produce was freely traded at urban markets or rural fairs. The volume of rural fair trade increased from 17.1 billion yuan in 1979 to 52.4 billion in 1985; urban fair trade exploded from 1.2 billion yuan to 18.1 billion yuan during 1979–1985.[13]

To summarize the features of production responsibility: (1) Legal ownership of land, fixed productive assets, large tools, and draft animals was vested in the production team; (2) planners informed the teams of state quotas and prices, but left the decisions on compliance with the team; and (3) the team, in turn, chose either to meet the production goals directly or to contract all or part of the fixed production assigned to it by the state to smaller units (work groups consisting of three to six households, individual households, or individual peasants).[14] The power to make production and income distribution choices on collective land injected an element of private property rights in households and individuals.

The system of rural responsibility decentralized agricultural decision making from Beijing to rural communes, and through the communes to individual household farming teams. Before 1978, central authorities dictated what to plant, regardless of the climate and local growing conditions. After 1978, local production brigades and teams assumed this authority and were given control over management procedures and the distribution of their own products and cash income. Freedom to choose which crops to grow was still constrained by planning directives, land transactions were forbidden, and agricultural workers still lacked geographical mobility.

Incentives in agriculture markedly increased. The marginal tax rate on above-quota production was zero because peasants paid no taxes on their receipts from free-market sales. During 1980, new instructions enlarged private plots and abolished restrictions on their use in many provinces. Certain taxes on livestock were abolished, and produce grown on private plots was free of tax. The new orders also removed all restrictions on individual livestock breeding, household sideline occupations, and rural trade fairs. Rural industry mushroomed.

The responsibility system fostered the development of so-called "specialized households," which constituted about one-tenth of rural households by 1984. These families and individuals owned their own tractors and trucks and could enter into contractual arrangements to plough fields, transport goods for members of their own team or brigade, sell their services to outside parties, and set up rural processing and other sideline industries.

Despite their enjoyment of rising incomes between 1979 and 1982, peasants remained reluctant to make capital investments in agriculture, fearing that the party might retrench on these reforms at a moment's notice. Recognizing this dilemma, the party issued a document in early 1983 to reassure peasants about the permanence of reforms and urged that contract periods be granted to households for fifteen years to encourage capital investment in the contracted plots. Despite a constitutional prohibition on the private ownership of land, the document even viewed transfers of contracted land among peasant households as a positive concomitant of specialization and commercialization. By the end of 1985, these long-term leases became inheritable as a matter of practice.

To summarize, Deng Xiaoping decollectivized agriculture. Individuals, families, or households contracted to farm portions of the collective field, and, after meeting state quotas, they were free to dispose of any surplus as they saw fit. Purely private plots doubled to constitute 15 percent of China's total cultivated area. Peasants were allowed to engage in the capitalist act of hiring their fellow peasants as laborers. Private markets for agricultural produce were legalized.

If China's leaders took a few additional steps, it would literally bring about a completely .free market in agriculture. All that remains is for the state to end purchase quotas; eliminate state-set prices; permit private wholesale and retail distribution throughout the country; free up the agricultural input markets for machinery, electricity, fuel, chemical fertilizers, and pesticides; and permit the conversion of the contracted portions of collective fields from leasehold form into outright private ownership with no restrictions on transfer. "The only socialist aspect of this [the present] system is that land remains collective property; peasants can use it but not sell it."[15] Such steps would require constitutional change. I am not aware that these reforms were actively discussed in party and government circles; rather, my purpose in enumerating them is to show the scope of rural reform compared with the Maoist era and what further steps could still be taken to bring about additional gains in efficiency.

Results of Agricultural Reforms

Since 1978, agricultural production recorded significant gains. Between 1978 and 1985, gross agricultural output value (GAOV) rose 96.6 percent, or nearly doubled in seven years.[16] An indication of how dramatic these gains were is that it took twenty-three years for the index (1952 = 100) to reach 202.1; by 1978, the index stood at 229.6. Seven years later it reached 451.5. Additional data, derived from a survey of over 30,000 peasant households in 600 counties, revealed that rural per capita incomes increased in real terms by 98.5 percent, or at an average annual rate of 14.7 percent.[17] Peasant living standards rose in five years by more than the total gain that occurred between 1952 and 1977.

By every measure, agricultural productivity registered sharp gains. Grain yields rose from 304.7 million tons in 1978 to 407.3 million tons in 1984, with a decline to 379.1 million tons in 1985. The fact that sown area in grain in 1985 was 95.6 percent of that in 1978 suggests a rise in efficiency. Responding to market forces, farmers shifted land from grain production to cash crops; sown area devoted to industrial crops increased 55 percent over 1978. Land allocated to such cash crops as melons and vegetables jumped 51.8 percent. Between 1978 and 1985, cotton output rose from 2.16 to 4.15 million tons; oil-bearing crops from 5.22 to 15.78 million tons; sugar cane from 21.1 to 51.5 million tons; beef, pork, and mutton from 8.6 to 17.6 million tons; and aquatic products from 4.7 to 7.1 million tons.[18] In terms of per capita output, the gains were equally impressive: grain rose from 704 pounds to 806 pounds, cotton from 4.4 to 8.8 pounds, oil-bearing crops from 12.1 to 33.6 pounds, and animal protein from 19.9 to 37.3 pounds.[19] Compared with the average annual percentage increase in output during 1952–1978, the annual rate of growth between 1979 and 1983 was fourfold for cotton, sixfold for oil-bearing crops, threefold for sugar cane and beets, double for tea, and threefold for pork, beef and mutton.

Good weather also played a role. The bumper years of 1982, 1983, and 1984 enjoyed especially good weather. Although the overall average between 1978 and 1984 was exceptionally high by Chinese historical standards, bad weather during 1980 and 1981 reduced output by 3.5 and 1.4 percent, respectively.[20]

Grain output grew so rapidly that China sharply curtailed grain imports. In 1984, grain exports reached record levels of 3.4 million tons, and China became a net cotton exporter for the first time. For a rare moment in Chinese history, the peasants enjoyed surpluses, not shortages.

Rising rural incomes coupled with improved incentives sharply increased the demand for agricultural machinery, fertilizer, and irrigation. The total horsepower of agricultural machinery in use rose from 159.7 to 284.3 million horsepower. The number of harvesters nearly doubled from 18,987 to 34,573, trucks more than quintupled from 73,770 to 429,554, and motor fishing boats multiplied from 47,176 to 172,582. Consumption of chemical fertilizer rose from 8.8 to 17.7 million tons, and electricity consumption increased from 253 hundred million kilowatt hours to 509 hundred million.[21]

Now that cash crops were more profitable and agricultural policies more liberal, an increasing number of production teams and households diverted land from grain production to cash crops. During 1982–1984, grain harvests reached record levels despite a change in land use patterns. In 1985, however, grain output slumped by 28 million tons.[22] Reduction in grain acreage was 300 percent higher than the average for the preceding six years.

Some regions had been hit by natural disasters. But the fall in grain production also reflected rational decisions by peasants. Other crops offered higher returns because their prices were free to reflect market situations in full (some grain was still procured at below-market prices during 1985), or because they required fewer expensive inputs of fuel, chemical products, or machinery, for which the government had raised prices. Moreover, in 1985 the state reduced its grain quota to 75 million tons from 1984's considerably higher target of 117 million tons. Another factor was the growth of rural industries, which siphoned labor off the land.[23] In 1985, rural industries contributed about 18 percent of gross domestic product, compared with only 13 percent in 1983, thus causing official alarm over the runaway rural industrial boom.[24]

The responsibility system had a positive short-run effect on the growth of agricultural output and improved rural incomes. But much of the improvement in peasant incomes was traceable to higher procurement prices. Through 1978, total state revenue and expenditure were largely in balance. China ran six consecutive deficits beginning in 1979.[25] In 1979 and 1980, deficits ran 15 and 12 percent of total receipts respectively. These deficits were financed, in part, through bank notes; in turn, an expanding currency issue fueled inflation. The price level remained stable between 131 and 136 (1950 = 100) during 1965–1978, but rose sharply by Chinese standards to 150 by 1981.[26] Inflation became a serious economic and political problem in the 1980s.

Nor did the state pass the full increase in agricultural prices to urban consumers. State subsidies to urban residents grew substantially from 1978 on, allowing the retail network to hold down prices. Urban subsidies for rationed cereals soared from about 4 billion yuan in 1978 to more than 10 billion yuan in 1981. This increase allowed the continued distribution of rationed cereals to urban consumers at prices unchanged since 1965, despite a 45 percent rise in the average procurement price for grains during the first three years of the responsibility system.[27]

In 1978, agriculture contributed 27.8 percent of the combined gross output value of agriculture and industry; by 1985, its share was 34.3 percent. The share contributed by light industry remained virtually unchanged. The entire increase was borne by heavy industry, whose share declined from 41.1 to 35 percent.[28] Thus Chinese leaders succeeded in shifting the emphasis from heavy industry to agriculture and improved rural living standards.

How did rising rural incomes translate into improved levels of consumption? Successive surveys of rural households revealed sharp rises in living standards. A rural construction boom reduced arable land since 1978 to a considerable extent (peasants are allowed to build and own private homes on collective land). Floor-space per capita increased from 109.3 to 158.3 square feet between 1978 and 1985. During that seven-year interval marking the operation of the responsibility system, per capita peasant net income increased from 133 to 398 yuan, grain consumption from 547 to 567 pounds, edible oils from 4.4 to 8.8 pounds, meat from 12.8 to 24.3 pounds, and equally dramatic gains were recorded for poultry, eggs, seafood, sugar, chemical fiber cloth, and woolen cloth. Possession of consumer durables exploded: Bicycles per 100 peasant households rose from 30.7 to 80.6, sewing machines from 19.8 to 43.2, radios from 17.4 to 54.2, clocks and watches from 51.7 to 163.6, and television sets from none to 11.6.[29]

Savings deposits of commune members increased from 5.6 billion yuan to 56.5 billion yuan, a tenfold increase in seven years.[30] Peasants thus had more money to spend and to save.

The effects of rural economic policy innovations substantially narrowed the persistently wide gap between urban and rural incomes.[31] Ratios of urban to rural per capita ownership of consumer durables declined.

The concept that land ownership could be separated from its use reintroduced incentives into the countryside. Peasants could keep what they produced after meeting reduced quotas for which they were paid higher prices, thus drastically reducing the implicit tax of below-market-price procurement. As household contracts to work collective fields increased to 15 years, a de facto system of private land ownership became widespread. How far rural productivity growth will grow ultimately depends on the availability of technology and other inputs.

Much of the increase in income since 1978 was due to higher prices for commodities sold to the state. Increased sideline income also contributed substantial gains. But after the state increased procurement prices 40 percent between 1978 and 1981, it granted only modest additional increases of 6.7 percent for 1982 and 1983. The objective of restoring and maintaining budgetary balance is likely to hold down future increases in procurement prices.

Personal income gains in agriculture in the future depend on expanding output. Increasing output depends on improved relative prices, the revival of private marketing opportunities, increased inter-regional specialization in production, increased flows of inputs from the modern sector at market prices, and further improvement in individual incentives. Investment in agriculture will have to increase.[32] Inefficiencies in the grain-procurement system will have to be reduced. Peasants spend considerable time and effort in both selling and buying grain because they must deal with the state monopoly, not to mention the potential for corruption that remains in any rigid, indifferent bureaucratic system.[33] If China is to use the price mechanism to achieve maximum efficiency in agricultural production and marketing, it must make enormous investments in infrastructure—in transport, storage, and processing facilities, and in market information. It must also reduce the proportion of farm sales controlled by the state's marketing apparatus, which, until now, has impeded the growth of a market economy and imposed strains on budget expenditure.[34]

INDUSTRIAL REFORMS

Upon Mao's death, the initial changes made in the industrial sector were primarily readjustments of the centrally planned administrative command system in the form of decentralized administrative controls—not structural reforms, as in agriculture (in the latter case, a de facto system of private property rights was created). During the 1980s, structural reforms increasingly came into play, but China remained a long way from a competitive market economy.

In 1985, state-owned enterprises accounted for 70 percent of gross urban industrial output, collectively owned enterprises (largely rural) about 28 percent, and private enterprises less than 1 percent.[35] Excluding the value of retail sales made by peasants to urban residents, publicly owned firms accounted for 40 percent of retail sales, and collectively owned firms about 37 percent. But the total yuan value of retail sales by individually owned businesses increased more than 300 times during

1978–1985, from 210 million yuan to 66.1 billion yuan; in proportional terms, its share rose from virtually zero to 15.3 percent.[36] The 3 million urban residents who were privately employed constituted less than 3 percent of the urban labor force. These statistics demonstrate that state ownership and planning remained dominant in the mid-1980s, but that private ownership and economic activity grew by leaps and bounds each year. If these growth rates persist, the total value of retail sales by individuals in 1990 will surpass those of state-owned and collectively owned units, marking a phenomenal turnaround in China's retail sales system.

In 1984, Chinese economist Yu Guangyuan released a collection of essays under the title *China's Socialist Modernization*, which was aimed at mobilizing the reform wing of the party. In the lead essay, Li Chengrui and Zhang Zhuoyuan assessed the damage suffered by the economy during the Cultural Revolution, quantified the achievements of the interim recovery measures taken between October 1976 and December 1978, and identified the problems that remained. But the main purpose of their essay was to explain the policies adopted in December 1978 by the Third Plenum of the 11th Central Committee of the Chinese Communist Party for "readjusting, restructuring, consolidating, and improving the economy" through December 1980.[37] (The essay and book were originally scheduled for publication in 1981, but were delayed due to internal disagreements on industrial reform.)

In brief, the Third Plenum signalled a serious attempt at fundamental change. Since the adoption of the policies approved during the Third Plenum in 1978, China has undertaken a bewildering variety of experiments and reforms in industrial enterprises. The innovations started on an extremely small scale, primarily in experiment-happy Sichuan Province, and then spread rapidly throughout the country. The reforms included campaigns to eliminate losses in state-owned enterprises, the substitution of income taxes for the remission of profits to the state, and expanding local managerial decision-making authority. The reforms did not encompass comprehensive price or labor reform.

Experiments were conducted to expand the decision-making power of state-owned enterprises as a prelude to more thorough industrial reform and reorganization.[38] In October 1978, even before the Third Plenum, six enterprises in Sichuan launched the experiment. The experiment sought to analyze the economic effects of letting managers plan production according to market demand, marketing production directly, retaining profits, investing profits in new capacity, and controlling personnel affairs. In 1979, coverage was expanded to 100 firms. Most were local state-owned units; the rest were transport and communications enterprises under central government management.

The experiments replaced central allocation of inputs and purchase of outputs with the following features. (1) After meeting a government-specified output target, the enterprise could produce and market additional merchandise in response to market demand. (2) An enterprise could market its above-target output and any new products it developed. (3) An enterprise could retain 3–5 percent of the profits it made according to the state plan, as well as an additional 15–20 percent of profits from above-plan sales. (4) An enterprise could retain 60 percent of depreciation funds for technical renovation and innovation. (5) An enterprise could pay its workers and staff a production bonus of 17 percent of standard total wages. (6) Enterprises could appoint middle management without interference from higher state bodies. (7) Interest on working capital was set at zero for quota sales and at low rates for above-quota production, but at high rates to finance excess inventory.

The experimental enterprises increased output value in 1979 over 1978 by 14.9 percent, general profits by 33.5 percent, and profits turned over to the state by 24.2 percent; the corresponding figures for non-reformed enterprises were 3.2, 6.9, and 14.6 percent, respectively.

In July 1979, the State Council issued five documents on various aspects of this new policy and authorized the inclusion of an additional 4,000 enterprises throughout the country. By April 1980, 3,300 enterprises were enjoying new powers of management. They accounted for 8 percent of the 42,000 enterprises included in the state budget, and produced one-third of their output. By June, the number of enterprises had doubled to 6,600. Constituting 16 percent of total enterprises, they produced 60 percent of the total value of output and earned 70 percent of total profits. Comparing the decentralized with the nonreformed state-operated enterprises, we find that in 1980 the gross value of output grew at 6.8 percent compared with 4.8 percent, profit grew 11.8 percent compared with a decline of 4.6 percent, and the profit they remitted to the state increased 7.4 percent compared with a decline of 12.1 percent.

Buoyed by success, the state broadened its experiments to encompass both the replacement of profit delivery to the state by tax payments and the introduction of complete enterprise autonomy, in which each business undertook independent accounting and assumed sole responsibility for its own profits and losses. The State Economic Commission requested that every province, municipality, and autonomous region select one or more state-owned enterprises to join the experiment. In 1980, 191 enterprises took part.

Seeking to foster competition, the State Council passed ten provisions on October 17, 1980, to prevent regional monopolization and other barriers to entry. Key regulations included disallowing exclusive rights to produce and market individual commodities; competitive bidding in construction, production, and management projects; payments for transfer of know-how or inventions; some fluctuations of prices within a state-fixed range for certain products; regulation through market conditions of supply and demand; and the elimination of state commercial unified procurement of consumer goods. By 1981, the original six Sichuan experimental enterprises numbered 30,000.

Accompanying experimental attempts to restructure industry were such measures as allowing the emergence of locally owned collective enterprises, and individual enterprises with private capital in 20 provinces, municipalities, and autonomous regions.[39] Between 1978 and 1980, the number of private-household-owned enterprises increased from 150,000 to 400,000. Other new economic institutions included joint state-private enterprises with private shareholders who received dividends from profits. Producers' cooperatives were authorized to pool their capital and establish enterprises with responsibility for profits and losses. The state also approved such purely private-sector developments as household-level service firms, which were permitted to employ small numbers of laborers without officially "exploiting" labor.

During 1983 and 1984, the state adopted further reforms.[40] These included reducing the number of cadres in factory leadership positions; training for and testing of enterprise managers; further expanding autonomy, thus allowing the sale of most above-quota output directly to users, the negotiating of prices within a 20 percent limit, the choosing of suppliers of materials, the disposing of idle fixed assets, and the exercising of greater control over labor; striving to eliminate losses at state-operated enterprises, including firing managers for failure to meet targets; substituting income taxes for remission of profit to the state; eliminating ceilings on bonuses; and no longer allocating working capital as grants through the state budget. The achievements in each of these reforms initially often fell far short of the announcements, but the new policies clearly signaled Deng's determination to shift from planning to greater reliance on market forces.

On June 1, 1983, the handing over of profits to the state was officially replaced by a profits-based bookkeeping system of taxpaying enterprises. Within three months, some 90 percent of all 60,527 industrial and commercial enterprises were making initial tax payments. In the same year, the head of the State Economic Commission announced that subsidies to state enterprises losing money would be cut off (the economic equivalent of free exit). But this was easier said than done as subsidies to financially strapped state enterprises actually increased after the announcement. To ensure that managers were operating their plants efficiently, measures were implemented to crack the "iron rice bowl"—a practice that guaranteed employment regardless of the employee's contribution to productivity. Managers were authorized to sign renewable contracts with new workers that linked pay with performance, and to dismiss loafers, slackers and other nonproductive staff.[41]

Liberal reform progressed to the point that thousands of different products and goods were being produced partly or entirely outside the state plan and sold at floating or free prices. Provisions announced in November 1984, in the wake of the 12th Central Committee release of "Reform of the Economic Structure" on October 20, 1984, reduced the scope of mandatory planning and allocation of key agricultural products and major industrial products such as coal, petroleum, steel and non ferrous metals, chemicals, large electrical and mechanical equipment, and military products. The decision of the Party Central Committee in October 1984 was a mandate for more thorough price reform, taking the form of a three-to-five-year phase-in of price adjustments for such key materials as coal, oil, and other raw materials. The objective of price reform was to replicate the decision-making structure and environment of a capitalist economy, thus marking a decisive break with the Soviet model of a command economy controlled by a central bureaucracy.

In order for price reform to foster maximum efficiency, new market mechanisms had to be created to replace the unified state-distribution system. Experiments in comprehensive reform began in 1983 in Chongqing, the largest city in reform-happy Sichuan, and several cities in other provinces. The trial cities tested such innovations as local fiscal authority and the establishment of alternatives to the exchange of goods and services outside the state distribution system. A significant test was the opening of a new wholesale trading center in Chongqing in January 1984. The products trade center consisted of an eight-floor exhibition hall, offices, and meeting rooms in which any enterprise could display its products for sale, selling directly to any buyer and buying, in turn, from any seller, without state involvement. Except for a handful of products sold at state-set prices, all products could change hands at floating or free prices, with volume discounts and payments made by cash or check. Since the opening of this trade center, four additional such centers have sprung up in Chongqing, with similar ones in Shanghai, Tianjin, and Canton.[42]

Chongqing was home to other free-market experiments as well. Minsheng Shipping Company, once China's largest conglomerate, was nationalized in 1949. In 1984, the company was authorized to resume operations as a private corporation under the direction of the late founder's son.[43] Minsheng became the first large-scale private enterprise in China since the Communist revolution. Chinese leaders hoped that Minsheng would improve shipping efficiency and service, forcing state-owned agencies to increase their efficiency. Minsheng received the right to hire and fire workers, set business targets, and remain free of government intervention save for the payment of taxes. Staff members held shares and participated in the firm's profits and losses. The revival of Minsheng Shipping Company exemplified the growing attempts by China to utilize the skills of its former capitalists for economic advancement.

In January 1985, Chinese authorities released Deng Xiaoping's October 1984 speech celebrating China's 35th anniversary. With this speech, entitled "Building China with Socialist Characteristics," Deng gave his reform movement greater impetus. To eliminate the budget drain from consumer subsidies, about $7.5 billion in 1984, the state announced plans to increase the cost of basic foods, rent, fuel, health care, and other publicly supplied consumer goods. Other venerables of Chinese socialism were cast aside: The traditional two-hour lunch break was cut in half, and the rigid wage system for government workers was replaced by merit increases. Again, implementation of these reforms often lagged behind the issuing of directives, but they represented the sustained effort to cause prices to better reflect relative scarcities.

China certified these urban industrial reforms at the Third Plenary Session of the 12th Central Committee of the Communist Party of China on October 20, 1984, in its "Reform of the Economic Structure" document. Regulation through the market was compatible with socialist public ownership. "Levers" of price, tax, credit, and wages replaced central allocation of resources. To assist the process of socialist modernization, the document called for full enterprise autonomy, incentives to increase labor productivity, less planning, a rational price system, reform of the tax, financial, and banking systems, competition, consumer sovereignty in the marketplace, the rule of law, the trimming of bureaucracy and overstaffing, wage differentials to reflect differences in skill, outright acceptance of unequal distribution of income, expansion of the place of the individual economy, contracting out the work of state-owned enterprises to individuals and small-scale collectives, the opening of China to foreign investment, and the replacement old party comrades with younger professionals.

China remained far from a truly competitive, private-enterprise economy through the end of 1985. Managers at state-owned enterprises did not enjoy anything near full autonomy, free entry and exit in every market, free purchase and marketing of all commodities, autonomy in foreign trade, and full flexibility to vary prices. However, compared with 1978, factory managers no longer conducted their operations under a regime of mandatory central planning; rather, a system of nonbinding instructive planning prevailed.

Discussion of political reforms accompanied market reforms. Renewed attention was given to the principle of rule by law and strict enforcement of laws to replace the past system that depended on the personal whims of rule by man. The legal reforms that required attention included civil law, finance, banking, statistics, accounting, contracts, patents, and taxation, although progress was slow in implementation. Other objectives of institutional reform included decentralizing economic authority over tax collection and expenditure to local governments, restricting ministries and bureaus from interfering in enterprise decisions, and trimming the bureaucracy. Beijing alone was home to 600,000 state cadres, about whom incredible stories were told of overstaffing, redundancy of organizations, inefficiency, and corruption.[44]

Economic Results of Industrial Reform

The state extended the responsibility system from agriculture to industry to attain several goals. These included balancing development by increasing light industry and slowing down heavy industry; breaking the bottleneck caused by limited energy resources;[45] and increasing factory productivity.[46]

The composition of output shifted markedly from heavy to light industry. The share of heavy industry fell from 41 percent of the total gross output value of agriculture and industry in 1978 to 35 percent in 1985; light industry remained constant at about 31 percent; and agriculture showed a marked gain from 28 to 34 percent.[47] Following the rehabilitation of the economy in 1952, coal output increased in the twenty-six years through 1978 from 66 million tons to 618 million, crude oil from 120,000 to 10,405,000 tons, pig iron from 1.93 to 34.8 million tons, and steel from 1.35 to 31.8 million tons. During 1978–1985, production of these heavy industrial items increased only modestly. In contrast, the production of consumer goods grew by leaps and bounds. The output of bicycles quadrupled and sewing machines doubled; and whole new industries erupted, producing cameras, household washing machines and refrigerators, and electric fans. Overall, light industrial output value more than doubled in constant value terms over this seven-year period, whereas heavy industrial output rose only 73 percent. The production of agricultural inputs also rose markedly.[48]

Changes in the composition of output were reflected in patterns of investment. Investment in "productive" construction fell from 79 to less than 57 percent of total capital construction; the share going to "nonproductive" construction, chiefly residential buildings, rose from 21 to 43 percent. Heavy industry watched its share of total investment fall from 49 to 36 percent.[49]

Although the Chinese changed the structure of industrial operations, industrial efficiency lagged. Between 1978 and 1982, for example, a 37 percent increase in fixed assets, an 18 percent increase in working capital, and a 16 percent increase in workers and employees were required to expand output by 26 percent. The productivity of fixed and working capital continued their downward trend, although labor productivity showed a modest gain.[50]

China suffered an overinvestment crisis in 1982, when actual capital construction outlays exceeded the plan by 11 billion yuan, an overrun of 25 percent. The year 1983 was worse: Investments exceeded planned targets by still larger amounts. Key state projects encountered difficulty in getting adequate steel and cement supplies; delays were inordinate. Many projects exceeded their budgetary estimates by upwards of 40 percent, thereby illustrating the difficulty of matching the policy pronouncements of China's reformist leaders with deeds.[51]

A World Bank study during 1980–1982 of two industrial enterprises—the Chongqing Clock and Watch Company and the Qingdao Forging Machinery Plant—concluded that Chinese enterprises tried to maximize total family income and benefits of workers, rather than profits, value added per worker, managerial income, or other objectives typically associated with capitalistic economies. Obstacles to greater efficiency included multiple leadership, a largely unreformed labor and wage system, and low profit margins on most products.[52]

To increase efficiency and labor productivity, the state granted wage and subsidy increases to workers and staff. In purely nominal terms, the total wage and salary bill (including fringe benefits) of workers and staff in state-owned enterprises more than doubled, and those in collective-owned enterprises tripled. In per-worker terms, the average wage rose from 614 to 1,148 yuan, or 87 percent, between 1978 and 1985. (During 1978–1985, the general index of cost of living for staff and workers rose 34.2 percent.) Of this increase (comparing 1985 with 1980), about half was due to a general rise in the salary schedule, 23 percent was due to increased bonuses and over-fulfilled piecework quota wages, and 21 percent was due to increased subsidies to offset increased retail prices.[53] The official index of the cost of living of urban workers increased 17 percent during 1978–1983. Thus real urban per capita income rose in the neighborhood of 40 percent.

In addition to wage and salary increases, state subsidies to urban residents grew substantially. Price subsidies and fringe benefits in 1983 were worth about 1,000 yuan per worker—twice the level of 1978, which was virtually equivalent to explicit wages.[54] Higher wages and subsidies raised per capita consumption of urban residents by about 27 percent.[55] Through 1985, peasant gains in income and living standards increased at higher rates than those of urban residents, but urban living standards remained nearly two and one-half times higher.

COMMERCIAL, FINANCIAL, FISCAL, AND MONETARY REFORMS

During the early 1960s, Mao's doctrine of self-reliance reflected autarkic policies. This doctrine could not last; the early 1970s witnessed imports of major plants, notably in the chemical sectors. However, foreign trade remained an afterthought of Chinese policy until Deng Xiaoping's rise to power.[56]

Since 1978, Chinese leaders have complemented agricultural and industrial reforms with several commercial, investment, and trade reforms. China previously depended heavily on its surplus in trade with Hong Kong to cover its trade deficit with the United States, Western Europe, and Japan. It began a search for foreign capital that included international borrowing and a concerted effort to attract direct foreign investment to China, especially advanced technologies. Opening China to foreign investment was a radical departure from the past. In 1979–1980, China promulgated its joint-venture code, gave Guangdong and Fujian Provinces greater autonomy in matters of foreign trade and investment, and formally designated four cities as Special Economic Zones (SEZs), an idea borrowed from the successful experiences of "export processing zones" in other developing countries.

The objective of such zones is to delimit special area that receive exemptions of customs duty and various preferential conditions to attract foreign investors to set up factories whose products are mainly for export, thereby earning foreign exchange. Indeed, the Chinese researched a number of existing zones in preparation for establishing their own, including Sri Lanka and the Phillipines, which, in turn, reflected the prior experience in Taiwan (see Chapter 6).[57] The SEZ was an especially suitable vehicle with which to take advantage of the capital, technology, and entrepreneurial know-how available in neighboring Hong Kong and among overseas Chinese who wanted to assist China's development.

Within the zones, foreign-owned enterprises and joint ventures managed by foreigners or overseas Chinese and their boards of directors produced goods for export. Local Chinese government intervention was minimized. Foreigners were subject to income taxes and property rents, but, by and large, the zones were intended to simulate Hong Kong's free-market system. The zones constituted enclaves of capitalism within China, with an outward orientation.

The four initial zones were Shenzhen and Zhuhai (which are respectively adjacent to Hong Kong and Portuguese-administered Macao), Shantou, also in Guangdong Province, and Xiamen, which is the old treaty port of Amoy, in Fujian Province. The National People's Congress approved guidelines for the first two in August 1980 and for the latter two in October 1980. Hainan Island, roughly the size of Taiwan, was turned into an SEZ in 1981.

Shenzhen was divided into several sections, of which the western section, Shekou, was earmarked for industrial development. As of January 31, 1982, about 1,000 foreign contracts to invest in Shenzhen were signed at an estimated value of $1.57 billion. Hong Kong investors accounted for 91 percent, with overseas Chinese and other foreign investors contributing the remaining 5.5 percent and 3.5 percent, respectively.[58] Shenzhen became a boom area. Annual revenue in 1981 was five times that collected in 1978, and total industrial output grew at double-digit rates.

Hong Kong is short of land and labor. The SEZ was a convenient marriage between the abundant land and manual labor in China and the capital, technology, and entrepreneurial know-how in Hong Kong. Tourism and real estate, largely catering to Hong Kong Chinese and visitors to Hong Kong, constituted 78 percent of early investment. Most of the residential units were purchased by Hong Kong residents for the benefit of relatives in China, who were then free to take up residence in Shenzhen with its higher living standards; other units were acquired as retirement or holiday homes and as temporary business premises.[59]

Investment in the other three zones has lagged. They were less conveniently located for Hong Kong businessmen and seriously lacked infrastructural facilities. For three years after Xiamen opened its SEZ, the response to the zone was feeble.[60] In November 1983, Premier Zhao Ziyang visited Xiamen, urging zone administrators to seek investments in technology and knowledge-intensive industries.[61] He viewed these "windows on the world" as vehicles to modernize China's obsolete industrial plant. In February 1984, elder statesman Deng Xiaoping himself visited three of the zones, including Xiamen. In March, the boundary of the zone was enlarged from the 1 square miles section of Huli to include the entire 48 square mile island of Xiamen. In 1984, Xiamen authorities opened a modern port and airport, and finished a half-dozen factory buildings in Xiamen's Huli industrial district. Xiamen International Airport handles flights from Beijing, Shanghai, Canton, and Hong Kong, with plans for Manila, Japan, and Southeast Asia (assuming the zone's own airline, Xiamen Aviation Company, gets off the ground). Shipping berths were constructed in Xiamen's deep-water harbor. By mid-1984, foreign investors had signed contracts for 82 projects worth a total of $385 million, including such American giants as Eastman Kodak, R.J. Reynolds, and Coca-Cola.

Xiamen, like other zones, offered foreign capitalists three-to-five-year tax holidays, followed by a flat corporate income tax rate of 15 percent. Within limits, foreign businessmen received the right to hire and fire workers. Reflecting Deng's new emphasis on the individual economy, privately run shops and restaurants opened along the main business street in late 1984.

The state's impetus to foreign investment produced dramatic results in 1984. Between January and September, $1.66 billion in foreign investments was recorded—a figure double that for the same period in 1983. Investment agreements worth $1.91 billion were also signed.[62]

In the summer of 1984, China extended the concept of the Special Economic Zone to fourteen coastal cities to accelerate foreign trade and investment. The cities ranged from Dalian in the far north to Beihei on China's extreme southern coast. The coastal cities were granted more economic decision-making power, with authority to offer investors low tax rates and other investment incentives, including the right of foreign bankers to open branches that provide such financial services as taking deposits and making loans to local Chinese entrepreneurs. The fourteen cities announced plans to create special "economic-technological development districts" to accommodate foreign factories.[63] Between January and September 1984, authorities in the fourteen cities signed 420 contracts with investors worth $880 million, which was one and one-half times the total value of all foreign investment in these cities in the last five years put together.[64] The fourteen cities held a joint exhibition in Hong Kong in November 1984 and claimed to sign contracts exceeding $1 billion.

Investment regulations in these cities mirrored those in the four SEZs. Foreign investors paid a 15 percent income tax rate, which compared favorably with applicable rates of 30–50 percent elsewhere in China, and were allowed to establish wholly owned enterprises free of state control and to remit earnings outside China tax-free. The central government announced plans to develop infrastructure in seven of the coastal cities, especially airports, roads, and utilities. Extension of the SEZ principle to the coastal cities fostered competition among the privileged economic units: Shenzhen promised investors additional concessions such as longer tax breaks and lower land-use fees to maintain its attractiveness.

The inclusion of fourteen additional coastal cities and Hainan Island under the SEZ umbrella encountered exceptionally stormy economic weather. Although Shenzhen's gross industrial output value reached $461 million in 1984, more than 20 times that of 1979, much of it reflected construction, thus causing the leaders disappointment over the low quality and volume of export-oriented investment. Indeed, rather than earning foreign exchange, the SEZs were consumers of state foreign-exchange support.[65] Disenchanted with the lack of progress in reaching its goals for SEZs, China announced in July 1985 a delay in plans to develop ten of the fourteen coastal cities. Only Shanghai, Tianjin, Dalian, and Guangzhou were scheduled to receive scarce foreign exchange to develop international trade facilities.[66]

The experience of Hainan Island, in particular, soured Beijing on the rapid expansion of SEZs and coastal cities. The island became an enormous foreign-exchange black market. Between January 1984 and March 1985, it imported vehicles worth $1.5 billion, about 43 times its official foreign-exchange quota. These purchases were largely intended for resale to other parts of China that lacked large-scale import privileges.[67]

Problems with the SEZs led Deng Xiaoping to comment on June 29, 1985, that Shenzhen was just "an experiment," rather than a centerpiece of his economic reforms. Deng's comments were prompted by growing reports of corruption highlighting such practices as smuggling, embezzlement, bribery, and fraudulent shipments. Reports surfaced that relatives of top Beijing officials and retired cadres with influential connections had set up shop in Shenzhen. Retail sales, property development, and infrastructure development continued to overshadow the development of domestic industries with foreign cooperation for export markets. Less than 20 percent of Shenzhen's industrial output was exported. Most found its way into internal Chinese markets.[68] The future expansion of SEZ facilities on Hainan Island and in the coastal cities was in doubt at the end of 1985. The optimism of summer 1984 gave way to a bleak winter a year and a half later, as the fourteen coastal cities temporarily became four.

China's new outward orientation resulted in a major increase in foreign investment and trade. Foreign investment in the zones and coastal cities surpassed the several billion dollar level. Reflecting China's inward-looking policies, total foreign trade stagnated at meager levels of $2 billion in 1952, $3.1 billion in 1957, and $4.3 billion in 1965. By 1978, it reached $20.6 billion. From that point, trade grew by leaps and bounds, expanding to $49.8 billion in 1984 and $59.2 billion in 1985.[69] (Exports are valued at free on board [f.o.b.], exclusive of customs, insurance, and freight, whereas imports are valued at c.i.f, which includes customs, insurance, and freight.) China enjoyed a trade surplus during the four years from 1980 to 1983; foreign-exchange reserves grew from $2.3 billion to $14.3 billion over that period.[70] The years 1984 and 1985, however, were another story. In 1984, China posted a $9.5 billion trade deficit followed, in 1985, by a $7.6 billion trade deficit. At the end of 1985, China held only $11.9 billion in foreign-exchange reserves.[71] (Taiwan, by contrast, held US$44 billion at the end of 1986.)

Rising peasant incomes unleashed pent-up demands for consumer goods that China's domestic industries could not supply. Because foreign-exchange reserves were steadily rising, import controls were relaxed from 1982 to fill this demand. Import volume surged from the second half of 1984, reflecting massive flows of consumer goods and increased purchases of foreign equipment and machinery by autonomous enterprises with retained earnings. Foreign-exchange holdings dropped 28 percent in just seven months from peak holdings of $17 billion in July 1984 to $12.3 billion. In addition, the official Renminbi exchange rate was devalued from US$1 = 2.05 yuan to $1 = 2.8 yuan in March 1985. By November 1985 the rate had steadily declined to $1 = 3.19 yuan, where it remained fixed until the next summer. On July 5, 1986, the People's Bank of China posted a new devalued rate of $1 = 3.69 yuan. The foreign-exchange drain continued throughout 1985, as reserves fell to as low as $8 billion, but successive devaluations finally stemmed the outflow in 1986. This decline represented a 50 percent exhaustion of foreign exchange, which had taken four years to build up, in just over one year.[72]

Financial Reforms

Economic deregulation required financial and budgetary reform. Instead of receiving capital grants from and remitting all their profits to the state, autonomous enterprises were required to borrow from banks and pay taxes. These changes brought financial, budgetary, and monetary policies into play, which hitherto had little independent role in the previous closed system of state allocations. In Chinese economic phraseology, finance became a lever for economic readjustment and growth.

Deng's main objection to leftist policy was overinvestment in capital construction in the face of declining returns to investment. The use of capital did not reflect its true value or scarcity. A priority was to reduce the high rate of capital investment to levels that could sustain fast growth with efficient results. Apart from cutting down on capital construction investments, new policies included using bank loans in place of state appropriations. Banks were instructed to consider the viability of each loan application as well as the repayment of principal and interest, thus allocating scarce credit to those enterprises that promised to use capital efficiently. Returns to investment were to become the basis for credit. But putting these changes into full practice was no easy task.

Initial experiments were conducted in 1979 and 1980 in the textile and other light industries as well as in tourism in Beijing, Shanghai, and Guangdong Province.[73] Variable time limits were applied to heavy and light industrial enterprises, interest rates varied across industries, and severe penalties were imposed for overdue payment. These experiments eliminated false overreporting of capital requirements (inasmuch as interest and principal had to be repaid), fostered more efficient utilization of existing facilities, curtailed reckless spending (of the state's funds), and encouraged economizing on capital (rather than rushing to spend the state's funds by year's end to secure future allocations).

China's several state-owned banks—the People's Bank of China, the Agricultural Bank of China, and the Bank of China—began to extend medium- and short-term credits for equipment and working capital. Capital construction investment in state-owned enterprises was increasingly financed by long-term credits from the Construction Bank. The old method of state financial appropriations applied more and more only to governmental units that had nothing to sell such as administration, health, national defense, and scientific research.

Other bank reforms included trust and investment business, domestic insurance, loans based on market need rather than planned quotas, variable interest rates to lure savings and rationalize loans, development of specialized services, financial autonomy for branch offices, business accounting within banks, and profit sharing.[74] These reforms represented partial movement from state control over banking. Full deregulation would include complete bank loan autonomy, independent setting of interest rates, treating banks as independent enterprises instead of state agencies, and introducing competition to a network of state-run banks.

On an experimental basis, China announced on December 22, 1984, that four foreign bank branches in Shanghai—the Hongkong and Shanghai Banking Corporation, the Standard Chartered Bank, the Hongkong-based Bank of East Asia, and the Overseas Chinese Banking Corporation of Singapore—were allowed to accept deposits and make loans in foreign currency in Shanghai beginning December 1, 1984.[75] Although the four banks were authorized to accept foreign currency deposits by joint ventures, foreign enterprises, and overseas Chinese firms, and could make foreign currency loans to them, demand for these services remained limited. Foreign banks have sought without success the right to engage in domestic deposit taking and lending, and to freely buy and sell foreign exchange.[76]

Other banking and credit policies became more liberal. Enterprises and specialist households were given the freedom to engage in cash transactions, and exemption from transactions that had to go through the People's Bank of China more than tripled from 30 yuan to 100 yuan. Check-clearing was diversified to include checks issued outside Beijing and those issued by foreign banks.[77] In December 1984, the Industrial and Commercial Bank of China opened checking accounts for residents in the Xuhui district of Shanghai, a revival of personal checking after its absence for more than thirty years. Checks could be used in restaurants and shops and to pay rent, taxis, and other bills.[78] Interest rates on individual deposits were increased to promote saving, and specialist banks were free to fluctuate rates within specified guidelines. Despite these reforms, state control over banking remained comprehensive. Progress in implementing urban, industrial, and commercial reforms was notably slower than the rapid diffusion of the responsibility system in agriculture.

Fiscal and Tax Policies

The original concept underlying taxation in socialist China under Mao Zedong's leadership was that taxation was unnecessary because the state had the right to the property of state-owned enterprises through taking its net profits. Profitable enterprises supplied revenue and losing enterprises received subsidies. Deng Xiaoping judged this approach destructive of incentives to efficient bookkeeping and management. His emphasis on enterprise autonomy, allowing enterprises to retain a portion of their profits, along with the resurrection of private corporations, joint state-private ventures, the operation of foreign-owned enterprises in China, and the individual economy (2.3 million urban residents were self-employed in 1983 compared with 150,000 in 1978), encouraged changes in taxation. As the state, in effect, gradually began to disown the economy, it no longer had the right to all the profits of private enterprises.

In keeping with tried-and-true practices, several areas were designated for tax experiments—Sichuan, Hubei, Shanghai, and Liuzhou.[79] The first test took place in 1980 in Liuzhou, which is located in the distant Guangxi Zhuang Autonomous Region. It combined the switch to enterprise autonomy with the replacement of profit remission to the state by taxation. The experiment encompassed a value-added tax on machinery (paid on the portion of value added after deducting the cost of material inputs); rising tax rates on different levels of profitability, ranging from none on products sold at a profit of less than 15 percent to a 0.6 percent levy imposed on each additional 1 percent increase in profitability; a straight 50 percent tax on state-owned enterprise profits; and fees charged for the use of fixed assets and working capital.

Tax reform became a priority. Apart from implementing systems of enterprise taxes, the measures included an income tax law for joint ventures with Chinese and foreign investment, individual income taxes, and taxation in the Special Economic Zones and coastal cities. For joint ventures, the law adopted in September 1980 levied a proportional 30 percent national tax and a local surtax of 10 percent (for a total 33 percent rate) on joint venture profits. However, joint ventures received preferential treatment in the form of tax remission in the first year of operation and a 50 percent reduction in the second and third years, a 40 percent refund of income tax paid on reinvested profits, accelerated depreciation, and additional benefits for investments in remote, undeveloped regions.

The individual income tax law applied to everyone residing in China for one year or more. First a monthly fixed allowance of 800 yuan per household was subtracted thus exempting most low-income Chinese from the levy; then a series of graduated rates ranging from 5 to 45 percent was imposed on wages and salaries. The tax on remuneration for personal services, royalties, interest, dividends, bonuses, rents, and other kinds of income was set at a low, flat rate of 20 percent. Twenty percent of income from personal services and leasing property was deductible as business expenses. Where possible, taxes were withheld at the source and remitted directly to the state; others filed a personal return at year's end.[80] Such categories of income as prizes, interest on savings deposits, welfare benefits, insurance indemnities, severance pay, and other categories specifically designated by the Ministry of Finance were tax free.

Of course, the purpose of taxation was to collect enough money for the state to pay its bills. For historical reasons, China's budgeteers feared inflation more than any other economic adversity, and therefore took great pains to maintain overall budgetary balance. They believed that fiscal deficits brought overissue of bank notes and rising prices. The principle of budget balance also extended to provincial and local governments.

During the readjustment years of 1979 and 1980, the state ran consecutive deficits of 17.1 and 12.8 billion yuan. These deficits were financed by drawing down past accumulated surpluses of 8 billion yuan and an overdraft of 9 billion yuan from the People's Bank of China in 1979, and through 8 billion yuan in bank borrowings and 4.8 billion yuan from state treasury bonds in 1980.[81] In effect, a portion of the deficits was financed by printing money, thus increasing the money supply and driving up prices. Inflation was 6 percent in both 1979 and 1980, well exceeding the long-term, post-1952 level of less than 2 percent. By 1981, the large deficits had diminished, although smaller deficits persisted. It should be noted that much of China's long-run success in maintaining stable prices took the form of repressed inflation, in which the state resorted to coupons, rationing, and queues to distribute goods for which excess demand existed at the low state-set official prices.

In general, China was averse to large-scale foreign borrowing.[82] China borrowed heavily from the Soviet Union to finance the development of heavy industry in the 1950s but repaid all loans within five years after the Sino-Soviet break in 1959, well ahead of schedule. Deng Xiaoping's drive toward modernization reopened China to foreign capital and technology, but foreign borrowing was slow to materialize. Indeed, between 1983 and 1984, China reduced its foreign debt from $3 billion to $1 billion by repaying existing loans ahead of schedule. After running trade deficits in 1982 and 1983, they ran consecutive balance-of-trade surpluses the following two years to strengthen foreign-exchange holdings. The Chinese preferred concessional loans from foreign governments in addition to the World Bank and International Monetary Fund.

Money and Banking

Recent years brought the reemergence of personal checking, relaxed restrictions on cash transactions, greater rationality of prices, enhanced incentives to work, decentralization of public finance and investment decisions, open courtship of overseas funds by special zones and coastal cities, and prospects for growing financial deregulation and private competition. As a result, monetary policy was no longer purely passive.

The implementation of liberal economic reforms made instruments of monetary control—such as targeting interest rates, adjusting the exchange rate, determining liquid assets requirements, and other regulatory measures—relevant to the level of prices and credit. As more goods and services were freely traded without price controls, private demand for credit and cash influenced prices.

The inadequacies of China's newly reformed monetary system lay behind the explosion in money supply and the sharp drop in foreign reserves from the middle of 1984 through early 1985, both of which forced Chinese authorities to induce a slowdown in the economy.[83] Prior to 1979, China's banking system was based on the Soviet model, in which the banking system served largely as a channel through which the state managed and allocated funds within a closed regime of fixed prices and state allocations. China's economy was disproportionately cash based: Individuals did not hold checking accounts and the bulk of bank deposits consisted of deposits made by enterprises and institutions. The state-owned People's Bank of China literally financed government deficits by printing money. Thus, banking arrangements in China during 1949–1979 were basically an extension of the government's fiscal operations, rather than a true banking system that functioned in market economies.

Recall that the government granted enterprises greater autonomy in their investments and output decisions. This reform required changing the pre-1979 system of complete central control of bank credit and deposits. Since 1979, the government moved to replace state-budget financing of economic activity with bank lending, instructing banks to issue loans on the basis of economic considerations in place of former state directives. Similarly, the People's Construction Bank replaced state appropriations as the means of financing capital construction investment.

In September 1983, China attempted to establish a true central bank. It separated the central banking and commercial banking activities of the People's Bank of China by splitting them between the Industrial and Commercial Bank, which, since 1984, held responsibility for commercial banking activities, and a new People's Bank of China, which acted as a central bank to oversee the operations of the whole banking sector. The four state-owned banks (the Industrial and Commercial Bank, the Agricultural Bank of China, the Bank of China, and the People's Construction Bank of China) were required to maintain reserve deposits with the PBOC equal to 10 percent of their outstanding deposits, on which they earned interest.

The PBOC, the central bank, used interest rates as a tool or "lever" of monetary policy to raise or lower the price of credit and varied rates in response to changes in economic conditions. This policy was a major departure from the pre-1979 system, under which interest rates were rigidly fixed for long periods of time. These changes changed the Chinese monetary system away from the Soviet model to one that began to take on the form of an orthodox Western monetary system.

However, the primitive level of development of China's financial system, in which checks are rarely used and most transactions are in cash, made it difficult to control the growth of money supply by controlling the monetary base (cash in circulation and bank reserves)—the approach taken by most Western central banks—and thus the overall level of prices. The problem was that large increases in the demand for currency were accommodated through an expansion of the monetary base by central bank injection of cash into the banking system. Thus cash requirements dictated the size of the monetary base and bank reserves rather than the monetary base determining the overall money supply in a conventional monetary system, where the cash-to-deposit ratio is typically less than 10 percent.

The inability of the PBOC to control the growth of money and credit was clearly revealed beginning in late 1984. The explosive increase in currency in circulation from 50 to 80 billion yuan in the fourth quarter of 1984 was due to a massive increase in the public's demand for currency (instead of deposits) and to sharply higher lending by specialized banks. Enterprises utilized their autonomy to grant massive increases in salaries and bonuses to workers; the nation's total wage bill rose 46 percent and bonuses increased more than 50 percent in the fourth quarter. In addition, provincial banks used their new independence to lend indiscriminately in capital construction, for which the state was partly to blame, having announced that credit extension limits of specialized banks in 1985 would be based on the value of total outstanding loans at the end of 1984. Total bank lending grew 30 percent in 1984, most occurring in the fourth quarter.

Enterprises drew down their bank deposits to pay the huge bonus payments to workers in cash. With bank lending sharply up and bank deposits sharply down, the PBOC was forced to increase lending to the banking system as a whole by issuing more currency to the banks. Cash in circulation surged 49 percent in 1984, mostly in the fourth quarter.

Inflation surged at 11 percent in 1984.[84] The supply of inputs, goods, and services failed to keep pace with the growth of money, thus bringing sharply higher prices. To reduce currency in circulation, the government instituted strict controls on credit extension by the specialized banks, raised bank deposit interest rates, implemented a tight fiscal policy to decrease its budget deficit, fully implemented a 55 percent tax on enterprise profits, introduced a progressive tax on worker bonuses, and spent several billion dollars of foreign exchange by importing consumer durables to absorb excess currency in circulation. Indeed, reserves dropped from $16.7 billion to $11.4 billion between September 1984 and March 1985. The tighter controls instituted to rein in runaway money growth and rising controls went against the general spirit of liberalizing reform of the economy. As the economy develops in a more market-oriented fashion, the PBOC will need to develop tools of monetary control to avoid problems of boom and bust and inflation.

NOTES

1. Reported in *Time* (January 14, 1985), p. 36.
2. *Decision of the Central Committee of the Communist Party of China on Reform of the Economic Structure* (Adopted by the 12th Central Committee of the Communist Party of China at Its Third Plenary Session on October 20, 1984), reprinted in *Beijing Review* 27, no. 44 (October 29, 1984).
3. *Wall Street Journal* (December 10, 1984); and *Peninsula Times-Tribune* (December 22, 1984).
4. Liu Guoguang and Wang Ruisun, "Restructuring of the Economy," in Yu Guangyuan, ed., *China's Socialist Modernization* (Beijing: Foreign Languages Press, 1984), p. 99.
5. Zhao Ziyang was elevated in August 1980 to the post of premier, the highest state position.
6. The *Far Eastern Economic Review* (December 13, 1984), featured a cover story by Robert Delfs on Chinese economic reforms subtitled "China Goes to Market," from which the title of this chapter is taken. On this point see pp. 72–73 of that cover story.
7. Li Chengrui and Zhang Zhuoyuan, "An Outline of Economic Development (1977–1980)," in Yu Guangyuan, ed., *China's Socialist Modernization,* p. 41.
8. The production responsibility system and other reforms in Chinese agriculture have received considerable scholarly attention. Details are found in Dwight Perkins and Shahid Yusuf, *Rural Development in China* (Baltimore and London: Johns Hopkins University Press for the World Bank, 1984), pp. 80–83; Kenneth R. Walker, "Chinese Agriculture During the Period of the Readjustment, 1978–83," *The China Quarterly,* no. 100 (December 1984), pp. 784–789; Graham E. Johnson, "The Production Responsibility System in Chi-

nese Agriculture: Some Examples from Guangdong," *Pacific Affairs* 55, no. 3 (Fall 1982), pp. 430–451; Lee Travers, "Post-1978 Rural Economic Policy and Peasant Income in China," *The China Quarterly,* no. 98 (June 1984), pp. 241–243; Audrey Donnithorne, "The Chinese Economy Today," *Journal of Northeast Asian Studies* 2, no. 3 (September 1983), pp. 18–19; Jan S. Prybyla, "Where Is China's Economy Headed?" *Journal of Northeast Asian Studies* 1, no. 4 (December 1982), pp. 17–19; and Frederick W. Crook, "The Reform of the Commune System and the Rise of the Township-Collective-Household System," in *China's Economy Looks Toward the Year 2000. Volume 1. The Four Modernizations,* Selected Papers Submitted to the Joint Economic Committee, Congress of the United States, May 21, 1986 (Washington, D.C.: Government Printing Office, 1986), pp. 354–375.

9. Lee Travers, "Post-1978 Rural Economic Policy and Peasant Income in China," p. 241.

10. Kenneth R. Walker, "Chinese Agriculture During the Period of the Readjustment, 1978-83," pp. 784–785.

11. See Lee Travers, "Post-1978 Rural Economic Policy and Peasant Income in China," p. 242. See also W. Klatt, "The Staff of Life: Living Standards in China, 1977-81," *The China Quarterly,* no. 93 (March 1983), pp. 33–37. Despite the sharp increase in farmgate prices, Klatt maintains that agriculture suffered an unfavorable "terms of trade" in 1981, because farm inputs and manufactured goods carried a heavy markup between the factory and the countryside.

12. Robert Delfs, "Back to the Market," *Far Eastern Economic Review* (May 30, 1985), pp. 77–79.

13. *China: A Statistical Survey in 1986,* compiled by the State Statistical Bureau, PRC (Hong Kong: Produced by the Longman Group for New World Press and China Statistical Information and Consultancy Service Center, 1986), p. 93. In 1985, gross agricultural output value was 458 billion yuan, which means that 15.4 percent of GAOV was sold in urban and rural fairs.

14. Graham Johnson, in "The Production Responsibility System in Chinese Agriculture," pp. 436–439, identified six broad forms of rural responsibility. These included (1) specialized contracting with remuneration linked to output, in which specific tasks were contracted through competitive bidding to specialist work groups; (2) contracting production for work groups with renumeration linked to output, in which the production team specified the amounts of labor, investment, and output, awarded bonuses for above-quota production, and levied fines for failure to meet contract levels; (3) linking remuneration to the output of each laborer, in which all allocation, accounting, and distribution were undertaken at the team level; (4) fixing output quotas for each household; (5) assigning full responsibility to the households, with permanent assignment of draft animals and tools; and (6) short-term contracts for field work.

15. David Zweig, "Opposition to Change in Rural China," *Asian Survey* 23, no. 7 (July 1983), p. 884.

16. *China: A Statistical Survey in 1986,* p. 9.

17. *Far Eastern Economic Review* (December 13, 1984), p. 66.

18. *Statistical Yearbook of China 1985,* compiled by the State Statistical Bureau, PRC (Hong Kong: Economic Information and Agency, 1985), pp. 255–258, 266–267, 270; and *China: A Statistical Survey in 1986,* pp. 4, 37–40.

19. *China: A Statistical Survey in 1986,* p. 41.

20. Kenneth R. Walker, "Chinese Agriculture During the Period of the Readjustment, 1978-83," p. 789.

21. *Statistical Yearbook of China 1985,* pp. 275–277, 281; and *China: A Statistical Survey in 1986,* pp. 44–45.

22. *The Economist* (January 18, 1986), p. 30.

23. David Bonavia, "Reaping Only What Is Sown," *Far Eastern Economic Review* (January 2, 1986), pp. 28–29. See also Robert Hsu, "Grain Procurement and Distribution in China's Rural Areas," *Asian Survey* 24, no. 12 (December 1984), pp. 1237–1240. Hsu discusses other peasant ploys to take advantage of opportunities for illicit gain, such as abuse of government grain resales to buy return-sale or disaster-relief grain or borrowing grain from the government at low prices and then reselling the same grain to the state at higher prices as negotiated-price gain.

24. Robert Delfs, "China's Fear of Flying," *Far Eastern Economic Review* (December 5, 1985), pp. 64–65.

25. *Statistical Yearbook of China 1985,* p. 523.

26. Ibid., p. 530.

27. Nicholas R. Lardy, "Consumption and Living Standards in China, 1978–83," *The China Quarterly,* no. 100 (December 1984), p. 862.

28. *China: A Statistical Survey in 1986,* p. 9.

29. Ibid., pp. 110–112.

30. Ibid., p. 113.

31. Paul B. Trescott, "Incentives Versus Equality: What Does China's Recent Experience Show?" *World Development* 13, no. 2 (1985), pp. 205–217.

32. Nicholas R. Lardy, "Consumption and Living Standards in China, 1978–83," pp. 863–864.

33. Robert Hsu, "Grain Procurement and Distribution in China's Rural Areas," pp. 1235–1236, 1241–1244.

34. Kenneth R. Walker, "Chinese Agriculture During the Period of the Readjustment, 1978–83," pp. 800–802.

35. *China: A Statistical Survey in 1986,* p. 50.

36. Ibid., p. 89.

37. Li Chengrui and Wang Ruisun, "Restructuring of the Economy," pp. 3–71.

38. Ibid., p. 46. See also Robert Michael Field, "Changes in Chinese Industry Since 1978," *The China Quarterly,* no. 100 (December 1984), pp. 742–750.

39. Li Chengrui and Zhang Zhuoyuan, "An Outline of Economic Development (1977–1980)," p. 50.

40. Robert Michael Field, "Changes in Chinese Industry Since 1978," pp. 756–760.

41. "China," *Asia Yearbook 1984* (published by the *Far Eastern Economic Review*), pp. 152–153. See also *Far Eastern Economic Review* (December 13, 1984), p. 72; and Donald Zagoria, "China's Quiet Revolution," *Foreign Affairs* (Spring 1984), p. 885.

42. *Far Eastern Economic Review* (December 13, 1984), p. 79.

43. *Wall Street Journal* (August 10, 1984).

44. Hong-yung Lee, "Deng Xiaoping's Reform of the Chinese Bureaucracy," *Journal of Northeast Asian Studies* 1, no. 2 (June 1982), pp. 21–35.

45. Shortages of electricity periodically affected the operation of as many as one-third of the factories in the country. See Shigeru Ishikawa, "China's Economic Growth Since 1949—An Assessment," *The China Quarterly,* no. 94 (June 1983), p. 246.

46. Joyce Kallgren, "China in 1983: The Turmoil of Modernization," *Asian Survey* 24, no. 1 (January 1984), pp. 71–73.

47. *China: A Statistical Survey in 1986*, p. 9.

48. Ibid., pp. 9, 53–57.

49. Ibid., pp. 76–77.

50. Robert Michael Field, "Changes in Chinese Industry Since 1978," pp. 750–756. Setting 1952 = 100 as the index of overall labor productivity, we find that the index increased from 266 in 1978 to 338 in 1984 for a gain of 27 percent in six years. See *China: A Statistics Survey in 1985*, p. 57.

51. Hsin Chang, "The 1982–83 Overinvestment Crisis in China," *Asian Survey* 24, no. 12 (December 1984), pp. 1276–1281.

52. William Byrd et al., *Recent Chinese Economic Reforms: Studies of Two Industrial Enterprises*, World Bank Staff Working Papers, No. 652 (Washington, D.C.: World Bank, 1984).

53. *China: A Statistical Survey in 1986*, p. 105.

54. Nicholas R. Lardy, "Consumption and Living Standards in China, 1978–83," pp. 857–863.

55. Derived from *Statistical Yearbook of China 1985*, p. 552.

56. Y. Y. Kueh and Christopher Howe, "China's International Trade: Policy and Organizational Change and Their Place in the 'Economic Readjustment,'" *The China Quarterly*, no. 100 (December 1984), pp. 813–848.

57. Clyde D. Stoltenberg, "China's Special Economic Zones: Their Development and Prospects," *Asian Survey* 24, no. 6 (June 1984), pp. 637–654; and George Fitting, "Export Processing Zones in Taiwan and the People's Republic of China," *Asian Survey* 22, no. 8 (August 1982), pp. 732–744. Fitting states that the laws governing the operation of the zones in Guangdong and Fujian closely follow the pioneering lead of Taipei.

58. Y. C. Jao, "Hong Kong's Role in Financing China's Modernization," in A. J. Youngson, ed., *China and Hong Kong: The Economic Nexus* (Hong Kong: Oxford University Press, 1983), p. 50.

59. Ibid., p. 52.

60. Andrew Tanzer, "Karl Marx Must Be Spinning in his Grave," *Forbes* (November 19, 1984), pp. 258–261.

61. Andrew Tanzer, "Growing Pains," *Far Eastern Economic Review* (October 11, 1984), pp. 98–100.

62. *Beijing Review* 27, no. 52 (December 24, 1984), pp. 10–12.

63. *Wall Street Journal* (June 27, 1984).

64. *Beijing Review* 27, no. 50 (December 10, 1984), pp. 16–17.

65. Robert Delfs, "Changing the Pattern," *Far Eastern Economic Review* (May 9, 1985), pp. 70–71.

66. *Far Eastern Economic Review* (July 25, 1985), p. 10.

67. Ibid. (August 22, 1985), pp. 100–101.

68. Ibid. (September 19, 1985), pp. 61–63.

69. *Statistical Yearbook of China 1985*, p. 508; and *Wall Street Journal* (January 23, 1986).

70. *Statistical Yearbook of China 1985*, p. 527.

71. *China: A Statistical Survey in 1986*, p. 87.

72. See the June 27, 1985 (p. 110), August 22, 1985 (pp. 100–101), and July 17, 1986 (pp. 50–51) editions of the *Far Eastern Economic Review*. The sequence of sharp devaluations in the wake of Deng Ziaoping's economic reforms suggests that China's currency was grossly overvalued in the 1970s

and early 1980s. Thus, even though per capita output rose sharply during 1978–1985, income per person in U.S. dollar terms fell during that period. Hence it is reasonable to suppose that the value of China's national income was overstated in U.S. dollar terms for part of the postwar period.

73. Xu Yi and Chen Baosen, "Finance," in Yu Guangyuan, ed., *China's Socialist Modernization,* p. 468.

74. Yang Peixin, "Banking," in Yu Guangyuan, ed., *China's Socialist Modernization,* pp. 420–421.

75. *Far Eastern Economic Review* (January 10, 1985), pp. 50–53.

76. Ibid. (April 25, 1985), pp. 70–71.

77. Ibid. (January 10, 1985), pp. 50–53.

78. *Beijing Review* 27, no. 51 (December 17, 1984), p. 11.

79. Xu Yi and Chen Baosen, "Finance," pp. 515–518.

80. Ibid., pp. 520–521.

81. Ibid., pp. 452–453 and Ma Hong, *New Strategy for China's Economy* (Beijing: New World Press, 1983), pp. 76–77.

82. Paul D. Reynolds, *China's International Banking and Financial System* (New York: Praeger Publishers, 1982), pp. 107–111.

83. This section draws from John G. Greenwood, "People's Republic of China: Problems of Monetary Control," *Asian Monetary Monitor* 9, no. 4 (July–August 1985), pp. 13–21.

84. M. T. Teng, "A Chinese Styled Socialist Economy: Economic Performance from 1979 to 1985 and the Prospect of the Future to 1990," mimeo (November 1985), p. 7. M. T. Teng is professor of economics at Anhui University in Hefei, China, but wrote the paper as Distinguished Visiting Professor at Winthrop College, Rock Hill, South Carolina.

PART II

TAIWAN

5

PEOPLE, RESOURCES, AND POLITICS

Taiwan is provincial home to 19 million people of Chinese background. It has a checkered history. Its historically popular name, Formosa, came from its encounter with Portuguese traders who named it "Beautiful Island." Although settled by a small number of mainland Chinese immigrants, it was not incorporated into the united Chinese empire until late in the sixteenth century during the Ming Dynasty. Following its defeat in the Sino-Japanese War, China ceded the island to Japan in 1895, but reacquired it in 1945 at the conclusion of World War II. The civil war between Chiang Kai-shek's Nationalist forces and Mao Zedong's Communist armies brought increased attention to Taiwan. Facing certain defeat, the Nationalist government and armies fled in 1948 to Taiwan, where they set up a "temporary" provisional government. They also imposed authoritarian rule over the native Taiwanese. Throughout the 1950s, behind the protective shield of the U.S. aid program and the Seventh Fleet, the Nationalist government planned for a triumphant return to the mainland.

By the 1980s, mainlanders had been diminished to a bare 15 percent of the population of Taiwan. Talk of recovering the mainland was idle rhetoric. In place of past military and political dreams, the leaders of Taiwan focused their energies on turning the island into a prosperous, independent economy. They succeeded: Per capita income rose from a low, low $70 at the end of World War II to surpass $3,000 in 1985. Real gross national product grew at the astounding annual average rate of 8.2 percent in the 1950s, 9.1 percent in the 1960s, and 10 percent in the 1970s, a thirty-year annual average of 9.2 percent. Although growth decelerated during the recent world recession to 5.7 percent in 1981 and 3.3 percent in 1982, it recovered to 7.9 percent in 1983 and

103

10.5 percent in 1984. After a somewhat slower 5.1 percent growth in 1985, it spurted to double-digit levels again in 1986. By 1986, real GNP was more than fifteen times that of 1952. The whole country was literally transformed from poor to middle-income in just one generation.[1]

As mainland China established diplomatic ties with more nations, including the United States in 1979, Taiwan became politically isolated. Mainland China replaced Taiwan as China's official member in the World Bank and the International Monetary Fund. Taiwan was not allowed to use its political name, the Republic of China, in the 1984 Olympic Games. Despite diplomatic adversity, Taiwan remains among the world's top twenty exporters and substantially expanded its external economic relationships during the 1980s. The country's external assets reached $44 billion at the end of 1986, following several years of record trade surpluses. Taiwan's foreign assets in 1986 quadrupled those of the mainland's with but one-fiftieth of the population. These foreign assets back its currency and have enabled it to purchase weapons for security on a cash-and-carry basis. Taiwan's economic links with other nations have thrived despite the shock of the United States' withdrawal of diplomatic recognition in 1979.

PHYSICAL SETTING, RESOURCES, AND POPULATION

Taiwan consists of one large semi-tropical island and a few adjacent small islands, lying astride the Tropic of Cancer. Taiwan is situated 100 miles east of mainland China, 700 miles south of Japan, and 200 miles north of the Philippine Islands. The air route connecting Tokyo, Taipei, and Hong Kong is known in Asia as the "golden triangle" due to its heavy traffic and profitability. Taiwan's total land area is about 36,000 square kilometers (13,800 square miles). About one-third the size of Virginia, it supports a population that exceeded 19 million in 1985, a population density considerably higher than that of South Korea, Japan, Puerto Rico, Belgium, and Holland, which demographers regard as among the most densely populated nations in the world. The island's shape is roughly that of a long oval, running 240 miles from north to south and stretching 98 miles from west to east at its broadest point.[2]

Taiwan is a mountainous island, with two-thirds of its area consisting of rugged mountains. Only about one-fourth of the land is arable. Its climate consists of alternating periods of wetness and dryness. The dry and rainy seasons occur in the north and in the south at opposite times. In the north, the rainy season is from October to March; in the south, it lasts from April to September. Rainfall in the north generally falls at a moderate rate. The south, in contrast, suffers frequent thunderstorms and typhoons that cause floods, destroy houses, damage crops, and injure persons. However, the island's overall favorable climate for agriculture permits multiple cropping and year-round farming.

Various soil groups support different land-use patterns, including fish culture along the coast, inland sugar cane, rice cultivation, citrus fruit, traditional vegetable farming and animal husbandry, and forestry. The organic content of the soils is regarded as normal, and the soils are neither excessively acidic or alkaline. They react favorably to nitrogen, phosphorus, and potash fertilizers.

Taiwan has few mineral resources. Its main reserves are inferior quality coal, exceptionally high-quality marble, natural gas, and limited amounts of gold, sulphur, copper, petroleum, and salt. Its chief resources are agricultural rather than mineral, and manufacturers must import the bulk of their industrial raw materials.

The Chinese were the first people to settle Taiwan.[3] Early pioneers, made up of South Fujianese and Hakkas, arrived from Fujian Province (the Taiwanese dialect is akin to that of Fujian). Under the East India Company, the Dutch governed Taiwan between 1624 and 1662; they were expelled under the leadership of Koxinga (Cheng Cheng-kung), who ruled the island as a Chinese nationalist until 1683, when the Manchu government restored the island to imperial rule. From 1683 to 1891, Taiwan was increasingly sinicized, and some preliminary steps in the process of modernization were undertaken. By the turn of the twentieth century, the population had reached 3 million.

Taiwan's rising importance to China was reflected in its political status. It grew in administrative prominence from an imperial prefecture with three districts to a "province" in 1885, becoming China's twentieth province. It consisted of three prefectures, eleven districts, and several smaller administrative units resembling those in post–World War II Taiwan.

After the two Opium Wars in the mid-nineteenth century, China assigned key leaders to strengthen Taiwan's defense to fend off coastal incursions by the Japanese and French. Early projects included a railroad line, shipping and bunkering provisions, the installation of telegram and postal services, and the introduction of such staple export crops as rice, sugar, camphor, cotton, and tea.

Japan occupied Taiwan from 1895 to 1945. During this half-century, the Japanese developed the power industry, built a network of railways and highways, and improved the infrastructure for their own economic goals.[4] However, allied bombing and the lack of maintenance during World War II destroyed much of this infrastructure. In addition, repatriation of Japanese personnel at the end of the war reduced the number of skilled and managerial personnel on the island, thus posing a severe obstacle to industrial rehabilitation efforts.

THE POLITICAL SYSTEM OF TAIWAN

For nearly four decades, the Kuomintang Party, the armed forces, Generalissimo Chiang Kai-shek (who died on April 5, 1975), and his son and successor as president, Chiang Ching-kuo, exercised political power. Although locally born Taiwanese ascended to an increasing share of middle-level and top government positions, the mainlanders who fled China in 1948 remained in charge. Taiwan has a formal written constitution with a division of powers among the executive, legislative, and judicial branches of government, and elections were regularly held for members of the legislature and local government offices. But the existence of a Western-style constitution should not mask the reality that the Kuomintang exercised a firm grip on political life and the formulation of economic policy. No opposition was ever allowed to mount a serious challenge to the Kuomintang.

Chiang Kai-shek arrived in Taipei from the Chinese mainland on December 10, 1949, when the political fortunes of the Nationalists were at their lowest ebb.[5] The United States prepared itself for a Communist takeover of the island. Taiwan suffered from low production, rife inflation, inadequate housing and other facilities, and no apparent way to handle the more than 1 million mainlanders who accompanied their leader. The Nationalists imposed their rule over an unfriendly local population, who were treated more as conquered enemies than as liberated compatriots by governors that Chiang sent to take over from Japan in late 1945. The first governor, Chen Yi, was renowned for his corrupt, predatory, and oppressive rule, evicting Taiwanese from Japanese-abandoned homes to accommodate mainland VIPs, and using excessive force to put down uprisings in early 1947 that embittered mainlander-indigenous Taiwanese relationships for years to come.

The Nationalist government declared a "period of national emergency," through which it justified authoritarian rule. The harsh reality of Nationalist rule sharply contrasted with the government's official ideology, which was based on Dr. Sun Yat-sen's "Three Principles of the People" of nationalism, democracy, and improving the people's livelihood. Democracy was nowhere to be found in Taiwan throughout the early phases of Nationalist rule.

The Nationalists survived an early crisis through the unintended, but good, fortune brought by the outbreak of the Korean War in 1950. Overnight Taiwan became an important U.S. base in containing Communist expansion in Asia. Resumption of U.S. military and economic assistance enabled Chiang's government to surmount its immediate economic and political crises. The Korean War gave the Nationalists a new lease on life.

The Kuomintang Party ran Taiwan from 1950 through 1985 as a virtual one-party state, although an opposition was allowed to exist and steadily received greater freedom to contest political office in the 1970s and 1980s. The opposition confined itself largely to calls for more democracy, offering little in the way of alternative economic policies. The Kuomintang controlled policy decisions on economic, political, and social issues. It developed a well-organized party structure in Taiwan, mounting frequent drives to recruit new members. Mainlanders consistently dominated key party and government positions, but by the 1970s increasing numbers of Taiwanese had been brought into top posts. Many old Nationalist generals passed from the scene and the emphasis shifted to civilian preoccupations, particularly in matters of economic policy. However, the Kuomintang was never compelled to answer to an independent, democratically elected legislature on matters of public policy.

Like the Chinese Communist Party on mainland China, the Nationalist Party on Taiwan maintained an official ideology—namely: the doctrines of its founding father, Dr. Sun Yat-sen, who wrote the *San Min Chu I*, or the *Three Principles of the People*. Political education in Taiwan to this day stresses its symbols and interpretations. Nationalism, the first principle, is identified with patriotism; democracy, the second, symbolizes political modernity. People's livelihood, variously translated as "socialism" or the "welfare state," was equated in recent times with private-enterprise-oriented development and a better life for the people. The Nationalists also endorsed the values expressed in Confucian philosophy.

The Constitution and Structure of Government

The constitution of the Republic of China was adopted by the National Assembly on December 25, 1946, and declared effective one year later. Unfortunately for the Nationalists, the Communists were winning the civil war and Chiang's new constitution applied only to the small island of Taiwan, which became the permanent home of his government.

The document provided for five branches of government: legislative, executive, judicial, examination, and control. The first three are self-explanatory, resembling a standard Western presidential system in which the usual attempts are made at separation of powers and checks and balances. The examination and control branches were throwbacks to imperial history, reflecting the Confucian-based system of testing by which the emperor selected his officials and a board by which corrupt officials were censored. Given the virtually unlimited powers of the president, who also heads the Nationalist Party, the executive branch proposed policies that the legislature routinely approved.

Over the years, Taiwan's rulers suspended some of the provisions of the constitution due to the island's "emergency" situation. For example, the constitution limits the president to two terms, but Chiang Kai-shek enjoyed five terms—to accommodate his continued presidency, the Judicial branch ruled that this limiting provision be suspended.

The constitution also enumerated "temporary provisions effective during the period of communist rebellion," which were adopted on April 18, 1948, and amended in 1966 and 1975. These provisions permitted the president to take "emergency measures" to protect the security of the state or to cope with any serious financial or economic crisis, repealed the two-term restriction for the president, and authorized him to take necessary measures to mobilize the people and to implement elections once the mainland was recovered.

Chapter II of the constitution, paralleling that in mainland China, enumerated specific rights of the people, including freedom of residence, speech, publication, privacy, religion, assembly, due process, election, and access to public employment; it also imposed the duties of universal military service and paying taxes. Chapter II, Article 23, specifically stated: "All the freedoms and rights enumerated in the preceding Article shall not be restricted by law except by such as may be necessary to prevent infringement upon the freedoms of other persons, to avert an imminent crisis, to maintain social order or to advance public welfare." Thus, the rights of Taiwanese can be suspended under these conditions. This article is remarkably similar to Chapter Two, Article 51, of the Constitution of mainland China: "The exercise by citizens of the People's Republic of China of their freedoms and rights may not infringe upon the interests of the state, or society and of the collective, or upon the lawful freedoms and rights of other citizens." The difference between the two is not in the language but in the application of specific policies. The Taiwanese have enjoyed a large measure of economic freedom that their mainland counterparts have been denied.

Since the establishment of the "temporary capital" of the government of the Republic of China in Taipei in December 1949, the island has supported dual government: the claimant for the whole of the Chinese mainland (including some skeletal administrations for mainland provinces) and the practical government of Taiwan. Of the original 2,961 elected National Assembly members in 1947, only 955 remained by 1985; similarly, the legislative chamber contracted from 760 to 251.[6] Supplementary elections were held in Taiwan in 1969, 1972, 1973, 1976, 1980, and 1983, placing 91 locally elected members in the National Assembly and 78 in the Legislative Yuan.

The "national" government is disproportionately populated by elders. In 1985, the average age of original members of the two elected assemblies was 80 and 78 respectively, whereas new members averaged 50 and 47. Elections to local county and municipal offices encountered no such problems, as these duties fell entirely within the scope of Taiwan Province. Political activity and participation at the provincial level and below was clearly in local hands, but major policies and budgetary allocations remained in the hands of national officials.

Through 1985, the island lived under a state of emergency. Martial law placed restrictions on freedom of action, imposed some censorship upon the press, and curtailed full-fledged economic liberalism. Security remained an overriding concern of the leadership, dictating the development of a well-organized system of surveillance. Given an armed force of some 600,000, about one in every twelve adults was directly involved in national defense and internal security. The military had a major say in land use, which explains why some land use was uneconomical. The large defense burden consumed nearly 10 percent of gross national product.

To summarize, because it occupied Taiwan at the close of World War II, the Nationalist government imposed an authoritarian regime that maintained political stability. Free from periodic electoral and interest group pressures, party and government officials were able to take a long-run view of the economy. The economic, fiscal, trade, and monetary policies they adopted were conducive to both rapid economic growth and a rising standard of living.

STRATEGY FOR ECONOMIC DEVELOPMENT

Economic policy in Taiwan was divided into two distinct phases. Phase one held sway during 1949–1958. Its central features were a comprehensive land reform program, cessation of the inflation that had contributed to the Nationalists' downfall on the mainland, and the development of local industry behind a wall of government tariffs and other restrictions on free trade. Security interests and political survival were paramount. This period included considerable state direction and interference in the economy, although the scope and extent of state control never approached anything like mainland China's regime of comprehensive central planning. Throughout this first phase, Taiwan depended heavily on U.S. financial assistance.

Phase two of Taiwan's economic policy began with a series of commercial, industrial, investment, and tax reforms that were implemented during 1958–1962 and were steadily augmented through 1985. These reforms transformed Taiwan's economy into a predominantly private-enterprise, competitive market economy. Public policy dictated that the creation and distribution of wealth was to reside largely in the private sector, except for those activities and public programs the government deemed necessary to provide, such as defense, transport, social services, and major public works.[7] This chapter describes the initial phase of economic policy; the next analyzes the causes and consequences of the post-1958 period of liberal reform.

The central features of government policy during the 1950s were agricultural development and land reform, monetary stabilization and reform, encouragement of national savings to finance industrial investment, job creation to reduce unemployment, and placement of public finances on a sound footing. It also prepared for the day when U.S. economic aid might be reduced and phased out.

LAND REFORM

During Taiwan's colonial era, the island's agricultural economy was developed to support Japan's industrialization program.[8] Just prior to World War II, about two-thirds of the labor force was engaged in farming, which produced about 35 percent of the national income.

Three crops—rice, sweet potatoes, and sugar cane—generated about 85 percent of the total value of agricultural output and consumed over 80 percent of the total crop area. Early farming was largely traditional, relying on intensive labor and farm-produced fertilizers. Between 1895 and 1910, the value of farm output grew about 1.9 percent per year. Output increases doubled to an annual growth rate of 3.8 percent during 1910–1940 due to improvements in technology (new strains of rice, chemical fertilizer, and irrigation) and an increase in multiple cropping (more intensive use of limited land).

World War II's disruptions reduced output sharply, but the era of colonial rule developed a relatively modern agricultural sector with experience in labor-intensive methods, modern technology, and a system of drainage and irrigation. The Japanese also developed a set of rural institutions that disseminated knowledge, extension and credit services, and marketing of both inputs and outputs. The knowledge of how to achieve relatively high crop yields and the human investments made prior to 1949 were somewhat immune from wartime destruction, thus giving the island's population a boost during the immediate period of postwar recovery.

The Kuomintang occupied a largely agrarian economy, with over half the population engaged in primary production and 44 percent of the national income contributed by that sector. By 1958, agriculture's contribution to national income had fallen to 30 percent (and continued falling to about 7 percent by 1985).[9] Land was unequally owned. Before land reform in 1949, 36 percent of all farm families were owners, 39 percent tenants, and 25 percent part-owners; moreover, about a tenth of the farm population owned 60 percent of the land, while some two-fifths possessed a mere 5 percent. After land reform, 60 percent of all farm families owned their land outright, and the proportion of purely tenant farmers fell by more than half to 17 percent. The number of families owning small- and medium-sized plots grew dramatically as big absentee landlords virtually disappeared. Within a decade, Taiwan was transformed into an island of family-owned farms.[10]

Land reform combined the political motive of securing the Nationalists' political base in the countryside with the economic motive of increasing agricultural output by improving individual farming incentives through enlarging private ownership. The Nationalists had lost the mainland to the Communist Party, a peasant-based movement, which stressed agrarian reform by distributing landlords' estates to the tillers. Chiang's government failed utterly on the mainland in its limited land reform efforts when coping with landlords, thus abetting Communist advances in rural areas, and was determined not to fail twice.

The land reform process was undertaken in three steps: (1) the rent reduction program; (2) the sale of public land to cultivators and tenants; and (3) the Land-to-the-Tiller Program, which limited land ownership by current tenants.[11]

To promote agricultural incentives and output, farm rents were reduced from an effective 50 percent in most fertile areas to a maximum of 37.5 percent of the annual yield of the major crops, thus increasing after-rent returns to the 43 percent of total farm households that were affected (on 29 percent of the total land area). The rent reduction program also authorized additional reductions due to crop failures, eliminated advance payments, stipulated the legal registration of leases, and assigned to tenants first option to purchase land from its owners. Falling rents reduced land values between 20 to 40 percent, making land ownership a less attractive proposition. Higher yields and lower rents increased tenant farm income by 81 percent between 1949 and 1952, thus enabling many tenants to purchase land put up for sale by their landlords.

The second stage of the land reform program was the sale of public lands, some 411,000 acres that was formerly owned by the Japanese, with priority given to leased tenants on these lands and to landless tenants. The average size of each parcel was 2.5 acres. Prices were set at 2.5 times the value of the annual yield of the main crops, with payments in kind stretched out over ten years. About 35 percent of these public lands was sold by 1953, with another 43 percent sold during the next five years. In all, about one-fifth of all farm families became owners through this program, which embraced about 8 percent of Taiwan's arable land.

The third stage was by far the boldest, stipulating compulsory sale of land by landlords. The Land-to-the-Tiller Program, promulgated in 1953, limited land ownership by current landlords to a maximum of about 7.4 acres; any excess was confiscated by the government. In all, about 519,000 acres of land were redistributed, constituting about one-quarter of total arable land. By 1955, Taiwan's land tenancy system had been converted into a regime of owner-operators. This massive intervention in the rural sector presumed that farmers would improve the productivity of their land if they owned it themselves.

Landlords received a purchase price for their land of 2.5 times the annual yield of the main crops. They collected 70 percent of their payment in land bonds denominated in terms of the purchasing power of rice and sweet potatoes, which yielded a 4 percent annual interest rate, and 30 percent in shares of stock in four government enterprises previously owned by the Japanese. Since the average market value of rice fields was between 4 to 6 times annual yields, the land reform program affected the distribution of wealth. It reduced the future income streams of landlords as it simultaneously enhanced that of the tenants who became owner-operators.

The incentive effects of land reform resulted in more intensive use of the land as well as more labor input and multiple cropping, inasmuch as owners got the full fruits of their extra efforts. Many farmers shifted production from rice to such higher valued crops as vegetables, fruits, poultry, and livestock, because they were no longer under obligation to deliver rice for rental payment.

Agricultural output recovered sharply between 1946 and 1953, increasing by 10 percent a year. An end to wartime disruption along with incentive-enhancing reforms increased the multiple crop index and the average number of man-days per agricultural worker by more than 50 percent; the value of current inputs grew 27 percent a year. Output rose from half its prewar peak in 1946 to surpass the 1939 peak by 1952.[12]

Agricultural output grew at an annual rate exceeding 4 percent through the balance of the 1950s, but fruits, livestock, and vegetables significantly exceeded the overall rate. More intensive use of land and labor, a major increase in fertilizer and other inputs, and the beginnings of mechanization stimulated higher output. By 1960, however, off-farm activities increased in importance as industrial development provided working opportunities outside agriculture, converting a portion of the agricultural population into commuters and seasonal workers.

Agricultural Pricing Policy

Agricultural pricing policy accomplished three objectives. In the short run, it helped finance public spending and transferred capital from agriculture to the rest of the economy. Over the long run, it fostered agricultural diversification.

Rice production was strictly controlled.[13] By various methods of compulsory rice collection, the government controlled both the supply and the price of rice. It purchased rice at below-market rates, thus collecting a hidden rice tax. It also offered guaranteed prices for sugar cane, corn, mushrooms, asparagus, and products other than rice to stimulate diversification.

During the 1950s, the share of rice under government control amounted to 62 percent of the total. The Taiwan Provincial Food Bureau governed the production, distribution, and marketing of rice. It stipulated that taxes on paddy fields be paid in rice. In addition, compulsory rice purchasing by the government was made at two-thirds of the wholesale market price. Second, until its abolition in 1972, the government operated a rice-fertilizer barter program in which the government supplied 2.2 pounds of chemical fertilizer for a specified quantity of rice to the advantage of the government. Nearly half of the hidden rice tax was imposed through the barter scheme. Finally, the government extended short-term production loans to farmers in exchange for rice, with the rice price set at the government's below-market, official-purchase price.

The implicit rice tax was a major mechanism for transferring capital from agriculture to the rest of the economy. It equaled in value all income taxes collected between 1952 and 1960. In the late 1960s, the rice tax became insignificant as the government raised the official purchase price to the market price and as tax receipts from industrial growth accelerated.

MONETARY REFORM

Taiwan's leaders believed that the downfall of the Nationalist government on the mainland was caused by hyperinflation, which destroyed public confidence in the leaders' ability to govern.[14] Taiwan experienced periodic bouts of inflation during the 1950s, which resurrected these fears. Because of limited tax revenues, government spending in 1947 and 1948 was largely financed by printing currency. Currency in circulation rose 3.2 times by the end of 1947 and 26.5 times by the end of 1948, and it soared to 99 times by mid-1949. Prices exploded. Between 1946 and 1948, prices rose at an annual rate of about 500 percent and then accelerated to about 3,000 percent in the first half of 1949.[15]

To ensure that the Kuomintang did not repeat its monetary and political debacle on the mainland, stern measures were taken to arrest inflation and maintain stable prices. Through the 1970s, the Bank of Taiwan issued no bank note larger than 100 yuan (about $2.50) to minimize even the symbolic appearance of depreciating currency that characterized the postwar hyperinflation, when wheelbarrows of high-denomination notes were required to purchase small amounts of simple necessities.

The New Taiwan Dollar Reform was put into effect on June 15, 1949. The old Taiwan currency was devalued at a rate of 40,000 to 1, and the value of the New Taiwan dollar was linked to the U.S. dollar at a rate of NT$5 to US$1. The reform mandated 100 percent backing in gold, silver, or foreign exchange, and the issue of currency was legally capped at NT$200 million.

The immediate effect was positive. Inflation slowed to 300 percent in 1950, but the scheme broke down as the Bank of Taiwan continued to issue currency to finance government deficits. Within six months, it nearly reached the cap of NT$200 million, prompting a rapid depreciation of the new currency and a rise in the price of the U.S. dollar in the black market. Under pressure from budget deficits, the ceiling was abolished. New Taiwan currency in circulation reached $267 million by December 1950, pushing the black market price to NT$16 to US$1.

The statutory limit on currency issue was no match for government spending pressures. A related attempt to stabilize the exchange rate and strengthen confidence in New Taiwan dollars by means of a gold savings-deposit program and the free sale of gold and foreign exchange also lasted only until December 27, 1950, when the foreign assets of the Bank of Taiwan faced exhaustion. The government restricted the free buying and selling of gold and foreign currencies, and it banned the importation of luxury goods. Importers were required to put up substantial deposits of local currency when applying for import exchange allocations, which became a method of freezing large amounts of currency for considerable periods of time.

The successful key to price stability lay in an overhaul of interest rate policy. Taiwan's financial system was dominated by government-owned banks. To combat inflation in the late 1940s, government officials imposed injudicious and injurious controls on interest rates in the belief that low interest rates would hold down costs. These controls kept nominal interest rates so low in the face of inflation that depositors received negative interest and borrowers paid negative interest. As a result, savings stopped flowing into the banking system and banks accommodated rising loan demand by creating new money and credit, thus aggravating inflation.

Finally realizing that changing the name and denomination of the currency would not cure inflation, the authorities raised interest rates. In March 1950, the Bank of Taiwan introduced a special system of Preferential Interest Rates Savings Deposits. It offered an interest rate of 7 percent on one-month savings deposits, which compounded to an annual rate of 125 percent. Total time and savings deposits in the banking system rose from NT$6 million in March 1950 to NT$28 million by June; inflation fell from 10.3 percent a month during the first quarter of 1950 to 0.4 percent monthly rise in wholesale prices during the second quarter.

Flushed with success, the government cut the monthly interest rate to 3.5 percent in July and to 3 percent in October, thus prompting the public to reduce savings and withdraw deposits in anticipation of a return to negative rates of interest. A 65 percent increase in prices between August 1950 and February 1951 redirected the government to increase the monthly rate to 4.2 percent. Money poured back into the banks. By March 1952, deposits reached NT$541 million, up sharply from NT$26 million in December 1950. As prices stabilized, the rate was cut to 2 percent in November 1952, and in 1953 preferential deposits were introduced for longer terms.

Between 1953 and 1958, the government created an increasing number of fixed-time deposits that matured in six months or one year, with rates set above the monthly accounts. Responding to higher returns in a climate of reduced inflation, depositors lengthened their maturities. In 1957, the monthly scheme was abolished, two-year deposits were offered to the public, and interest rates were further reduced. By the end of 1958, the government suspended the preferential interest rate scheme.

Inflation was arrested over a twelve-year period. Between 1952 and 1960, the annual increase in prices was 8.8 percent. It dropped to 2 percent in 1961 and then averaged about 3 percent during the 1960s.

Why was it necessary for the government to make periodic upward and downward adjustments in interest rates? Taiwan did not (and still does not) have a free-market banking system that would automatically solve the problem of insufficient savings and excess demand for credit by raising deposit and lending interest rates until supply of and demand for credit came into balance. Negative interest rates have the dual effect of (1) destroying the real purchasing power of deposits, thus discouraging saving, and (2) enabling borrowers to repay loans in cheap money, thus encouraging borrowing. To encourage savings, and to ration scarce credit to more efficient borrowers, the government resorted to raising interest rates. It substituted its judgments for the market by adjusting interest rates on the basis of its leaders' subjective assessments of future price inflation. Sometimes they overestimated the public's confidence in price stability and cut interest rates too sharply.

FOREIGN-EXCHANGE POLICY

The Korean War strengthened military ties between the United States and the Taiwan government. Billions of dollars in foreign economic and military aid poured into the island. During the 1950s, U.S. aid financed approximately 40 percent of Taiwan's import bill. Aid financed 49 percent of public enterprise investment in infrastructure, especially electricity, transportation, and communications, and 32 percent of private enterprise manufacturing investment. U.S. aid was equivalent to more than 30 percent of domestic investment each year before 1960, sometimes reaching more than 50 percent (falling sharply from 31 to 7 percent between 1962 and 1963). Although external assistance was critical in financing investment during the 1950s, it also induced the island's leaders to put off the implementation of economic policies that would produce self-sustaining long-run growth.

The huge volume of foreign aid allowed the financial authorities to grossly overvalue Taiwan's currency. An overvalued currency subsidized domestic consumers, including the government, who purchased imports at less than half of world prices. Each N.T. dollar bought more U.S. dollars, thus commanding greater international purchasing power. Taiwan took advantage of massive foreign aid to embark on a policy of import substitution by encouraging the development of indigenous industries producing for the local market.

These nascent industries could not compete with imports made artificially cheap by an overvalued currency. Thus the government established a maze of tariffs and quotas to protect local industries from foreign competition. But an overvalued exchange rate was a dual-edged sword; it reduced the competitiveness of Taiwanese manufactured goods in overseas markets, inasmuch as production costs in N.T. dollars were translated into excessively high U.S. dollars in international trading prices. Only foreign aid allowed the government to maintain an overvalued exchange rate and still acquire needed foreign exchange, because trade was not an important source of foreign earnings.

An overvalued currency harms the competitiveness of exports in world markets and cheapens imports. These circumstances lead invariably to a balance-of-payments problem, which motivates the government to impose a variety of tariff and nontariff restrictions on imports. Protection, imposed either to preserve scarce foreign exchange or to assist the growth of import substitutes, typically results in inefficient production because producers are spared the test of market competition. Thus the price of domestic inputs into locally produced goods rises above least-cost levels.

A correctly valued exchange rate equates domestic and world prices. A correct exchange rate is one that prevails under conditions of free trade: no restrictions of any sort on imports and exports. Under free trade, buyers and sellers conduct their exchanges in domestic or world markets on a least-cost basis, and each country exploits its comparative advantage in any good or service. Economic efficiency is maximized.

In 1949, when the monetary reform was put into effect, a simple exchange rate was adopted.[16] Those exchanging foreign for domestic currency were given a portion in cash at the official rate of US$1 = NT$5 and a portion in exchange settlement certificates (ESCs) of equivalent value. ESCs were freely negotiable in the market; they could also be sold to the Bank of Taiwan at the official rate. However, continued deficits in the balance of trade and rising applications for foreign exchange at the same official NT$5 = US$1 rate outgrew the supply. The government was repeatedly compelled to devalue the official supply price of ESCs, thus effectively devaluing the currency.

In addition, the government introduced a complicated multiple exchange rate system. Imports of goods by the public sector, and of plants, raw materials, and other designated inputs, were given a preferential lower rate; other goods were assigned a higher ESC rate. Export earnings of sugar, rice, and salt were given a lower ESC rate than private export earnings.

The NT$5 to US$1 rate was grossly unrealistic. In 1953, the government installed a basic exchange rate of NT$15.55 = US$1. To spur exports, the government allowed exporters to receive exchange surrender certificates for 50 to 80 percent of their exchange proceeds surrendered to the Bank of Taiwan in addition to the official buying rate of NT$15.55. These certificates could be freely sold on the market to importers who could use them to acquire foreign-exchange import allocations.

This policy constituted an effective devaluation of the N.T. dollar. In April 1958, exporters were awarded exchange certificates representing the full amount of their exchange earnings surrendered to the government. The basic exchange rate plus the market price of the certificates represented the current market evaluation of one unit of foreign exchange earned by exporters. In August 1960, the market price of the exchange certificates was taken as a guidepost to fix a new uniform exchange rate of NT$40 = US$1 (which was largely maintained through 1985 within a 10 percent range).

The foreign-exchange condition shifted from scarcity to abundance in 1963 after the government abolished the ESC system. In its place, it established a straightforward rigidly pegged system under which the Central Bank and the Bank of Taiwan passively accepted all earnings of foreign exchange at the official NT$40 rate. Until the currency was allowed to float in 1979, Taiwan maintained a gold-standard rule, balance-of-payments, fixed exchange rate monetary system. Increases and decreases in the balance of payments, through multiple credit expansion and contraction, determined the overall level of prices and economic activity. Sustained balance-of-payments surpluses supported credit expansion and economic growth, but overly rapid internal price increases produced the opposite effect.

In effect, monetary policy was converted in the 1950s from a system of artificially imposed interest rates, extensive import controls, and a complicated foreign-exchange rate regime into a balance-of-payments monetary system linked to the U.S. dollar.

BUDGETARY POLICY

The effort to eliminate budget deficits, which were financed by the printing presses in the late 1940s with destructive inflationary effects, complemented the other two dimensions of combatting inflation through monetary reform and manipulation of interest rates. As Former Minister of Finance K.T. Li wrote, "Mindful of the fresh [1950] painful lesson of a vicious unarrested inflation of the currency, our financial authorities have made painstaking efforts to maintain a balanced budget in spite of all sorts of difficulties. Consequently, the inflationary issue of bank notes was forsaken as a method of meeting government deficits and a firm foundation was laid for economic stability."[17]

Budget balance in the 1950s was achieved through watchful control of spending and U.S. financial assistance, not by increases in taxation, which might have deterred economic growth. K.T. Li noted that "placing too much emphasis on increasing tax revenue is detrimental to economic development, and without economic development there can be little increase in national income. Only when national income is on the rise can the people afford to pay more taxes."[18] Thus financial authorities pursued a conservative budgetary policy, predicated on low tax rates as a means of stimulating growth.

U.S. aid played a major role in balancing the budget throughout the 1950s. Excluding U.S. aid, the government ran deficits of 11.3 percent of public spending in 1951, 5.2 percent in 1956, and 7.2 percent in 1961, with an overall average of 4.6 percent during the decade. (The deficit disappeared in 1963.) Foreign transfers converted these deficits into a net surplus every year, thereby financing public investment in infrastructure.

At no time did overall government spending get out of control. Excluding U.S.-supplied counterpart funds, spending financed from domestic sources generally averaged 19 percent of GNP from 1951 to 1961. Holding down government spending made it possible to maintain light taxation. Compared with Western countries, total spending on social and health services, pension payments, and massive defense outlays remained remarkably low. The tradition of family responsibility for its members and the emphasis on thrift in Chinese culture were sources of both social services and private household savings.

The share of total tax revenue of GNP remained stable at around 14 to 15 percent in the 1950s. Anxious to improve conditions of production and capital formation in the private sector, import tariffs were gradually reduced in the spirit of trade liberalization, and receipts from income and profits taxes were depressed by means of low rates and tax rebates. Most households paid no income taxes. Tax rates were kept moderate except for rather high incomes, but the existence of loopholes and evasion moderated the statutory high rates. Business income tax rates were kept low, ranging from 5 to 25 percent, but specific rebates and exemptions further lowered even that modest burden. In place of high tax rates on income and profits, the government relied heavily on the hidden rice tax.

The structure of taxation in the 1950s emphasized indirect taxes to minimize the harm to incentives caused by high rates of direct taxation. The income tax was particularly low; the business income tax and individual income tax combined constituted only 1.5 percent and 1.6 percent of GNP. In contrast, customs supplied nearly one-quarter of receipts and internal indirect taxes, such as the commodity tax, stamp tax, salt tax, business registration tax, and slaughter tax; and revenue from government monopolies provided half of tax collections. Overall, tax revenues extracted only 10 percent of GNP in 1951–1955 and 11.7 percent in 1956–1960. This tax system effectively encouraged work, savings, and investment. Light taxation enabled the industrial sector to retain a large part of its profits for further investment.

During the 1950s, the sum of government consumption spending plus investment in public corporations and government enterprises amounted to about 30 percent of GNP. Approximately three-quarters of every public consumption dollar went to defense and administration, with the balance spent on such services as education, health, transport, and communication. The public sector also contributed about half of the total fixed capital formation.

To summarize, fiscal policy in the 1950s was generally in harmony with monetary policy. Maintaining high interest rates with a regime of low taxes and limited public spending stimulated private savings and encouraged efficiency in investment. The avoidance of government debt eliminated the threat of inflationary public finance, which had plagued the Nationalists on the mainland and during its first few years on Taiwan.

ECONOMIC PLANNING AND DEVELOPMENT

The extent of reliance on economic planning and the manner of implementation vary across countries. Taiwan's planning apparatus took the form of a checklist of private targets and public investments in infrastructure on government enterprises. Beginning in 1953, when the island completed its initial recovery from wartime disruption, the leadership drew up a succession of four-year plans. The first plan was launched largely as a means of making effective use of U.S. economic aid. Since then, the planning mechanism focused on overall economic strategy or specific objectives. At no time was it ever intended to replace or even distort the role played by private enterprise within the context of a free economy. The chief activities of the planners were to develop reliable and comprehensive statistical data on the economy, leaving implementation firmly within the operating ministries. The government encouraged private firms to develop new industries, rather than to undertake direct control of industrial development.[19]

The objectives in early plans were to promote agriculture and initiate industrial production, foster a climate of economic stability, curtail deficits in the balance of payments, and gradually develop a transportation infrastructure. Like other developing countries, Taiwan was an agriculturally based economy, with 60 percent of the population living on farms. In the process of industrialization, the government sought to maintain a firm agricultural base, which explains the early importance attached to land reform measures. Rising agricultural production supplied raw materials for industrial processing of foodstuffs, which became Taiwan's first major export industry. Rural prosperity simultaneously expanded the market for domestic industrial production and provided the savings to finance industrial development. The industrial sector complemented agriculture by supplying fertilizer, pesticides, and farm machinery.

Industrial Development

In 1952, Taiwan's industrial sector was small; the existing industrial capacity was largely under government control, having been seized from its former Japanese owners, and most private production was of traditional products.[20] Within three decades Taiwan's economy underwent a dramatic transformation, in which agriculture's contribution to national output declined from 36 to 7 percent while that of industry increased from 18 to 50 percent.[21]

As previously described, Taiwan's economy under Japanese rule was largely that of an agricultural appendage to Japan's economy, supplying sugar and rice and receiving industrial goods in return. A small food-processing industry arose behind a wall of tariff protection (mostly in sugar refining, rice, and pineapples), generating about a fifth of national income and providing more than half of all industrial employment by 1930. As Taiwan grew in strategic importance to Japan prior to World War II, Japan undertook investments in power, transport, and such basic industries as cement, pulp, and paper, fertilizer, petroleum refining, and metallurgy. By 1940, some 310,000 Japanese were residing in Taiwan and directing its industrial development.

Allied bombing destroyed three-fourths of Taiwan's industrial capacity, two-thirds of its power-generating facilities, and one-half of its transportation network. With Japan's surrender, about 30,000 skilled technicians and administrators were repatriated to Japan. Recovery of Taiwan by China meant that the island's producers had to shift their exports from Japan to mainland China's internal markets and, cut off from Japanese industrial products, to begin producing such essential consumer items as textiles, leather goods, and soap. Skilled personnel in the arriving Nationalist ranks replaced the departed Japanese. Once inflation was controlled and wartime disruption repaired, the government turned its attention to the development of a coherent economic policy and selected the method of import-substitution industrialization.

The early stages of Taiwan's industrial development were characterized by a shortage of capital, technology, and natural resources; most daily necessities were imported. A persistent balance-of-payments deficit was covered by U.S. aid. Taiwan's chief productive asset was an abundant, relatively unskilled, but hardworking labor force. To exploit its labor resources, the government encouraged small-scale, labor-intensive, import-substituting industries that required little capital or skilled labor and could be set up almost overnight. Its goals were to provide jobs quickly, to stem the outflow of foreign exchange that financed essential consumer imports, and to improve the balance-of-payments position.

A policy of import substitution requires a more activist government than does a free-trade policy. The government imposed import licensing, protective tariffs to minimize foreign competition, multiple exchange rate schemes, and exchange controls to ensure that import-substitution industries had first claim on scarce foreign exchange; it also allocated credit on a preferential basis. The producer goods industries that were taken over from the Japanese and run by government corporations (chemicals, fertilizer, and petroleum products) received direct subsidies and preferential interest rates. The overall objectives of the import-substitution policy were to acquire foreign exchange to finance public-sector infrastructure, to maintain existing industry, and to expand consumer goods industries through protection.

As a consequence of the gradual exhaustion of the protected domestic market by the mid- to late 1950s, the process of primary import substitution began to slow down. The annual growth rate of industrial output declined between 1953 and 1958. The domestic market for the products of these import-substituting, labor-intensive industries was largely saturated, and further growth depended on new market outlets overseas. One tactic would be for the government to shift its policy toward further expansion of more capital- and technology-intensive durable consumer and capital goods industries, a policy known as secondary import substitution. As Taiwan possessed abundant manpower but lacked advanced technology, major foreign-exchange reserves to import machinery and equipment, and a large domestic market to benefit from economies of scale, there was little sense in pursuing the second strategy.

Taiwan's initial industrialization efforts unfolded against a backdrop of declining inflation, high real interest rates to encourage saving, low tax rates to encourage investment, the development of physical infrastructure in transportation and power, and investment in human capital (education and farmers' associations). In addition, Taiwan refrained from building up public enterprises, which often become "white elephants" that typify most planning regimes under policies of import substitution. Except for projects that had to be undertaken by the government, most investment projects with promising prospects were reserved for the private sector.

How did the primary import-substitution phase of development fare in Taiwan? First, the overall trade orientation of the economy declined sharply from the prewar period and remained at relatively low levels during the 1950s. Between 1952 and 1957, the share of consumer goods in total imports fell from 19.8 to 6.6 percent. Imported consumer goods constituted only about 5 percent of the total domestic supply by the late 1950s.

Within the manufacturing sector, the complete dominance of food processing in the immediate prewar period (73 percent of total output in 1936–1940) gave way to the import-replacing industries of textiles, rubber and leather goods, wood products, and bicycles, which constituted 66 percent of output by 1954.

During the 1950s, annual growth rates of manufacturing output averaged 10 percent and employment 6 percent. However, the growth rates declined in the second half of the 1950s as domestic markets became saturated. Pressure mounted for the organization of domestic cartels to resist price cutting, while others sought export subsidies in the form of tax rebates to redress the discrimination against exports caused by the overvalued exchange rate. These pressures brought major changes in policy beginning in 1958.

ECONOMIC PERFORMANCE

It is difficult to judge Taiwan's first phase of development on its own, as it was really a prelude to the major steps taken since 1958 that transformed the island into an international economic and trading power. Under the military and economic crisis conditions that prevailed in the late 1940s and early 1950s, Taiwan's leaders successfully put the economy on a sound basis, assisted by roughly $1.5 billion in U.S. aid. The economy absorbed about 400,000 workers in the 1950s. The number of unemployed remained at or under 194,000 between 1953 and 1958. Also during the 1950s, the economy stayed in a state of surplus labor; thus real wages rose slowly, remaining at a subsistence level. Real wages took off only when a condition of full employment was reached in the late 1960s.

Since 1964, and annually since 1970, the government has conducted periodic surveys on family income distribution.[22] Earlier private estimates were conducted by university professors. These data show that the income share of the richest 20 percent of families fell from 61.4 to 51 percent between 1953 and 1959, whereas the income share of the poorest 20 percent rose from 3 to 5.7 percent. Thus the ratio of the income share of the richest one-fifth to the poorest one-fifth declined from 20 to 9 during the first phase of development. Agricultural reforms in concert with the first import-substitution phase of industrialization improved income distribution in Taiwan. But it must be stressed that, apart from land reform measures, the improved distribution of income did not stem from policies of high taxation or the redistribution of income through transfers or expanding public social spending; rather, it took place as a result of economic growth in agriculture and industry, which provided new job opportunities.

Overall economic growth was dramatic during the 1950s, averaging 8.2 percent. The gross domestic product increased from NT$17.2 billion to NT$51.5 billion between 1952 and 1959—a 69 percent increase in real terms. Per capita income increased from NT$2,009 to NT$4,754 or, in real terms, about 33 percent. With industrial growth averaging 8.9 percent in 1953–1958, the industrial production index doubled between 1952 and 1959: Annual growth rates registered 25, 6, 13, 4, 13, 9, and 12 percent in the seven years beginning 1953; and industry increased its share of gross national product from 17 to 25 percent.[23]

During the same period, gross domestic capital formation increased from a very modest NT$2.6 billion to NT$9.8 billion in 1959; of this total, U.S. aid, foreign capital, and loans supplied between one-third and one-half.

The number of students enrolled in school nearly doubled from 1,187,858 to 2,204,759. Deaths from communicable diseases fell by one-quarter, reflecting improvements in the economy and in health care personnel and facilities. Food intake improved in quality and quantity. Prices doubled between 1952 and 1961, but stabilized at low levels during the next decade.

Yet these figures, however impressive, pale against the exceptional performance turned in by Taiwan's economy since 1961, which is the subject of the next chapter.

NOTES

1. For a capsule summary of Taiwan's postwar development, see Ramon H. Myers, "The Economic Transformation of the Republic of China on Taiwan," *The China Quarterly,* no. 99 (September 1984), pp. 500–528.

2. Paul K.T. Sih, "The Physical Setting of Taiwan," in Paul K.T. Sih, ed., *Taiwan in Modern Times* (New York: St. John's University Press, 1973), pp. 1–20.

3. A useful summary of the origin of Taiwan's population appears in Paul K.T. Sih, "Introduction," in Paul K.T. Sih, ed., *Taiwan in Modern Times*, pp. vii–xix.

4. An excellent treatment of the colonial period in Taiwan is found in Samuel P.S. Ho, *Economic Development of Taiwan 1860–1970* (New Haven and London: Yale University Press, 1978).

5. This section on Taiwan's political system draws from Richard L. Walker, "Taiwan's Movement into Political Modernity: 1945–1972," in Paul K.T. Sih, ed., *Taiwan in Modern Times*, pp. 359–396.

6. Alexander Ya-li Lu, "Future Domestic Developments in the Republic of China on Taiwan," *Asian Survey* 24, no. 11 (November 1985), p. 1089.

7. During a November 1984 visit to Taiwan, several government officials told me that, since 1978, some of their colleagues had visited mainland China where they participated in economic policy discussions resembling those that took place in Taiwan in 1958, when Taiwan's leaders implemented liberal economic reforms.

8. An excellent treatment of agriculture in Taiwan is found in Erik Thorbecke, "Agricultural Development," in Walter Galenson, ed., *Economic Growth and Structural Change in Taiwan: The Postwar Experience of the Republic of China* (Ithaca and London: Cornell University Press, 1979), pp. 132–205.

9. *Taiwan Statistical Data Book 1986* (Taipei: Council for Economic Planning and Development, Republic of China, 1986), p. 39.

10. Shirley W.Y. Kuo, Gustav Ranis, and John C.H. Fei, *The Taiwan Success Story: Rapid Growth with Improved Distribution in the Republic of China, 1952–1979* (Boulder, Colo.: Westview Press, 1981), pp. 51–53.

11. Erik Thorbecke, "Agricultural Development," pp. 172–176; Shirley W.Y. Kuo, Gustav Ranis, and John C.H. Fei, *The Taiwan Success Story*, pp. 48–55; and, Shirley W.Y. Kuo, *The Taiwan Economy in Transition* (Boulder, Colo.: Westview Press, 1983), pp. 26–29.

12. For the period up to 1967, see Erik Thorbecke, "Agricultural Development," pp. 171–184.

13. Ibid., pp. 178–181; Shirley W.Y. Kuo, Gustav Ranis, and John C.H. Fei, *The Taiwan Success Story*, pp. 56–60; and, Shirley W.Y. Kuo, *The Taiwan Economy in Transition*, pp. 30–41.

14. For extensive discussions of Taiwan's fiscal and monetary policies, see Erik Lundberg, "Fiscal and Monetary Policies," in Walter Galenson, ed., *Economic Growth and Structural Change in Taiwan*, pp. 263–307. From December 18 to 20, 1981, the Institute of Economics, Academia Sinica in Taiwan, convened a *Conference on Experiences and Lessons of Economic Development in Taiwan*. See Shoh-chieh Tsiang, "Monetary Policy of Taiwan," pp. 249–270; and Tzong-shian Yu and Ting-an Chen, "Fiscal Reforms and Economic Development," pp. 275–306.

15. Shirley W.Y. Kuo, Gustav Ranis, and John C.H. Fei, *The Taiwan Success Story*, p. 64.

16. Ibid., pp. 66–68.

17. K.T. Li, *The Experience of Dynamic Economic Growth on Taiwan* (Taipei: Mei Ya, 1976), p. 64.

18. Ibid., p. 470.

19. Kwoh-ting Li and Wan-an Yeh, "Economic Planning in the Republic of China," *Conference on Experiences and Lessons of Economic Development in Taiwan,* pp. 169–195.

20. Gustav Ranis, "Industrial Development," in Walter Galenson, ed., *Economic Growth and Structural Change in Taiwan,* pp. 206–62.

21. *Taiwan Statistical Data Book 1986,* p. 39.

22. Shirley W.Y. Kuo, *The Taiwan Economy in Transition,* pp. 93–106.

23. *Taiwan Statistical Data Book 1986,* pp. 1–2, 21, 27.

6

FROM IMPORT SUBSTITUTION
TO EXPORT PROMOTION

Beginning in 1958, government leaders in Taiwan switched their development strategy from an import-substitution policy for a limited domestic market to the development of labor-intensive, manufactured goods for export to world markets. International price competition replaced domestic subsidies and tariffs. Financial authorities reformed the exchange rate system to ensure correct valuation of the currency. They granted tax incentives to encourage foreign and domestic investment, including the establishment of special industrial estates or free-trade zones to expedite the production of goods for export. They also minimized costly labor regulations.

Several forces precipitated the change. First, the domestic market for nondurable consumer goods was gradually exhausted by the late 1950s, and such industries as textiles, paper, rubber goods, and soap faced excess capacity. Excess capacity jeopardized the goal of full employment as employers faced incentives to organize domestic cartels to resist price cutting, to seek costly export subsidies in the form of tax rebates to compensate for the bias against exports caused by the overvalued exchange rate, or try to switch from primary product to capital-intensive secondary import-substitution industries, which made little economic sense in labor-abundant Taiwan.

Second, in the late 1950s the U.S. government announced plans to phase out its massive economic assistance. If Taiwan was to earn foreign exchange, trade had to replace aid. Finally, by 1958 the Kuomintang, for practical purposes, abandoned its ambitions to recover the mainland; buoyed by the success of land reform, it concentrated on industrial policy. In sum, the pressures of a limited home market, continuing surplus labor, the rising costs of capital- and skill-intensive industries, and the loss of U.S. aid pushed government policy in favor of export promotion.

Security considerations remained paramount during the past quarter-century of trade and economic liberalization. Martial law was in force through the mid-1980s. National security concerns hindered changes in economic policy that stood to improve economic efficiency. These included letting market forces dictate the optimal size of farms, setting interest rates, establishing offshore banking, and abolishing all exchange controls, to name a few. Political leaders held that maintaining many family-owned farms fostered rural stability and ensured that the island could feed itself under emergency conditions. The government controlled the banking system to influence the allocation of credit and to prevent any recurrence of inflation. It accumulated massive reserves to pay for needed military hardware in cash. Exchange controls, although recently relaxed, were imposed to prevent a flight of capital. Both inertia and conservatism constrained the pace of liberalization. For reasons of national security, the government developed and operated such basic heavy industries as shipbuilding, steel, petrochemicals, energy, and transportation in the belief that the private sector would not and could not finance such enterprises.

Few Taiwanese economists doubt the economic benefits of market-enhancing reforms, but military and security considerations often over-rode their recommendations. Although the Kuomintang may have gone too far in letting national security hold back the pace of liberalization, Taiwan's political isolation and the mainland's preponderant numerical superiority in any future conflict warranted these concerns. Despite the constraint of national security, economic growth was still spectacular.

AN OVERVIEW OF DEVELOPMENT STRATEGY

Economic planning in Taiwan remained largely indicative, with the government setting major targets for output, investment, foreign trade, the balance of payments, social development, urban and regional de-velopment, infrastructure, public investment in several key heavy in-dustries, and the overall structure of the economy. Quantitative and qualitative targets were expressed in such terms as "maintain price stability," "promote exports," "expand infrastructure," "upgrade in-dustrial structure," "modernize agriculture," "improve living standards," "complete the Ten Major Development Projects," "enhance energy efficiency," and "strengthen manpower development." Apart from in-frastructure and the major development projects, primary responsibility for wealth and job creation was left to the private sector. Setting broad objectives in Taiwan bore no resemblance to mainland China's central planning regime, which tried to allocate inputs and outputs.

Until 1958, economic planning concentrated on postwar rehabilitation, agricultural reform, and the development of labor-intensive, import-substituting industries to conserve foreign exchange and create manufacturing jobs. During the 1960s, the emphasis switched to improving the investment climate, encouraging saving, establishing export-oriented industries, creating new jobs at a faster rate, developing new agricultural products, and promoting agricultural exports. The government enacted the Statute for Encouragement of Investment to attract foreign and domestic capital to key export industries. The succession of reforms that followed suit brought a condition of full employment by 1971.

In the 1970s, the government gave increased attention to infrastructural investment, eliminating transport bottlenecks, establishing intermediate goods industries, and developing government-owned and -operated basic, heavy industries. Industrial exports were the lynchpin of industrial policy.

The ten-year perspective plan adopted for the 1980s emphasized energy efficiency; judicious application of tax and financial incentives for high-technology industry concurrent with educational emphasis on science and technology; "twelve new projects" to complete the island's transportation network, improve farmland, accelerate agricultural mechanization, and develop cultural centers; and further liberalization in such areas as tariffs, imports, interest rates, exchange controls, freedom of travel, and tax rates. The 1980s were designated the decade of further liberalization and internationalization of the Taiwan economy.[1]

EXPORT PROMOTION POLICIES

By 1958 the investment climate had become gloomy and fundamental policy changes were required. The government had already reformed the currency, stabilizing the exchange rate at NT$40 to US$1. To compensate for distortions imposed on exporters, which characterized the prior import-substitution regime, the government took a number of concrete steps. It gradually liberalized, and finally abolished, the commodity import quota system. It reduced tariffs, relaxed import controls, granted three-year income-tax exemptions to certain categories of industries to stimulate investment, revised the income and company tax laws, eased controls over the establishment of factories, and instructed the Bank of Taiwan to raise interest rates. These steps preceded massive changes that took effect in 1960 with the promulgation of the Statute for Encouragement of Invesfment.

The government's third four-year plan (1961–1964) was dominated by the Nineteen-Point Economic Financial Reform.[2] Its basic objectives were to review and liberalize past control measures; give private business preferential treatment in the areas of taxation, foreign exchange, and financing; reform the tax system and tax administration to enhance capital formation; maintain a unitary exchange rate and liberalize trade; and encourage exports by more favorable settlement of foreign exchange earned by exporters.

Investment Incentives

The Statute for Encouragement of Investment fostered an improved business climate through specific incentives. Article 5 granted a five-year tax holiday to approved export-oriented ("productive") enterprises. The maximum rate of business tax on approved enterprises was cut from 32.5 percent to 18 percent, with provisions for deducting reinvested profits and 2 percent of annual export proceeds from taxable income. The stamp tax was waived or reduced. Seven percent of pretax profits could be set aside as a reserve against possible loss caused by exchange rate revision.

The government revised and expanded the scope of the investment statute in 1965, and also authorized the creation of duty-free, export-processing zones. The Kaohsiung Export Processing Zone was set up, within which no duties were imposed on imports. It and two additional zones grew so fast that by 1970 they were providing 7 percent of all manufacturing jobs and turning out a tenth of all exports. Between 1967 and 1970, they exported about $5.5 billion worth of goods, the equivalent of 70 percent of the country's favorable balance of trade over that period.[3] By 1980, 293 firms had invested $300 million, of which 88 percent came from foreign firms. In July 1980, 81,147 persons were employed in the three zones, which represented about 3 percent of the island's industrial labor force. During 1980, Taiwan shipped more than $200 million in goods into the zones. Thus, if persons employed in neighboring satellite industries outside the zone were included in the country, the job total would have been even higher.[4]

The new investment package refunded taxes to businessmen. As a percentage of total income, stamp, customs, and commodity taxes, annual refunds ranged from a low of 19 percent in 1963 to a high of 52.4 percent in 1973, with the annual average in the 30 percent range.[5] During 1971–1973, the total rebates on income, stamp, customs, and commodity taxes accounted for about half of the total revenue of the four business taxes. These annual refunds enabled firms to finance additional expansion from internal cash flow.

The 1960 investment statute was periodically augmented, giving Taiwan an extremely attractive investment climate. Overseas investors were accorded the same incentives and privileges given Chinese nationals, including 100 percent equity ownership, free remission of all profits and interest earnings, repatriation of investment capital after two years, and protection against government expropriation or requisition for twenty years.

Amendments to the investment statute went beyond the original five-year tax holiday. New investments in machinery and equipment qualified for an additional four years of tax exemption or accelerated depreciation. Capital-intensive or technology-intensive enterprises were allowed to defer the commencement date of their tax holidays for a period of one to four years. Once production targets were reached for an approved merger that enlarged capacity, 15 percent of business taxes were deductible for two years. All research and development expenditures could be charged to current operating expenses. Specifically designated industries were exempted from duty on imported machinery and equipment, or on inputs for manufacturing machinery and equipment if not available domestically. Duty paid on imported raw materials used in export products was refunded. Tax rates were limited to 22 percent on high-technology firms and 25 percent for other productive enterprises. Stock dividends were tax free if earnings were reinvested. Publicly-listed firms received a 15 percent income tax reduction for three years. Foreign executives and technicians living in Taiwan for six months or less in a taxable year were not taxed on salary or remuneration.

In addition to the three export processing zones at Kaohsiung, Nantze, and Taichung, the government established a science-based industrial park at Hsinchu in July 1979, which offered a reduction or exemption in land rentals for up to five years, the most favorable terms under any of the tax laws in the country, low-cost loans, government equity participation to reduce investor outlays, and the right to sell products manufactured in the park in the domestic market after taxation.[6]

Labor Regulations

Supply and demand for labor in the market, not government intervention, determined wage rates.[7] Although a minimum wage law was in effect since 1956, it was too low to affect actual rates paid. In 1956, the initial minimum was NT$10 a day for adult workers against the average manufacturing daily rate of NT$22. The minimum was raised to NT$15 in 1964 and to NT$20 in 1968, but average wages had already reached NT$50 and NT$64 in those years. By 1976, the statutory minimum was a mere 10 percent of the average manufacturing wage.

Trade unions exerted little impact on wages. One reason is that the government declared strikes illegal.[8] Another reason is that rapidly rising wages and growing job opportunities in a full employment economy, especially since 1971, diminished the potential benefits unions could have provided, even if they were free of state control.

Apart from a modest list of labor regulations—the government limited overtime work, stipulated rest days and annual holidays, banned night work for women and those under 16 years of age, required full leave pay for short-time military training, guaranteed eight weeks maternity leave with pay, and imposed mandatory insurance on all workers over 14 financed by a premium of 7 percent of workers' salaries—wage levels and fringe benefits were set in the market. Job placement was largely private, wages reflected prevailing rates in the area, merit dominated wage increases, and dismissals from work were extremely rare. Taiwan possessed a stable labor force, which enhanced the investment climate.

MONETARY POLICY AND BANKING

From the fixing of the New Taiwan dollar at the rate of NT$40 = US$1 in 1960 through 1979, Taiwan maintained the equivalent of a gold-standard rule, balance-of-payments, fixed exchange-rate monetary system, which was augmented by such discretionary measures as changing reserve requirements, raising deposit rates of interest in state-run banks to mop up excess money, and modifying restrictions on imports to permit funds to flow abroad.[9] Under a fixed-exchange-rate regime, Taiwan's domestic money supply was largely determined by the balance of payments (which includes the balance of merchandise trade, the sale of such invisibles as tourism, insurance, shipping, and financial services, and the movement of capital funds). Under a fixed rate, the banks and the government passively accepted the net outcomes of all overseas transactions. When Taiwan earned more foreign exchange than it used, the banks purchased the excess and thereby increased the New Taiwan dollar deposits held by the private sector. Conversely, any deficit in foreign exchange required the conversion of New Taiwan dollars into foreign currency to pay overseas bills, which contracted the money supply. Banks in Taiwan, as elsewhere, generated multiple credit creation (or contraction) on the basis of their liquid assets.

Improvements in Taiwan's external accounts were invariably associated with a domestic monetary expansion, which, by increasing domestic liquidity, tended to push up domestic costs and prices. Conversely, a deteriorating external balance of payments invariably resulted in a domestic monetary squeeze.

An ideal balance-of-payments, fixed-exchange-rate monetary system works as an automatic correction mechanism to determine increases or decreases in an economy's domestic money supply and the resultant level of income and employment. A favorable balance of payments results in an inflow of foreign exchange, an expansion of the domestic money supply (as foreign exchange is converted into domestic currency), a fall in domestic interest rates (due to greater availability of credit), and increased business activity. Rapid growth increases the demand for labor, which drives up costs and prices. Imports rise (because people have more money to spend) and exports decline (because local prices rise more rapidly than those of competitors). The economy automatically tends to deflate, thereby slowing down the rise in internal costs and prices and stimulating the production of goods for export at more competitive prices. The process repeats continuously. Through the balance of payments, the money supply, level of economic activity, and domestic cost/price structure are tied to the world economy. The long-term growth of credit and economic activity thus depends upon and reflects the balance of payments over time.

The process of adjustment under Taiwan's fixed-exchange-rate regime was not so efficient as this ideal model suggests. First, the presence of substantial tariffs and other barriers to the free movement of goods and services impeded the transmission of external price movements to the internal cost/price structure, thus slowing the rate at which the economy adjusted to world trading conditions. Second, capital controls restricted the export of foreign exchange, which could have counteracted sharp increases in the domestic money supply caused by massive trade surpluses. To cope with overrapid monetary growth, the government employed two discretionary measures. It periodically raised interest rates to soak up excess liquidity and eased import barriers to encourage spending abroad.

During the period 1960–1979, in which Taiwan pegged its currency, the trade balance was persistently in surplus.[10] As the new policy emphasizing exports took hold, the balance of payments abruptly improved in 1963 and 1964, thus sharply increasing the net foreign assets of the banking system. Domestic money supply, in turn, grew 28 and 32 percent, respectively. Concerned about inflation, the government permitted a one-time increase in imports of 30 percent in 1964–1965, which reduced the net foreign assets of the banking system and slowed domestic money growth.

Large trading surpluses in 1972 and 1973, purchased by the Central Bank at the fixed rate, increased the domestic money supply by 38 percent in 1972 and 49 percent in 1973. Prices rose a modest 7.3 percent in 1972 but shot up 40.3 percent in 1973. To cope with inflation, the Central Bank raised interest rates on time and savings deposits and relaxed restrictions on luxury imports. These two measures reduced money supply growth to 7 percent in 1974, thereby restoring stable prices in 1975.

Following the oil-induced worldwide recession of 1974–1975, Taiwan scored large trade surpluses in 1976, 1977, and 1978. These surpluses increased money supply growth by 29 percent in 1977 and 34 percent in 1978. To restrain domestic prices, controls on capital outflow were relaxed and tourist travel abroad was liberalized. On several occasions, the government adjusted the pegged rate; it revalued the exchange rate against the U.S. dollar to NT$38 in 1972 and NT$36 in 1978, thus letting the exchange rate bear a portion of the brunt of trade surpluses. However, it devalued back to NT$38 in 1981 to restore external competitiveness. Finally, since about 1980, and particularly since 1982, the government has abandoned its U.S. dollar pegged exchange rate. It started to manage the exchange rate of the N.T. dollar on a more ad hoc basis in an attempt to offset the large inflows of foreign exchange, which were producing disruptive expansions in domestic money and credit growth.

Since 1980, the Central Bank has pursued a quantity growth rule of money supply designed to accommodate noninflationary, high real growth. It has also adjusted reserve requirements, conducted modest open market operations in treasury bills, raised or lowered interest rates, eased or tightened import and capital controls, and acquired a growing stock of foreign assets to neutralize the persistent, large surpluses.

Growing trade surpluses, US$10 billion alone in 1984, brought Taiwan's accumulated foreign-exchange reserves to $22 billion in December 1985, equivalent to $1,162 per capita, or an extraordinary 38 percent of GNP. At the end of 1985, Taiwan held the sixth largest stock of reserves in the world after West Germany ($42.8 billion), Japan ($27.6 billion), the United States ($27.2 billion), Saudi Arabia ($25 billion) and France ($23 billion). Taiwan's reserves approximately doubled to $44 billion a year later. They quadrupled those of mainland China, despite the mainland's fifty-to-one numerical preponderance in population.

Responding to a rising trade balance, the Central Bank of China (CBC) began to purchase foreign assets—an action equivalent of exporting capital. By increasing its purchase of foreign assets, the CBC prevented the acquisition of foreign assets from being translated into a domestic monetary expansion. Since 1981, the CBC borrowed funds from the commercial banking system to purchase foreign exchange or add to official reserves, thus draining funds from the banking system. By sterilizing large trade surpluses in this manner, the CBC maintained a stable exchange rate. However, under the persistent pressure of a massive trade surplus during 1986, the New Taiwan Dollar appreciated against its U.S. counterpart, breaking through the NT$36 barrier for the first time in a quarter-century.

Augmenting sterilization of trade surpluses through public-sector acquisition of foreign assets, the government announced new regulations at the end of 1985 permitting financial institutions, corporations, and individuals to invest in foreign government securities and bank deposits. The purchase of equity shares in foreign private companies remained banned. Additional measures authorized three domestic banks to offer foreign currency deposits, and Taiwanese citizens traveling abroad could use more foreign funds.

The currency issue itself is a relatively small component of the overall money supply, especially compared with mainland China. By law, the local note issue enjoys 100 percent external backing in such forms as gold, foreign currencies, and other financial instruments. Taiwan's official reserves provided more than 100 percent backing. The New Taiwan dollar is literally as good as the U.S. dollar, although it is not freely convertible in unlimited quantities.

The modernization of the banking system failed to keep pace with the growth of trade and money supply. Under banking law, the Central Bank prescribed different maximum rates for different kinds of deposits. The Central Bank confirmed and enforced the spread of interest rates on different kinds of loans proposed by the Bankers' Association. Since commercial banks are mostly owned by the government, which appoints their top officers, competition among the commercial banks was restricted. Policy also stipulated that minimum loan rates exceed maximum deposit rates.

An official money market was established in 1976 to pave the way for more flexible interest rate movements and to channel financial savings to businesses. Money market instruments consist of commercial paper, bankers' acceptances, negotiable certificates of deposit, and treasury bills. Interest rates in these money market instruments were no longer subject to ceiling regulation. Since 1981, the value of outstanding money market instruments rose as a fraction of total banking loans: While bank loans grew about 20 percent in the early 1980s, bankers' acceptances increased 5.4 times, certificates of deposit by 2.4 times, and commercial paper 40 percent.

In March 1985 a serious bank scandal was disclosed to the public. This event resulted in the imprisonment of a member of the Legislative Yuan and of a prominent businessmen, the forced resignation of two cabinet officials, massive dismissals, and the discipline of more than two dozen officials in the Ministry of Finance.[11] This scandal was partly blamed on excessive government control over the banking system, thus pointing up the need for greater reform and liberalization.

BUDGETARY POLICY

Rampant inflation in mainland China during the late 1940s, which led to the downfall of the Nationalist government, ensured that the inflationary issue of bank notes would be forsaken as a method of financing government spending in Taiwan. Government policy consistently avoided deficits.

U.S. aid offset modest budget deficits in the 1950s. Between fiscal years 1954 and 1960, revenue and spending at all levels of government were in approximate balance, with three surplus and three deficit years. As the U.S. government weaned Taiwan from aid, Taiwan endured three consecutive deficits beginning in fiscal year 1961, largely due to the tax cuts that were enacted to enhance investment incentives and promote exports. However, since 1964, the public finances of the combined central, provincial, county, and municipal levels of government yielded surpluses for eighteen consecutive years. A deficit in 1982 was quickly restored to surplus the following year.

This picture is somewhat misleading inasmuch as the government counted proceeds from the issue of public bonds as part of revenues. However, public bonds remained exceptionally modest, contributing about 2–3 percentage points of net receipts. Excluding the proceeds of borrowing from net receipts, we find that tiny deficits materialized in fiscal years 1967, 1968, 1972, and 1977, with somewhat larger deficits in 1982 and 1983. Even with this method of calculation, taking one year with another, the budget was seen to be firmly in the black.[12]

The government used its accumulated surpluses to undertake a major expansion in infrastructure and direct investment in publicly owned heavy industries known as the "ten major construction projects" in the 1970s. These consisted of two major ports, construction of a new railroad and electrification of the west coast mainline, a new international airport for Taipei, two nuclear power plants, establishment of a petrochemical industry, construction of a large shipyard and steel mill, and completion of a north-south highway.[13] The total cost of these ten projects came to US$7 billion.

Estimates for the "twelve new construction projects" to be completed during the 1980s run in excess of US$10 billion. The government announced plans to construct an around-the-island railroad, three cross-island highways, new towns and housing projects, seacoast dikes and river levees; to widen existing highways and make other traffic improvements; to build cultural centers throughout the island; to expand the steel mill and Taichung harbor; and to improve farmland. It plans to finance 40 percent of the cost with taxes and other domestic revenue sources, with foreign and domestic loans supplying the balance.

Recall that tax reductions and rebates to industry since 1960 ran as high as 50 percent of total taxes collected from business. Taiwan achieved its objective of balanced budgets on the basis of low levels of taxation. It sought to keep increases in public spending in line with the overall growth rate of the economy. Strong economic growth since 1960 financed huge increases in public spending on the basis of a system of low taxes.

Between fiscal years 1961 and 1985, overall public spending ranged from a low of 18.2 to a high of 27.9 percent of GNP; in 12 of those 25 years, spending remained below 23 percent of GNP.[14] At no time did the public sector's claim on national output crowd out the private sector. A large, relatively stable share of the annual increase in GNP remained in private hands for consumption and investment.

In 1960, about three-fifths of government spending was allocated to defense and general administration. That figure fell below 40 percent in 1975, reaching a low of 34 percent in 1981. Correspondingly, expenditure on education, science, culture, communications, and social affairs relief rose sharply. The government was able to allocate increasing proportions of its steadily rising receipts for nondefense outlays aimed at improving the quality of life. In absolute terms, after adjusting for inflation, public outlays for education, science, culture, and social affairs relief have increased thirtyfold since 1960.

Financial authorities in Taiwan maintained a strict regime of low taxes. The tax burden, defined as receipts from all taxes (customs, commodity taxes, the income tax, stamp tax, business tax, harbor dues, license tax, land tax, slaughter tax, household tax, house tax, amusement tax, deeds tax, and the feast tax—the household tax was abolished in 1972 and the salt tax in 1978) and the revenue of government monopolies, rarely exceeded 20 percent of GNP. In the twenty-five fiscal years between 1961 and 1985, the tax burden averaged 17 percent of GNP.

Apart from tax and monopoly revenue, which constituted about 70 percent of all government revenues, the balance came from the profits of public enterprises and public utilities, issuance of public bonds, and miscellaneous fees and charges.[15]

In 1960, direct taxes (income, land, households, deeds, and property) contributed 22 percent of collections, whereas indirect taxes (customs duties and harbor charges on foreign trade and a variety of internal excises) accounted for 78 percent. By the mid-1980s, the ratio of direct to indirect taxes had increased to 37:63 as rising incomes and land values brought more people into the direct tax net, whereas lower tariffs had reduced customs receipts.[16] Still, the income tax supplied only about one-fifth of tax and monopoly revenues, or only about 14 percent of overall government revenues.

In general, government tax policy encouraged private savings and capital formation. Average tax rates on business were kept low, and these were further reduced through specific tax rebates and exemptions. Most households paid no personal income taxes through the 1970s. The income tax law allowed an individual to deduct from his or her gross consolidated income an allowance for support of dependents, property and land taxes, charitable contributions up to 20 percent of gross income, insurance premiums up to NT$4,000, medical costs, uninsured disaster losses, 20 percent of income from salaries and wages up to NT$9,000, and various kinds of interest and dividends up to NT$120,000.[17] Although the personal income tax imposed a top marginal rate of 60 percent on high incomes, the few that were affected paid an effective rate of tax below 35 percent.[18] Nor has auditing kept pace with evasion and multiple bookkeeping.[19] Some Chinese economists in Taiwan argue that a steeply graduated income tax system punishes industrious people, and "that reduced tax rates would help eliminate tax avoidance and thereby lend to increased tax revenues."[20] Responding to these arguments, the government reduced the top marginal tax rate from 60 to 50 percent in 1985.

Attempts to estimate the impact of taxation on income distribution concluded that direct taxes modestly reduced income inequality in Taiwan, but that rising wages and employment opportunities played a much more important role in evening overall income distribution.[21]

ECONOMIC PERFORMANCE

Producers who supplied internal markets in the 1950s turned to export markets after 1960. The bias in the 1950s against exporters was eliminated when Taiwan's overvalued currency was refixed in 1960 and thereafter maintained at an effectively free-market exchange rate. Exporters enjoyed the equivalent of a free-trade regime. Foreign and domestic investors received a variety of tax incentives. High real interest rates channeled household savings into business investment. The policy of export promotion yielded dramatic results, with real GNP rising 9.4 percent in the 1960s and 9.9 percent in the 1970s.

While agricultural production grew modestly, approximately doubling between 1960 and 1985, industrial production increased more than twentyfold.[22] In the two periods 1963-1972 and 1973-1985, the annual increase in agricultural production was 4 and 2 percent respectively, while annual industrial production grew 18.5 and 9.2 percent. Although agricultural efficiency in Taiwan was about double that on mainland China, the bulk of economic growth took the form of industrialization. Output in transportation and communications rose more than sevenfold.

Foreign trade spurred economic growth. The index of exports increased 205 times between 1960 and 1985; the index of imports rose 74 times. Exports increased almost ten times as fast as overall industrial production. For the periods 1963-1972 and 1973-1985, the average annual growth of exports was 29.9 and 19.6 percent, respectively.[23]

In 1960, primary and processed agricultural products constituted 68 percent of exports, while industrial goods made up 32 percent. By 1985, agriculture's contribution to exports fell to 6 percent, while industry's rose to 94 percent.[24] In less than one generation, Taiwan was transformed from a largely agricultural economy to an industrial one.

Taiwan remained heavily dependent on a few major export markets. In the mid-1980s, the United States took nearly half of all exports, with the balance going to Japan, Western Europe, and other Asian nations.

Effect of Exports on Growth and Employment

The switch in policy from import substitution to export promotion substantially opened the economy, increasing the role of foreign trade.[25] Exports as a share of GNP stood at 8.6 percent in 1952 and 11.2 percent in 1961, but thereafter rose sharply to surpass 50 percent in 1984.[26] Similarly, imports rose from 5.3 to about 39 percent of GNP during 1952-1984. Imports fell back to 33 percent of GNP in the recession year of 1985. The main imports were raw materials, machinery, and equipment for industry, constituting more than 90 percent of the total.

Dr. Shirley Kuo has disaggregated the growth in demand for Taiwan's production into the four categories of domestic demand, export growth, import substitution, and changes in technology.[27] According to her analysis, for the three five-year periods 1961-1966, 1966-1971, and 1971-1976, output expansion due to domestic demand rose 63.2, 51.4, and 34.7 percent respectively, while that due to export expansion increased 35, 45.9, and 67.7 percent. Expansion due to import substitution and changes in technology fell below zero. After the 1960s, the contribution of export expansion outweighed that of domestic expansion.

Export expansion created millions of new jobs. Even as higher productivity reduced the need for labor, sharply rising exports during the three periods 1961–1966, 1966–1971, and 1971–1976 generated net increases in employment of 377,000, 1,015,000, and 925,000, respectively. Between 1961 and 1976, the proportion of the labor force utilized in export producing and related businesses increased from 11.9 to 34 percent. Rapid expansion of exports created jobs quickly enough to allow the economy to reach full employment by 1971 and maintain that status throughout the 1970s and 1980s. Export growth sustained full employment despite steadily rising productivity and continuous migration from agricultural areas into the cities.

The labor force was successfully absorbed during the 1960s.[28] From an unemployment rate of 6 percent in the early 1960s, the rate fell and remained below 2 percent after 1968.[29] As Taiwan's economy changed from a state of surplus labor to full employment, real wages rose sharply. The annual growth in manufacturing real wages rose 2.7 percent in the 1950s, 6.2 percent in the 1960s, and 10.7 percent during the first eight years of the 1970s. Average earnings of workers in manufacturing in all industrial sectors more than doubled in real terms during 1974–1985.[30]

The distribution of national income shifted away from entrepreneurial income to compensation of employees. The wage share of national income rose from 43 to 61 percent between 1952 and 1985, while the fraction earned by entrepreneurs fell from 30 to 5 percent. Private income from property, representing interest, dividends, and rental payments, remained stable at about 20 percent. Thus the greater portion of rising national income was received by workers in the form of wages and salaries.[31]

The structure of the economy changed to reflect the prominent role of manufacturing for export. Employment in agriculture decreased from 51.4 percent of total employment in 1952 to less than 30 percent in 1979, while employment in the industrial sector increased from 20.4 to 41.8 percent during the same period.

Capital Formation

The various savings reforms and the restoration of domestic price stability, coupled with the innate Chinese propensity for thrift, worked their wonders. The average ratio of net domestic savings to national income from 1951 through 1959 was only 5 percent, and from 1960 to 1962 it was 8 percent. After U.S. aid was withdrawn, the domestic savings ratio jumped to 13 percent in 1963. Between 1967 and 1971, net domestic savings ranged from 20 to 27 percent. During 1972–1980, it exceeded 30 percent of national income every year, and it remained in the high 20s during 1981–1983, again exceeding 30 percent in 1984.[32]

Rising domestic savings helped finance sharp increases in gross fixed capital formation, which rose from 16 percent of gross domestic product in 1960 to 20 percent in 1967; it remained in the high 20s and low 30s since 1974. (Taiwan has no external debt to speak of.) The growth of new capital accumulation (the value of capital per worker doubled between 1965 and 1980) contributed to a steady rise in labor productivity.[33] During the entire period of Nationalist rule in Taiwan, factor productivity grew remarkably. New capital and technology, along with liberal rural and urban reforms, played a major role.

U.S. aid financed almost half of all investment before 1962. Almost no private capital flowed into Taiwan before 1961, but this situation changed dramatically after 1964. Private foreign investments from 1962 to 1969 came to $378 million. Foreign investment was about $150 million every year in the 1970s; it increased to $330 million in 1979, and to $466 million in 1980; and it remained strong during the 1980s. By 1976, exports by private foreign and overseas Chinese firms amounted to 29 percent of Taiwan's total exports and 82 percent of exported electronics and electrical products. Taiwan's receptivity to foreign direct investment helped expand and modernize its economy.

Standard of Living

Rising wages in industry fueled increases in per capita GNP by an average annual rate of 7.0 percent between 1961 and 1985.[34] An annual rate of 7.0 percent doubles per capita income every 9.9 years, which means that per capita income more than quadrupled in real (inflation-adjusted) terms between 1961 and 1984. In current U.S. dollars, per capita GNP reached $441 in 1971, $1,122 in 1976, and $2,269 in 1981; it then surpassed $3,000 in 1985. These figures dwarfed incomes in mainland China, which Beijing estimated for 1984 at $125 among 800 million peasants and $213 among 200 million urban residents at realistic (not overvalued) exchange rates; it also estimated the overall per capita income at almost exactly US$200 in 1985.[35]

Personal consumption tripled since 1963. In 1963, 48.9 percent of total spending by an average family was on food. That spending declined to 34.3 percent by 1983, and spending on education and recreation increased from 12.9 to 20.6 percent. Comparing 1983 with 1952 shows the dramatic enrichment of Taiwan's population: Life expectancy rose from 58.6 to 72.7 years; daily intake of calories increased from 2,078 to 2,749 (with protein intake up 56 percent); living space more than doubled from 75 to 189 square feet per capita (more than 80 percent of all the houses in Taiwan were built after World War II); telephones per 1,000 persons increased from 3.9 to 259 (and they work!), automobiles per 1,000 persons from 1.0 to 57.3 (which is one-fifth of all four-person households), the percentage of households with electricity from 45.2 to 99.7; and every household now has its own television set (compared with 1.4 per 100 households in 1964).[36]

Rising prosperity gave most families the opportunity to purchase a variety of consumer durables. In 1980, every 1,000 households owned

934 refrigerators, 172 air conditioners, 1,902 electric fans, 650 washing machines, 990 gas stoves, 980 electric cookers, 437 exhaust fans, 747 flush toilets, 618 enamel baths, 521 sewing machines, 273 cameras, 258 stereo sets, 443 recorders, and 783 motorcycles.[37] These statistics better fit an advanced industrial society than a developing country.

In addition to increased private consumption, government consumption expenditure grew more than fourfold in real terms between 1960 and 1985. The number of students enrolled in classes more than doubled, rising from 21 to 25 percent of the population. Higher education enjoyed a sixfold increase in faculty, and enrollment jumped from 35,000 to 428,000. Students studying abroad tripled.[38]

Health and medical care attained levels found in Western industrial democracies. Deaths due to communicable diseases fell from 248 in 1952 to less than 10 every year since 1972. Public and private medical care became widely available. The population per hospital bed declined from 2,686 in 1960 to 270 by 1985.[39]

Distribution of Income

Scholars worry a great deal about the effects of rapid economic growth on the distribution of national income. Rapid growth on Taiwan went hand in hand with greater equality in the distribution of income. The poorest quintiles of the population enjoyed increases in real household income more rapidly than the richest, thus narrowing the gap between rich and poor. Between 1964 and 1984, the share of personal income received by the lowest fifth of all households rose from 7.7 to 8.5 percent, while that enjoyed by the highest fifth fell from 41.1 to 37.3 percent. Thus the ratio of the highest fifth's income to that of the lowest fifth fell from 5.33 to 4.40.[40] Among developing countries, Taiwan is widely regarded as a low-inequality nation, thus refuting any claim that rapid economic and industrial growth necessarily creates growing gaps between rich and poor—gaps that foster social tension and political instability.

NOTES

1. For a comprehensive review of the challenges facing future economic development in Taiwan and the policies that are likely to be implemented, see Yuan-li Wu, *Becoming an Industrialized Nation: ROC's Development on Taiwan* (New York: Praeger Publishers, 1985).

2. Shirley W.Y. Kuo, *The Taiwan Economy in Transition* (Boulder, Colo.: Westview Press, 1983), pp. 300–309; Shirley W.Y. Kuo, Gustav Ranis, and John C.H. Fei, *The Taiwan Success Story: Rapid Growth with Improved Distribution in the Republic of China, 1952-1979* (Boulder, Colo.: Westview Press, 1981), pp. 73–83; K.T. Li, *The Experience of Dynamic Economic Growth on Taiwan* (Taipei and New York: Mei Ya, 1976), selected speeches; "A Brief Introduction to the Investment Climate in Taiwan, Republic of China," Industrial Development and Investment Center, Taipei, Taiwan, August 1984; and Ramon

H. Myers, "The Economic Transformation of the Republic of China on Taiwan, *The China Quarterly*, no. 99 (September 1984), pp. 500–528.

3. Ramon H. Myers, "The Economic Transformation of the Republic of China on Taiwan," pp. 518–519.

4. See George Fitting, "Export Processing Zones in Taiwan and the People's Republic of China," *Asian Survey* 22, no. 8 (August 1982), pp. 733–734. Fitting also examines the social impact of the zones on its predominantly female employees in terms of overcrowded housing, the difficulty of finding suitable marriage partners, and the limited power of these workers to bargain collectively for improvements in wages and working conditions. In particular, Fitting contends that unions work closely with the party and state security apparatus to maintain stability and investor confidence.

5. Shirley W.Y. Kuo, *The Taiwan Economy in Transition*, pp. 301–303.

6. Yuan-li Wu, *Becoming an Industrialized Nation*, pp. 41–42.

7. For a thorough review of the labor force and working conditions, see Walter Galenson, "The Labor Force, Wages, and Living Standards," in Walter Galenson, ed., *Economic Growth and Structural Change in Taiwan: The Postwar Experience of the Republic of China* (Ithaca and London: Cornell University Press, 1979), pp. 384–447.

8. Ibid., p. 428.

9. For a summary of Taiwan's monetary policy both pre- and post-1980, see John G. Greenwood, "Taiwan: A New Bull Market Signals the Limits to Sterilisation," *Asian Monetary Monitor* 10, no. 1 (January–February 1986), pp. 4–8.

10. S.C. Tsiang, "Monetary Policy of Taiwan," *Conference on Experiences and Lessons of Economic Development in Taiwan* (Taipei: Institute of Economics, Academia Sinica, December 18–20, 1981), pp. 258–261.

11. Alexander Ya-li Lu, "Future Domestic Developments in the Republic of China on Taiwan," *Asian Survey* 24, no. 11 (November 1985), pp. 1081–1082.

12. *Taiwan Statistical Data Book 1986* (Taipei: Council for Economic Planning and Development), pp. 161–163.

13. Ian M.D. Little, a prominent development economist, has questioned the economic efficiency of these massive government projects. See "An Economic Renaissance," in Walter Galenson, ed., *Economic Growth and Structural Change in Taiwan*, p. 506. Recent studies in Taiwan show that the rate of return on capital in private enterprises is around three times that of public enterprises. See Ramon H. Myers, "The Economic Transformation of the Republic of China on Taiwan," p. 526.

14. *Taiwan Statistical Data Book 1986*, p. 166.

15. Ibid., pp. 167–170.

16. Ibid., p. 171.

17. "Income Tax Law," Industrial Development and Investment Center, Taipei, Taiwan, February 1983, pp. 7–12.

18. Shirley W.Y. Kuo, Gustav Ranis, and John C.H. Fei, *The Taiwan Success Story*, pp. 138–139.

19. Erik Lundberg, "Fiscal and Monetary Policies," in Walter Galenson, ed., *Economic Growth and Structural Change in Taiwan*, p. 305.

20. Tzong-shian Yu and Ting-an Chen, "Fiscal Reforms and Economic Development," *Conference on Experiences and Lessons of Economic Development in Taiwan*, pp. 297–298.

21. Ibid., pp. 292–298; and Shirley W.Y. Kuo, Gustav Ranis, and John C.H. Fei, *The Taiwan Success Story*, pp. 137–141.

22. *Taiwan Statistical Data Book 1986*, p. 1.

23. Ibid.

24. Ibid., p. 207.

25. Shirley W.Y. Kuo, *The Taiwan Economy in Transition*, pp. 135–174.

26. *Taiwan Statistical Data Book 1986*, derived from pp. 23 and 203.

27. Shirley W.Y. Kuo, *The Taiwan Economy in Transition*, pp. 142–157.

28. Shirley W.Y. Kuo, Gustav Ranis, and John C.H. Fei, *The Taiwan Success Story*, pp. 19–23.

29. Walter Galenson, "The Labor Force, Wages, and Living Standards," p. 404.

30. *Taiwan Statistical Data Book 1986*, p. 18–19.

31. Ibid., p. 37; and Simon Kuznets, "Growth and Structural Shifts," in Walter Galenson, ed., *Economic Growth and Structural Change in Taiwan*, p. 99.

32. *Taiwan Statistical Data Book 1986*, p. 54.

33. Ramon H. Myers, "The Economic Transformation of the Republic of China on Taiwan," p. 511–512.

34. *Taiwan Statistical Data Book 1986*, pp. 28–29.

35. See *Wall Street Journal* (March 11, 1985). During my visit to Taiwan in August 1986, several high-level government officials communicated to me their speculations that the underground economy might add an additional $1,000 or even as much as $1,500 per capita to the official estimates, thus placing per capita income closer to $4,500.

36. *Economic Development, Taiwan, Republic of China* (Taipei: Ministry of Economic Affairs, April 1984), pp. 39–40. In the *Wall Street Journal* (September 29, 1986) it was reported that mainland China had 6.04 million telephone instruments in China at the end of 1985. The corresponding figure in Taiwan was 5.6 million, and they work much better!

37. Shirley W.Y. Kuo, *The Taiwan Economy in Transition*, p. 129.

38. *Taiwan Statistical Data Book 1986*, pp. 277, 279.

39. Ibid., pp. 293–295.

40. Ibid., pp. 59–60.

PART III
HONG KONG

7

ECONOMIC AND
POLITICAL SETTING

Since its founding in 1841, and especially during the period of postwar British colonial rule, Hong Kong was the world's closest approximation to a free-market, private-enterprise, capitalistic economic system. Its residents enjoyed the trading benefits of a free port, low taxes, and limited government intervention in their economic and social affairs. But the British colony's postwar future was always under a cloud, regulated by the precise date of midnight, June 30, 1997—the moment Britain's 99-year lease on the New Territories (90 percent of the colony) expires. Novelist Han Suyin best coined the phrase aptly describing Hong Kong as a "borrowed time, borrowed place," an entity with a perpetually uncertain future.

In 1982, Hong Kong's uncertain future leapt onto center stage. Chinese leaders Deng Xiaoping and Zhao Ziyang firmly indicated to British prime minister, Mrs. Margaret Thatcher, during her September visit to Beijing, that China would reclaim sovereignty and administrative authority over Hong Kong on July 1, 1997. On December 19, 1984, after two years of intense negotiations, the British and Chinese governments signed a joint declaration that determined Hong Kong's political future. On July 1, 1997, Hong Kong would be reincorporated into mainland China as a Special Administrative Region. In return for the British transfer of sovereignty, China guaranteed in writing that Hong Kong would retain considerable autonomy; in particular, the territory's more than 5 million residents could retain their present social, economic, and legal systems for an additional 50 years through 2047.

Economic policy did not change in 1982, nor in 1984. Yet anxieties over the colony's future shocked investors, factory owners, and workers.

Several banks failed. The stock, property, and financial markets were hit hard. Political uncertainty adversely affected business confidence. The double-digit growth rates of prior years yielded to disinvestment, capital outflow, and slower growth.

Hong Kong's modern economic history is thus divisible into two phrases: uninterrupted British rule through 1982 and the post-1982 era of increasing Chinese influence. In this sense, Hong Kong resembles mainland China and Taiwan, inasmuch as the economic development of each can be separated into two distinct phases. Unlike the leaders of mainland China and Taiwan, however, Hong Kong's leaders charted a steady course in economic policy. But maintaining policies of competition and free entry are not sufficient conditions of prosperity; political confidence in the future is also important. In the wake of Beijing's confidence-shattering announcement of September 1982, Hong Kong's economic growth slowed for the next three years. Despite written promises, investors have less confidence in Hong Kong's future under Chinese rule.

Hong Kong is widely regarded as the industrial world's single best example of the free-market-economy model of development.[1] Throughout its history, Hong Kong overcame many obstacles, and received almost no foreign aid in the process. Its land area is virtually resourceless, consisting largely of unproductive granitic rock formations. It suffers a population density that ranks it among the world's most overpopulated areas, and it is dependent on imports for the bulk of its food, raw materials, and all capital equipment. Located thousands of miles from its most important markets, Hong Kong historically was unable to control population movements across its borders. Through 1985, it was ruled by a colonial government that critics regarded as obsolete, antiquated, and inconsistent with the principles of independence and self-rule.

Yet despite these formidable obstacles, the rate of growth of the Hong Kong economy was so rapid in the post–World War II era that it took on an almost certain inevitability. And despite its anachronistic colonial administration, a secret-ballot referendum among local Chinese on the future of Hong Kong, if allowed, would likely produce a large majority vote favoring retention of the status quo under British rule.

PHYSICAL SETTING, POPULATION, AND RESOURCES

Hong Kong lies inside the tropics on the Southeast coast of China, adjoining the province of Guangdong.[2] It consists of a small part of the Chinese mainland and a scattering of offshore islands, the most important of which is Hong Kong Island. Including reclamations through 1985, the total land area of the colony was about 410 square miles. Hong Kong Island, Stonecutter's Island, Kowloon, and a number of small adjacent islands constituted about 10 percent; the New Territories, which consist of part of the mainland and more than 230 offshore islands, made up the balance.

Of the total land area, 9 percent was used for farming and 74.5 percent was marginal unproductive land. Built-up urban and rural lands made up the remaining 16.5 percent, within which most of Hong Kong's people lived and worked.[3]

As noted, Hong Kong remains one of the most densely populated places in the world.[4] Its overall density figure of 13,137 per square mile in 1985 included a wide variety of densities in individual areas. According to the 1981 census, the density for the metropolitan areas of Hong Kong Island, Kowloon, New Kowloon, and Tsuen Wan was 73,760 per square mile, but for the New Territories it was 2,051 per square mile. The most densely populated district was Sham Shui Po in New Kowloon, with 428,503 per square mile.

The total population at the end of 1985 was 5,466,900, almost evenly balanced between males and females. The 1981 census revealed that 57 percent were born in Hong Kong; the other 43 percent largely comprised refugees and immigrants from other countries, mainly China. About 98 percent of the population were classified as Chinese on the basis of place of origin and language, most having originated from Guangdong Province. Other Commonwealth citizens in residence numbered 64,800, consisting largely of British, Indian, Malaysian, Australian, Singaporean, and Canadian nationals. Non-Commonwealth residents numbered 97,200, of which the largest groups were Filipinos, Americans, Pakistanis, Japanese, Thais, and Portuguese.

The British physically occupied Hong Kong in early 1841, well before the Sino-British Treaty of Nanking (signed on August 29, 1842), legally transferred sovereignty and administrative control to Her Majesty's Government.[5] By the end of 1841, the population of Hong Kong stood at about 15,000, of whom only a minority was foreigners. The great majority were Chinese people of the surrounding region, attracted to Hong Kong for its employment and commercial opportunities, despite the prevalence of tropical diseases. Captain Charles Elliot, the de facto administrator of seized Hong Kong, announced that its Chinese residents would enjoy British protection but would be governed by traditional law. In addition, trade would be free of tariffs.

The Manchu government of China had discouraged and even forbidden the emigration of Chinese overseas. But this decaying dynasty was unable to enforce its edicts. Large numbers of Chinese continued to move into Hong Kong and through it to Southeast Asia, the United States, and elsewhere around the globe.

Throughout most of its history, Hong Kong willingly accepted political refugees and immigrants seeking freedom and opportunity. Several hundred thousand Chinese entered Hong Kong in the 1930s during the Sino-Japanese War. The Japanese forcibly deported large numbers of Chinese to China during their World War II occupation of Hong Kong in order to ease the local food problems, thereby reducing the population of Hong Kong to about one-third its prewar size of 1.8 million. But after Hong Kong's liberation from the Japanese in 1945, the deported Chinese returned at a rate approaching 100,000 a month. By the end of 1947, the population had regained its prewar size. Still another influx took place during the Chinese civil war of 1948 and 1949, when nearly half a million people, mainly from Guangdong Province, Shanghai, and other commercial centers, entered the colony. Aside from returning residents, immigrants, of which 700,000 were refugees, increased the population between 1945 and 1956 by approximately 1 million. Another flood of persons crossed the border in 1962, following three years of bad harvests. Several hundred thousand more Chinese entered during 1979 as the Cultural Revolution wound down; this influx coincided with the exodus of "boat people" from Vietnam, during which some 65,000 (mostly ethnically Chinese) refugees landed in Hong Kong.[6] For much of its postwar development, Hong Kong authorities were unable to restrict the arrival of new immigrants, thus making very difficult the implementation of such social programs as housing, schools, and health in an orderly manner.

The small colony of Hong Kong almost entirely lacks natural resources. Its mineral wealth is negligible, consisting of a modest amount of iron ore, building stone, kaolin clay, graphite, lead, and wolfram. Most of the activity in the mining and quarrying industry has concentrated on the production of building stone and sand. Only one-seventh of its land is arable; the colony, therefore, could not feed itself and throughout most of its history encountered difficulty in maintaining an adequate water supply. Almost all industrial materials, capital goods, and the vast majority of foodstuffs were imported.

Hong Kong sits on the edge of an eroded mountain chain that extends along the south coast of China, consisting mainly of sedimentary and granitic rocks. The hilly topography restricted agricultural activity. Indeed, the shortage of land was always one of Hong Kong's chief concerns. Upon its occupation by the British in 1841, the island had scarcely any flat land. Reporting on this condition, *The Times* (London) candidly remarked on December 17, 1844:

> The place has nothing to recommend it, if we except the excellent harbor. The site of the new town of Victoria . . . is most objectionable, there being scarcely level ground enough for the requisite buildings, and the high hills, which overhang the locality, shut out the southerly winds, and render the place exceedingly hot, close and uncomfortable.[7]

Lord Palmerston, Britain's Foreign Secretary at the onset of the Opium Wars, rebuked Captain Charles Elliot for his seizure of Hong Kong, which he contemptuously described as "a barren island with hardly a house upon it."[8]

The colony's British masters undertook reclamation within ten years of its occupation. In the postwar period, Hong Kong became one huge construction site as contractors literally moved mountains into the sea to create land for roads, factories, and cities. Builders transformed small rural villages into modern industrial towns in a few short years, providing housing and jobs for more than a million people.

Through much of Hong Kong's history, water shortages posed severe difficulties. There are no rivers and only a few large streams in the colony. Fulfillment of local water needs depended upon the collecting and storing of rainwater by systems of catchwaters and reservoirs, the bulk of which are located in the New Territories. This problem was complicated by the fact that the rainy season is concentrated in the five summer months from May to September; within these five months sufficient water must be caught to last throughout the winter. As wells and hillside streams proved insufficient to keep up with growing water requirements, the government built a large number of reservoirs and signed an agreement with China to purchase up to one-third of its fresh water consumption. Hong Kong also lacked coal, oil, or other internal sources of power.

From the standpoint of economic policy, the colony's internal market was too small to offer a solid base for economic expansion. Therefore, the government erected no tariff wall or other protectionist devices to shield Hong Kong's domestic industries from overseas competition.

AN ECONOMIC AND POLITICAL HISTORY SINCE 1841

Hong Kong became a British possession in 1841 for the simple purpose of trade with China. Although the British dominated foreign trade with China since the end of the eighteenth century, conditions at Canton were unsatisfactory, reflecting the conflicting viewpoints of two different civilizations.[9]

The Chinese regarded themselves as highly civilized, with little need for foreign imports. They stringently restricted foreign traders to a clearly defined trading season, excluded family members from Chinese soil, confined the traders to a small area, forbade them to enter the city of Canton or to learn Chinese, and arbitrarily varied shipping dues. Nonetheless, the lucrative opium trade brought foreign free traders who hoped to get rich quickly. To stem the outflow of silver from China that financed opium imports, the Chinese emperor appointed Lin Zexu (Lin Tse-hsu) to stamp out the opium trade. He surrounded the foreign factories and compelled all foreign traders to turn over their stocks of opium. The British community retired to Macau, and then took refuge on board ships in Hong Kong harbor in summer 1839.

The British sent an expeditionary force in June 1840 to back their demands for either a commercial treaty or the cession of a small island where the British could live free from threats under the security of their own flag. Hostilities alternated with negotiations until the Treaty of Nanjing, signed on August 29, 1842, ceded Hong Kong Island to Britain in perpetuity. It also opened five Chinese ports for trade. A supplementary treaty in October 1843 granted Chinese subjects free access to Hong Kong Island for trading purposes.

Two subsequent treaties filled out the territory of British Hong Kong. The Convention of Peking in 1860, which terminated the Second Anglo-Chinese War (1856–1858), ceded the Kowloon Peninsula, located directly across the harbor from Hong Kong Island, to Britain in perpetuity. The Sino-Japanese War of 1895 encouraged the British to augment their defensive position by demanding, and gaining control of, the territory north of Kowloon up to the Shum Chun River and 235 adjacent islands. In accordance with the terms of the Convention of Peking in 1898, China ceded sovereignty of these New Territories to Britain for a period of 99 years.

The early years of Hong Kong were difficult. Hong Kong attracted unruly elements, while fever and typhoons threatened life and property. Crime was rampant. Large Chinese inflows quickly turned Hong Kong into a British-run Chinese community, a surprising development given that few had anticipated that the Chinese people there would want to live under a foreign flag.

Colonial administration of Hong Kong followed normal British overseas practices, with a governor appointed from London assisted by nominated, not elected, Executive and Legislative Councils. British exclusivity in government gradually yielded to Chinese participation in both councils. On several occasions, local British residents pressed for self-government, but the home government rejected these demands in the fear that a small European community might use self-government to take unfair advantage of the Chinese majority.

From its beginning, Hong Kong developed as an entrepôt free port—as a mart and storehouse for goods in transit to Asia and the West.[10] This entrepôt activity diminished after World War II when the transition to an industrial economy took place.

In keeping with Hong Kong's entrepôt character, the first industrial venture was shipbuilding and repairing. A number of ancillary industries were then established to cater to the seafaring trade: a large graving dock, a sugar refinery, a rope factory, and other service activities. Until World War I the colony possessed a number of enterprises linked with the operation of the port, with few cottage industries. Hong Kong became the headquarters of the major merchant houses trading in the Far East. As a clearing house of trade between the East and the rest of the world, it developed specialized associated services, such as banking, insurance, accountancy, and legal services. It also developed a gold market. After World War I, the area of the entrepôt trade grew to cover much of the Far East and Southeast Asia.

Since World War II, manufacturing (largely export-oriented light industries) has been the mainstay of Hong Kong's economy, augmented by a myriad of servicing industries. Highly developed banking, insurance, and shipping systems created in the entrepôt era flourished in the 1960s, 1970s, and 1980s. In keeping with its free-port tradition, Hong Kong eschewed tariffs and other restrictions on the import of commercial goods.

Hong Kong's post–World War II transformation from a trading to an industrial economy was so dramatic that between 1938 and 1956 it successfully absorbed a doubling of its population. In the wake of the war, many of the factors that contribute to rapid industrial development were found in Hong Kong. The Communist revolution in China produced a massive influx of refugees, and an important injection of Shanghainese capital and entrepreneurial skill moving to the safe haven of Hong Kong. Chinese immigrants brought labor, new industrial techniques from the north, and capital seeking employment and security, thus facilitating the colony's transition from an entrepôt port to an industrial territory. Since 1950, the inflow of an additional million-plus Chinese has fueled a burgeoning economy with industrial workers, construction-site laborers, service personnel, stevedores, and coolies.[11]

THE POLITICAL GEOGRAPHY OF HONG KONG

From the end of World War II through July 1982, Hong Kong enjoyed remarkable political and economic stability. Local Chinese did not clamor for democracy, a British-style welfare state, or political independence. Meanwhile, China resisted political encroachment on Hong Kong. What made these circumstances possible?

One answer is found in Hong Kong's political geography.[12] Hong Kong's prosperity served mainland China's developmental interests, largely through China's foreign-exchange earnings, which had arisen from doing business in and with Hong Kong. Entrepreneurs from Britain and other countries benefited from commerce in Hong Kong. Finally, the local residents, many of them refugees from China, found personal opportunity for economic improvement—life in Hong Kong was materially good. They did not clamor for more state intervention in their personal lives; many fled an oppressive Communist government in order to obtain personal freedom in Hong Kong. Thus a tripod of consent—Britain, China, and the local people—fostered the economic haven of Hong Kong.

Apart from its political geography, the colony's economic policy makers knew that Hong Kong's economic resourcelessness dictated a heavy dependence on external trade. A small, open trading economy must remain externally competitive. The government believed that intervention would, if anything, adversely alter the cost/price structure of exports or imports to the detriment of Hong Kong. Accordingly, the government maintained a hands-off attitude toward the private sector, although other developing countries in similar circumstances have been less inclined to follow Hong Kong's example. Let's look at this confluence of forces in more detail.

China's Benefits from Hong Kong

Why did a Communist government in Beijing tolerate the existence of a foreign enclave on its doorstep for so many years? Indeed, this situation was one that demonstrated the success of a free-market economy compared with the disappointing performance of its own state-directed, state-controlled socialistic system.

Economic benefits must rank first in this calculation. Since the mid-1960s, receipts from Hong Kong, which ranged as high as $6 billion in 1983 alone, accounted for 30–40 percent of China's total earnings of foreign exchange.[13] China supplied Hong Kong with about 20 percent of its imports, a wide range of inexpensive consumer goods, oil products, the bulk of its food imports, and annually increasing quantities of fresh water. It bought less in return, leaving a balance-of-trade surplus that helped finance China's development policies. In 1982, 1983, and 1984, for example, imports from China into Hong Kong totaled HK$32.3 billion, HK$42.8 billion, and HK$55.8 billion respectively, while domestic exports to China during the same three years were a modest HK$3.8 billion, HK$6.2 billion, and HK$11.3 billion. (During 1982–1984, the average monthly exchange rate varied from US$1 = HK$6.07 to US$1 = HK$8.10.)[14] In addition, Hong Kong was the clearing house for remittances to China. Local and overseas companies and individuals remitted to their relatives and business associates upwards of US$100 million a year.

Hong Kong has the largest, deepest, and most modern port facilities along the China coast. It was an important redistribution center for goods made in China to the outside world. Each year, China exported several hundred million dollars' worth of goods through the port of Hong Kong to overseas destinations.

Apart from quantifiable economic and financial benefits, Hong Kong provided China with indirect—but tangible—benefits in the form of access to Western technology and modes of business management, a convenient center for trade contacts and financial negotiations, a training ground for thousands of Chinese technicians and service personnel, and a first-hand opportunity to observe the workings of a free-market economy. Since the advent of China's "Four Modernizations" campaign in 1978, Beijing has experimented with a variety of market incentives to improve the performance of its economy. The regime could learn about incentives from Hong Kong.

China's postwar relationship with Hong Kong was pragmatic in economic affairs. Ideological consistency dictated that Hong Kong, as a dependent capitalistic territory of a sovereign power on Chinese soil, should not have existed at all. But China allowed the British colony to exist and flourish because Hong Kong's prosperity served its own wider interests.

Furthermore, China is in the fourth millennium of its national history. Consolidating its power over the mainland and beginning the job of national economic reconstruction after 1949 were more important tasks for the Communist leadership than recovering Hong Kong. The half-century to 1997 is just the blink of an eye on China's time horizon. Why not let the British administration and people of Hong Kong develop the most modern city in Asia outside Japan? It would fall into China's hands sooner or later.

Britain's Relationship to Hong Kong

Apart from a few scattered offshore tax-haven islands and Gibraltar, Hong Kong became Britain's sole remaining major colony by the 1960s. The once majestic British empire, on which the sun never set, was no more. Since 1945, the Queen's ministers conferred independence on many British colonies, within the framework of the Commonwealth, largely through the process of self-government.

Local pressures on the British to hand over independence were missing in postwar Hong Kong for several reasons. First, China had ruled out national independence for Hong Kong as a feasible political option. Second, China's leaders regarded sovereignty as indivisible. And third, a large proportion of Hong Kong's residents were not Hong Kong born, but were refugees from the various provinces of China. Many of these refugees were politically acquiescent, seeking comfort and security; upon arriving in Hong Kong, they scrupulously disdained any form of political agitation. Besides, as most Hong Kong residents always presumed that their future would be determined by ministers in London and Beijing, there was little scope or point to local political activism. The only two serious political options were the maintenance of some form of British rule or a Chinese takeover. Therefore, most concentrated their efforts in economic, not political, activity.

What were Britain's benefits from administrative authority over Hong Kong? In the nineteenth century, Hong Kong served as one of a string of British naval stations around the world that provided bunkering and repair facilities. This strategic era passed, however, and the naval dockyard closed down. By the 1980s, there was no British fleet in the Far East and the British base in Hong Kong had become an isolated outpost. Only a small contingent of British-officered Gurkhas were present in the mid-1980s, largely to assist the police with internal security.

Hong Kong provided Britain with modest economic benefits, which were concentrated in a handful of trading companies and individuals. In general, Hong Kong was not a captive market for British goods, which were forced to compete with goods from other countries in Hong Kong's relatively free economy. Some funds flowed from Hong Kong to Britain in the form of pensions paid to retired Hong Kong civil servants living in Britain, dividends paid to British shareholders in Hong Kong firms, and payments for commercial facilities arranged through the city of London. British firms provided the railways and rapid transit carriages. The nationalized British Airways Corporation gained from Britain's authority to negotiate landing rights at Hong Kong's airport. Britain used its management of the colony's external affairs to grant landing rights in Hong Kong in exchange for preferential foreign routes to British Airways. Finally, expatriate British civil servants serving in the Hong Kong government enjoyed a great deal of local respect and an especially comfortable standard of living.

Compared to the few concentrated British interests with a direct stake in colonial rule, the vast majority of Britons were relatively uninformed about and indifferent to events in Hong Kong. Until the commencement of Sino-British negotiations in 1982, media coverage in Britain on Hong Kong affairs was virtually nonexistent. Since the signing of the Joint Declaration in late 1984, coverage on Hong Kong has disappeared again.

Britain's experience with Caribbean West Indians, Pakistanis, and Indians prompted it to lock the door on the sole large remaining class of overseas British passport holders in Hong Kong. To tighten immigration, Parliament passed the British Nationality Act of 1981.[15] Formerly known as citizens of the United Kingdom and Colonies, this Act reclassified 2.6 million British passport holders, largely Chinese, as British Dependent Territory Citizens. Stringent rules of patrilineality disqualified virtually all such citizens from applying for regular British citizenship, which brings with it the right of abode in Britain. There is an escape clause for Crown servants in a dependent territory to bypass the patrilineality rules, but the British government stated that this discretion would be exercised only sparingly. With the 1981 act, Britain effectively excluded its Hong Kong subjects from refuge.

Despite the apparent contradiction of the 1981 Nationality Act, British leaders claimed moral responsibility for the people of Hong Kong. No British prime minister wanted the responsibility of handing over 5 million people living in economic and personal freedom to the Chinese Communist Party.[16] It might have been easier to dispose of the colony if the local people had demonstrated any desire to live under Communist rule. But Hong Kong's people had resisted Maoist blandishments even when they were backed up by street agitation and occasional violence. Hong Kong residents were well informed about the different life-styles in Hong Kong and mainland China. Several million were born in China and voluntarily sought refuge in colonial Hong Kong; several hundred thousand risked their lives to escape. During the Sino-British negotiations over the future of Hong Kong, delegations of local Chinese repeatedly visited London, urging British ministers and members of Parliament to negotiate for some form of British presence in Hong Kong after 1997. Hong Kong people saw a continued British presence as the best guarantee of their freedoms.

The Local People

Rounding off this tripod of consent is the fact that the vast majority of Hong Kong Chinese were content with British administration, despite any personal dislike of or racial aversion to "barbarians" or foreign rulers. While China convulsed in periodic political campaigns, postwar Hong Kong remained remarkably free of serious outbreaks of rioting, strikes, or other forms of labor or political agitation. Few Chinese, barely 2 percent of the eligible electorate, ever voted in Urban Council elections, Hong Kong's only broadly elected body through 1982.

Why did the local Chinese population so readily accept this alien, "barbarian" colonial government? First, it was the only alternative to living on the Communist-ruled mainland. Second, life in Hong Kong was materially rewarding, with rapidly rising incomes. Finally, the Hong Kong government was exceptionally efficient. It housed nearly half the population in subsidized housing at below-market rents, provided a wide battery of medical and health services, and developed roads, communications, port facilities, waterworks, and public utilities of high qualilty, but without high taxes. A weekend visit to neighboring Canton in the 1980s revealed the gap separating Hong Kong's modernity and high living standards from China's backwardness and relative poverty.

HISTORICAL PRECEDENTS OF ECONOMIC AND FISCAL POLICY

Beginning with Captain Elliot's occupation of Hong Kong Island in 1841, the colonial government adhered to a set of free-market economic policies and conservative fiscal policies.[17] Hong Kong rigidly eschewed central planning, regulation of the private sector, budget deficits, high tax rates, industrial subsidies, costly labor regulations, and other instruments of state control. These policies were rooted in historical precedents of financial administration, a constitutional system of government, and the dogged application of an economic philosophy of nonintervention.

Hong Kong was a barren island with no large or established community entitled to political representation. It was established as a military, diplomatic, and trading station, not as a colonial settlement in the normal sense. For these purposes, the British secretary of state for war and the colonies imposed firm imperial control on the new colony. Self-government was never a feature of Hong Kong's development.

In practice, administrative absolutism meant that the colonial government did little more than maintain law and order and raise taxes to pay for the cost of a modest civil establishment and the necessary public works. Parliament instructed Hong Kong's governors to take from colonial resources all public expenditures except the salaries of only three principal officers in the colonial government. In 1855 the governor happily announced that Hong Kong had reached the objective of fiscal self-support, thus entrenching the doctrine and practice of balanced budgets.

Hong Kong, as a Crown Colony, was administered under colonial regulations. These regulations dated back to 1837 and served as "directions to Governors for general guidance given by the Crown through the Secretary of State for the Colonies," especially in financial and administrative matters.[18] In particular, the annual budget of each British colony required the secretary's approval well before the beginning of the financial year. It was the responsibility of the Colonial Office to see that colonies did not incur debt and impose a charge on the British Treasury.[19]

Colonial Office policy and the colonial regulations that applied to Hong Kong reflected the prevalent economic theories of nineteenth-century Britain, which stressed the passive role of government in the economy. Private individuals and companies, not the government, were responsible for the creation and distribution of wealth. Although the British Treasury ceased its oversight of colonial expenditures after 1870, Colonial Office approval was typically required until the 1930s, when convention began to replace the letter of the regulations and budget estimates were no longer submitted to the secretary of state before presentation to the local legislature. But the secretary retained powers of disallowance if he thought a colony's spending plans would cause recourse to the Exchequer.

Until financial autonomy was granted to the Hong Kong government in 1958, the colonial regulations provided the formal background against which Hong Kong's financial officers worked. The guiding principle was that all colonies should be self-supporting. Public finance in postwar Hong Kong was a direct offshoot of colonial tradition. The form and scope of the budget changed little since the granting of financial autonomy in 1958. Nineteenth-century values of economic liberalism influenced official thinking and practice in postwar Hong Kong.

CONSTITUTIONAL AND ADMINISTRATIVE FRAMEWORK

Until September 1985, Hong Kong never had any form of representative democracy.[20] Administrative and executive authority lay in the hands of appointed civil servants whose personnel, at the higher levels, were largely recruited from the United Kingdom, although the pace of localization accelerated in the 1970s. Through the early 1980s, neither periodic elections nor public opinion polls guided or constrained the administrative decisions of these appointed officials. Hong Kong political activity took the form of decision making by appointed officials, sometimes within the administration, often in consultation with one of a myriad of official advisory committees or, on occasion, through open solicitation of the public's views. Civil servants responsible for economic and budgetary policy were free of the electoral pressures for increased spending and higher taxes that prevailed in postwar Western industrial democracies.

Constitutional authority for making policy was concentrated in the governor, assisted, in practice, by his Executive Council. The governor's powers were defined by the *Letters Patent and Royal Instructions to the Governor of Hong Kong*. As representative of the queen, he was the head of government and constitutionally accepted his instructions from the secretary of state; in actuality, however, instructions were rarely given.

As chief executive, the governor held final responsibility for the administration of the colony. He made laws by and with the advice and consent of the Legislative Council. In the execution of his duties, the *Royal Instructions* stipulated that he shall consult with the Executive Council—his advisory body consisting of both *ex officio* members of government and other official and unofficial (nongovernment) persons appointed by the secretary of state on the governor's nomination. He was specifically empowered to act in opposition to advice given him by members of the Executive Council. No provision existed for formal voting in the advisory body; the governor sought to distill a consensus from the advice he was given and acted on this advice unless he had overwhelming reasons for not doing so. The Council met regularly, in confidence, and its proceedings were confidential, although many of its decisions were later announced. In January 1986, the Council included five *ex officio* high government officials—the governor, the chief secretary, the financial secretary, the attorney general, and the commander of British forces—and ten nominated members, of whom eight did not hold public office. These ten members were drawn largely from prominent business firms and the professions.

The *Letters Patent* also set forth the constitutional foundations of the governor's legislative authority. Clause VII stipulated that "the Governor, by and with the advice and consent of the Legislative Council, may make laws for the peace, order, and good government of the Colony." At the end of 1984, the Legislative Council consisted of the governor as its presiding officer, three *ex officio* high public officials, and forty-three nominated, hand-picked members, of whom thirty were not civil servants. A clear majority of the legislative councillors were drawn from the private sector.

In November 1984, the colonial government implemented a system of indirect elections to the Legislative Council.[21] Twelve members would be selected by an electoral college composed of members of various locally elected bodies (District Boards, Urban Council, Regional Council). Another 12 would be chosen by specific, functional constituencies. Of the 56 members of the Legislative Council, 24 would be elected, 22 would be appointed non-civil servants, and 10 would be high-ranking civil servants. *Ex officio* and nominated members still held a clear majority. The first elections under the completely new system of partially representative government were held in September 1985. The government also committed itself to a further review of representative government in 1987 (although Beijing expressed dismay in late 1985 over the rapid pace of political reform).[22]

Decisions of the legislature were typically consensual, with an occasional holdout or two among the appointed unofficial members. The Legislative Council rarely withheld consent from legislation proposed by the official bureaucracy. Proceedings in the legislature relied heavily upon British parliamentary procedure in which the government proposes and the legislature disposes. The norm was that official motions were overwhelmingly accepted, although members often used the forum to speak on topics of personal or public interest.

It is useful to summarize the colony's constitutional status at the heyday of British rule. All power was concentrated in the governor. None of his staff exercised specific constitutional power or authority, although the force of individual personalities often determined which branches of government were more influential than others. He was instructed, under the *Royal Instructions*, to consult his Executive Council in the exercise of his power and authorities, but he could lawfully override their advice. His legislative authority, under the *Letters Patent*, required majority votes in the legislative chamber; however, he could disallow proposed laws. In practice, he was never forced to do so. Serious differences of opinion were invariably reconciled before an official government measure was proposed to the Legislative Council. Non-civil-servant members of both councils were appointed on recommendation from the governor from among the most prominent members of the community. None of these officials was accountable to an electorate, nor did the job pay an official salary.

In sum, the economic and fiscal policies of the Hong Kong government were determined largely by the governor and his high-ranking subordinates, especially the financial secretary, who oversaw the operations of the Finance, Monetary Affairs, Trade and Industry, and Economic Services branches of the government. In addition to his responsibility for preparing the annual budget estimates, the financial secretary and his aides were heavily involved in the wide-ranging activities that bear upon the fiscal health of government and the economic health of the colony.

The Legal System

Generally speaking, the law of Hong Kong followed that of England and Wales; the common law and rules of equity were in force in Hong Kong through 1985 insofar as they were applicable to the circumstances of Hong Kong.[23] On occasion, laws were made to apply to Hong Kong by order of Her Majesty in Council, as expressed by Article IX of the *Letters Patent*. In practice, this was largely confined to matters affecting

Hong Kong's international position, such as civil aviation treaties. Local legislation, closely modeled on British or Commonwealth country statutes, augmented the common law. Cases from Commonwealth countries and the United States were quoted in the courts and considered with respect. The Hong Kong courts applied a doctrine of binding precedent similar to that adopted by the English courts. Appeals from Hong Kong courts could be lodged with the Privy Council in England, whose decisions were binding on Hong Kong courts. In short, Hong Kong residents enjoyed fundamental human rights protected under the rule of law. This condition contrasted with the colony's neighboring Communist giant, where all too often the capricious rule of man prevailed.

SUMMARY

Historical precedent shaped Hong Kong's economic and fiscal policies. The incentives and constraints that dictated budgetary policy derived from the letter and spirit of both the colonial regulations, with its emphasis on self-support and balanced budgets, and the doctrine that low taxes foster economic growth. In the case of economic policy, the free-port status of early Hong Kong discouraged an interventionist government—wealth creation resided in the private sector. Nonintervention and conservative fiscal practice remained the cornerstones of Hong Kong public policy during 1945–1985.

NOTES

1. The material in this chapter draws from two books I have written on Hong Kong. See *Value for Money: The Hong Kong Budgetary Process* (Stanford, Calif.: Hoover Press, 1976) and *Hong Kong: A Study in Economic Freedom* (Chicago: University of Chicago Press, 1979). In the first volume I analyzed the policymaking and budgetary practices within the Hong Kong government. In the second I presented a comprehensive treatment of politics and business in Hong Kong, showing the structure of the colony's free-market economy and documenting its remarkable economic growth.

2. Valuable descriptive material and statistics on Hong Kong are published in an annual report, of which the most recent edition used is *Hong Kong 1986: A Review of 1985* (Hong Kong: Government Printer, 1986). A convenient source of recent data is the *Hong Kong Monthly Digest of Statistics* (Hong Kong: Census and Statistics Department).

3. *Hong Kong 1986*, p. 83.

4. Ibid., pp. 268–269.

5. For an excellent political history of the founding and early years of Hong Kong, see G.B. Endacott, *Government and People in Hong Kong* (Hong Kong: Hong Kong University Press, 1964). A summary treatment appears in *Hong Kong 1986*, pp. 275–283.

6. David Bonavia, *Hong Kong 1997* (Hong Kong: South China Morning Post, 1983), pp. 63–66.

7. Cited in *Hong Kong Annual Report, 1957*, pp. 2–3.

8. *Hong Kong 1984*, p. 245.

9. *Hong Kong 1986*, pp. 276–277.

10. This section draws from Alvin Rabushka, *Hong Kong: A Study in Economic Freedom*, pp. 16–20.

11. David Bonavia, *Hong Kong 1997*, p. 76.

12. See Alvin Rabushka, *Hong Kong: A Study in Economic Freedom*, pp. 20–29. See also Norman J. Miners, *The Government and Politics of Hong Kong* (Hong Kong: Oxford University Press, 1975), pp. 1–46.

13. Derived from *Hong Kong Monthly Digest of Statistics* (November 1985), Tables 5.4 and 5.5, pp. 24–25. For a comprehensive review of the economic interdependence of China and Hong Kong, see A.J. Youngson, ed., *China and Hong Kong: The Economic Nexus* (Hong Kong: Oxford University Press, 1983), *passim*.

14. *Hong Kong Monthly Digest of Statistics* (November 1985), Table 9.16, p. 70.

15. Mary Lee, "A Backdoor to Britain," *Far Eastern Economic Review* (May 5, 1983), p. 14.

16. Leo Goodstadt, "The Hong Kong Question," *Euromoney* (July 1983), p. 113.

17. This section is summarized from Alvin Rabushka, *Value for Money*, pp. 12–37.

18. Sir Charles Jeffries, *The Colonial Office* (London: George Allen & Unwin Ltd., 1956), pp. 106–107.

19. See Brian L. Blakeley, *The Colonial Office, 1868–1892* (Durham: Duke University Press, 1972), pp. 135–149. The regulations that applied in early Hong Kong were *Rules and Regulations for Her Majesty's Colonial Service* (London: Her Majesty's Stationery Office, 1843).

20. See Alvin Rabushka, *Value for Money*, pp. 38–82. See also *Hong Kong 1985*, pp. 294–295.

21. "White Paper: The Further Development of Representative Government in Hong Kong" (November 1984).

22. Emily Lau and Philip Bowring, "Laying Down the Law," *Far Eastern Economic Review*, December 5, 1985, pp. 12–15. Xu Jiatun, director of Xinhua new agency (China's unofficial mission in Hong Kong), in an unprecedented local press conference on November 21, 1985, implicitly accused Britain of "having a tendency to deviate from the joint declaration." He also stated that the political system of the Special Administrative Region of Hong Kong was China's business and would be clearly stated in the Basic Law. Some Hong Kong residents interpreted Xu's remarks as calling for a halt to all political reforms until 1990, when the Basic Law comes into being.

23. *Hong Kong 1986*, pp. 28–33.

8

ECONOMIC POLICY
AND PERFORMANCE

The founding and development of Hong Kong were synonymous with trade. For 140 years, the territory's population lived and prospered on its trading wits. As the colony lacked most natural resources, it depended on imports for the bulk of its food, consumer goods, raw materials, capital goods, and fuels, which it paid for through exports and the sale of services. Trade was and is an everyday fact of life in Hong Kong. In 1985, for example, the total value of visible imports and exports amounted to 176 percent of the gross domestic product. Between 1975 and 1985, the annual real growth rate of domestic exports in real terms was about 10 percent, roughly twice the growth rate of world trade.[1] By the 1960s, Hong Kong had become one of the world's leading trading nations.

The economy of Hong Kong reflects its political geography as a trading city-state. Primary production from agriculture, fishing, mining, and quarrying contributed a relatively insignificant share to the GDP. Manufacturing accounted for 25 percent in 1984 (down from 28 percent in 1971), construction about 5 percent, and the tertiary services sectors (wholesale and retail trades, restaurants, and hotels; transport, storage, and communications; the financial and related business services sectors; and the community, social and personal services sector) about 62 percent. Financial, insurance, real estate, and the business services sector, which grew rapidly in the 1970s and 1980s, had contributed 16 percent of GDP by 1983.[2] Indeed, by the 1980s Hong Kong possessed the third largest gold market in the world.

Light manufacturing industries, producing mainly consumer goods for export, always predominated in Hong Kong. Within manufacturing, the most significant change was the textile industry's declining share

161

of net output and employment, which was matched by the relative expansion of the clothing, electrical and electronics, and professional and scientific equipment (including watches and clocks) industries. Hong Kong's industrialists quickly adopted new technologies.

In terms of employment, the manufacturing sector contributed 37 percent of all jobs in 1985 and the tertiary services sectors 53 percent; the remainder engaged in primary production. Although manufacturing steadily declined in the postwar era in its contribution to GDP, it still accounted for the largest share of the employed labor force.

ECONOMIC POLICY

Economic affairs in Hong Kong were always conducted in an environment of free enterprise.[3] Since the founding of Hong Kong in 1841, the government generally maintained a hands-off approach toward the private sector, a policy that was well suited to Hong Kong's exposed and dependent economic and political situation. The official view held that reliance on market forces brought the greatest measure of economic efficiency in the allocation of resources. Nor did the government try to dictate the structural development of the economy; in the sharpest possible contrast with the practice of central planning in mainland China, the Hong Kong government let individuals freely direct their resources to those areas of economic activity that yielded the highest return. It made no effort to plan for or favor any particular type of development.

It would be correct to describe Hong Kong's economy from 1945 through 1985 as a free-enterprise system. A regime of low tax rates provided incentives for workers to work and for entrepreneurs to invest. The activities of the government revolved around the provision of infrastructure, some social and economic services marked by a massive public housing program, and a stable legal and administrative framework. Hong Kong developed a modern, efficient seaport in which is located the world's third largest container port, a centrally located airport with a computerized cargo terminal, and excellent worldwide communications. The government maintained the colony's historical duty-free status, free of import tariffs. Revenue duties were levied only on tobacco, alcoholic liquors, methyl alcohol, some hydrocarbon oils, and the first registration of motor vehicles (except franchised buses).

Apart from providing the necessary infrastructure, either directly or through cooperation with privately owned public utility companies and autonomous bodies, the government neither protected nor subsidized manufacturers. Economic intervention was restricted to the pressure of social needs or emergencies.

Capital Movements

Hong Kong's free market extends to money. Apart from limitations on exchanges between English pounds sterling and the Hong Kong dollar, which vanished in the 1960s, the Hong Kong dollar was freely convertible into other currencies. Financial assets were easily transferable in and out of Hong Kong with minimum regulation or interference. Large capital inflows helped finance the colony's industrial development and transformed it into a major financial center. At the end of 1985, there were 143 licensed banks (with about 1,400 branches), 35 of which were locally incorporated, and 273 deposit-taking companies with total foreign currency and Hong Kong dollar assets of US$200 billion.[4]

Subsidies

Except for land grants in the mid-1970s to land-intensive industries that injected new technology into the economy, and the segregation of industrial land to protect it from the competition of other land users, no protection or government assistance was typically given to manufacturing industries, utilities, service industries, or private citizens. No attempt was made to distort factor prices to favor any particular type of development. Industries that lobbied for protection from market competition were routinely resisted.

Postwar financial secretaries resolutely opposed any system of subsidy that exempted any industry from paying the full costs of the resources it consumed; each also opposed subsidizing consumption for the well-to-do. In 1960, for example, Arthur Clarke rejected a proposal to rebate water charges for industry. Private motorists were subjected to a continuous series of price increases for parking meters, public garage charges to recover rising costs in full, and increased first-automobile registration charges. Housing subsidies for all but the lowest-income families were resisted on the grounds that building middle-income housing with taxpayers' funds would divert resources from a maximum housing effort for poor households.

Despite the lack of democracy, Hong Kong's appointed administrators gradually succumbed to pressures for increased social subsidies on lower- and middle-income households. In recent years, for example, the government established a home-ownership scheme that attempted to meet the needs of middle-income households. These middle-income groups are known in Hong Kong as the "sandwiched classes"—too rich to qualify for public housing and too poor to buy or rent expensive private accommodation. Spending on social programs steadily rose in absolute terms and as a share of GDP in the 1970s and early 1980s. This trend of rising public expenditure was reversed when revenues fell as a result of collapsing land values and declining economic activity in response to Beijing's announcement of the restoration of Chinese sovereignty in 1997.

General Business Requirements

The Hong Kong government always encouraged the setting up of private business enterprise. It steadfastly maintained the competitive market principles of free entry and exit, and unregulated prices in almost every line of production. The legal formalities required to set up a business were few and inexpensive. In 1984, the business registration ordinance imposed an annual fee of less than $65, which was waived in the case of very small businesses.[5] Incorporation fees were equally modest. Foreign corporations with branches in Hong Kong paid neither incorporation nor annual registration fees; their obligations were simply to file with the registrar of companies a copy of the company's charter, its by-laws, its annual financial statement, and the names of persons in Hong Kong who are authorized to receive notices served on the company.

Anyone who opened a factory or industrial undertaking that employed more than twenty persons had to comply, prior to registration, with fire service department safety standards and labor department standards for workers' safety. Approval was routinely quick in normal circumstances.

Hong Kong never discriminated between residents and nonresidents. Overseas investors could fully own local factories. At the end of 1980, overseas interests either fully or partly owned 460 factories. Overseas capital, of which U.S. firms had the largest percentage, employed 87,000 workers, or 10 percent of the manufacturing work force.

Employment and Labor Unions

Market conditions, reflected in the supply and demand for labor, determined wage rates. There was no statutory minimum wage in Hong Kong, nor did trade unions appreciably affect wages and working conditions.

Hong Kong labor was chiefly engaged in small enterprises. At the end of 1980, only 40 factories employed over 1,000 workers and only 1,500 employed 100 or more. Conversely, 28,000 factories had fewer than 49 employees each; of these factories, 20,000 were virtual household operations employing fewer than ten workers.

Labor was highly mobile in Hong Kong's geographically compact, light industrial economy. The labor force was mobile between industries and trades; rigid craft demarcation did not prevail, nor was entry protected by trade unions. In the absence of a statutory minimum wage, earnings fluctuated with overall economic activity, although it was customary to award each worker an extra month's salary at the Chinese New Year. Loyalties to firms were less important than remuneration and other benefits; workers responded rationally and quickly to alternative opportunities.

Labor legislation consisted chiefly of the Factories and Industrial Undertakings Ordinance, the Employment Ordinance, and the Workmen's Compensation Ordinance. The first imposed no restrictions on the working hours of men aged eighteen and over in industry, but altogether banned employment of children under fifteen in industry and limited overtime to 200 hours per year for children and women aged fifteen to seventeen. Adult women were limited to a maximum of six eight-hour days per week.

The Employment Ordinance governed terms of employment for all full-time manual labor and nonmanual workers earning less than HK$2,000 (about US$250) per month. It stipulated rest days, statutory holidays, paid annual leave, and other entitlements. Lastly, the Workmen's Compensation Ordinance provided personal compensation from injury or death arising from work.

The economy experienced minimal interruptions compared with the disruptive strikes that have plagued Britain and other European industrial states. In 1980, only 37 work stoppages occurred, with 21,069 man-days of work lost from an annual total exceeding 200 million (a fraction of 1/10,000). Investors faced few problems with strikes, work stoppages, and worker grievances.

Manufacturing and Finance

The counterpart of employment and trade unions is manufacturing. Among all the ingredients that go into industry, land was perhaps the scarcest and most highly prized commodity in Hong Kong. All land in Hong Kong belonged to the British Crown, and freehold tenures, except for one historical instance (the Anglican church), were never granted. In the early years, Crown leases were granted for terms of 75, 99, or 999 years. They were finally standardized in the urban areas of Hong Kong Island and Kowloon south of Boundary Street to a term of 75 years, and were usually renewable for a further 75 years at a reassessed Crown rent. In the New Territories and in Kowloon north of Boundary Street, leases were written to expire on June 27, 1997, three days before the termination of the original 99-year lease that China granted to the British in 1898.

Apart from an occasional private land treaty for a particular developer, government generally made land available to private developers and industrialists through public auction, drawing no distinction between local and foreign residents. Land went to the highest bidder. Building covenants, attached to land sale conditions, required a specific minimum expenditure within a reasonable period of time. The covenant prevented any individual or company from acquiring enormous banks of undeveloped land.

Trade restrictions against Hong Kong were always of greatest concern to manufacturers in the garment and textile industries. The flow of Hong Kong-made merchandise was controlled largely through foreign governments' imposition of quantitative restrictions and import duties. Hong Kong was a member of the General Agreement on Trade and Tariffs (GATT) and did not accord preferential treatment to British and Commonwealth producers.[6] Both local and overseas exporters and importers received equal treatment.

The most comprehensive restrictions confronting Hong Kong were the quantitative limitations, imposed largely on its garments and textiles, specified by the Multi-Fibre Agreement (MFA), which was created under the auspices of GATT. The bulk of Hong Kong's garments and textile quotas to EEC countries and the United States were shipped under export quota restrictions. These worked as follows. Importing countries specified quantities of each category of textiles and garments annually acceptable; permissible growth rates in these quotas averaged about 6 percent a year. The quotas were then administered within Hong Kong by the Trade Department, which dispensed quota allocations on a formula basis.

Within Hong Kong itself, trade formalities were few and inexpensive. As a duty-free port, Hong Kong allowed the entry and exit of most raw materials, consumer goods, and commodities with only a registration charge. To raise revenues, it imposed duties only on liquors, manufactured tobacco, and hydrocarbon oils. A handful of items required import and export licenses for reasons of health, safety, or security. Certificates of origin were granted to manufacturers to qualify goods made in Hong Kong for entry under quotas, for generalized scheme-of-preferences tariff rates, or for Commonwealth preferences. Cars were not subject to duties, but a hefty first-registration fee was paid to the transport department. This fee was intended not so much for the purpose of raising revenue as for unclogging Hong Kong's congested roads by increasing the cost of private car ownership.

Finally, the government maintained statutory controls on rents and security of tenure for certain classes of accommodation since 1921.[7] The Landlord and Tenant Ordinance of 1947 restricted rents for both domestic and business premises by reference to prewar levels, while excluding from control new or substantially reconstructed buildings. Decontrol of prewar business premises took effect on July 1, 1984. Comprehensive rent-control legislation affecting postwar domestic premises in the private sector has been enforced since 1963 (except for the period between 1966 and 1970). The legislation provided security of tenure and controlled rent increases, but it applied neither to buildings certified for occupation after June 18, 1981, nor to new rentals after June 10, 1983, nor beginning December 19, 1985, to tenancies that had a rateable value above HK$30,000 as of June 10, 1983. The legislation excluded postwar office accommodation.

Government Economic Services

What part did government play in the operation of the Hong Kong economy? Its philosophy was noninterventionist, and its reliance on the private sector and the market mechanism extended even to public utilities and public transport: Electricity, gas, telephone services, buses, ferries, and tramways were lodged in private hands, although they derived monopoly franchise rights under an ordinance that requires the provision of adequate services and governmental approval of fare increases. Government, however, did intervene in such areas as provision of water, land ownership, public housing, operation of the airport, the railways, and the underground mass transit, and regulated banking, rents, pollution emissions, labor conditions, the rice trade, fish marketing, and other activities.

Government's management style followed the doctrine of economic self-support, except when it had overriding social reasons not to do so—as in the case of such specific subsidies as low-income housing, education, health care, and transfer payments. These social exceptions aside, the government operated its economic services on a commercial basis. The airport and railways, for example, were historically net contributors to government receipts. Once the government determined that it had to provide a service to achieve certain social or economic objectives, either because the service could not be found in the private sector or because these were common facilities that only the public sector could provide (e.g., water supplies), it tried to conduct its affairs with minimum cost to the general taxpayer. Hong Kong's annual budgets are full of explanations for the application of commercial practices to the provision of waterworks, car parks, the post office, and other public economic services.

Sir John Cowperthwaite, financial secretary from 1961 to 1971, cogently expressed the heart of the government's economic policy: "One trouble is that when Government gets into a business it tends to make it uneconomic for anyone else."[8] "For I still believe that, in the long run, the aggregate of the decisions of individual businessmen, exercizing individual judgment in a free economy, even if often mistaken, is likely to do less harm than the centralized decisions of a Government." And what was so magical about the private sector to Cowperthwaite? "It has to be recognized, and it is recognized over a large part of our daily life, that the community's scarce resources can be efficiently allocated only by the price mechanism."[9] This was the same recognition that the Central Committee of the Chinese Communist Party officially pronounced in its pivotal manifesto of October 20, 1984, on price reform.

BUDGETARY POLICY

The principles of self-support and balanced budgets in the colonial regulations applied equally to a financially independent Hong Kong.[10] The government followed a fiscal policy to avoid systematic deficits and, if possible, to accumulate reserves; this approach permitted sustained government expenditure on agreed-upon programs over a long recession without serious cutbacks and, in the process, earned interest to meet current expenses. Except for a small deficit in the immediate postwar budget, the public finances enjoyed a surplus in thirty-two of the thirty-five years through 1982. (This string of budget surpluses gave way to three successive deficits in the aftermath of Beijing's confidence-shattering announcement in 1982 that it would terminate British rule in 1997.) These surpluses were obtained after all capital expenditures other than a trivial amount financed by borrowing had been charged against current receipts; the government traditionally financed its entire public works program and other capital investments from current receipts. In 1982, the general revenue balance stood at about HK$19 billion, which was more than half of the government's total projected expenditures for both current and capital outlays for the 1982–1983 fiscal year.[11] In a world of chronic public debt, deficit financing, and foreign borrowing, existence of these massive reserves reflected a uniquely conservative fiscal policy.

Taxation

Financial authorities in Hong Kong consistently stressed one tenet of tax policy: Low standard rates of direct taxation facilitate rapid economic growth. The postwar experience of Hong Kong demonstrated that it was possible to finance an ambitious program of public expenditure on housing, education, health, welfare, and other social and community services from revenue yields based on rapid economic growth, without recourse to high tax rates.

Their words merit reiteration. In his outgoing year in 1960, Arthur Clarke cautioned that "we would do well to delay an increase in our direct taxation rate [12.5 percent], the low level of which is such an incentive to our expanding economy, on which in turn we depend for increasing revenue."[12] His successor, Sir John Cowperthwaite, asserted the same principle in 1964: "That revenue has increased in this way is in no small measure, I am convinced, due to our low tax policy which has helped to generate an economic expansion in the face of unfavorable circumstances. . . . Economic expansion remains the door to social progress and I am convinced that low taxation can in general produce a greater growth in revenue than can tax increases."[13]

Through 1985, Hong Kong did not levy an overall income tax; instead, it levied four separate direct taxes on profits, salaries, property, and interest. The tax rate on corporate profits was 18.5 (16.5 until 1984) percent and 17 (15 until 1984) percent on unincorporated business profits, after deducting all expenses incurred in producing income. The salaries tax was more complicated. It was imposed on a sliding rate scale, ranging from a maximum of 5 percent on the first assessable HK$10,000 to 25 percent on taxable income exceeding HK$50,000. The total tax due could not exceed the standard rate of 17 (15 until 1984) percent of gross income; at some point in the income ladder, the marginal rate dropped from 25 to 17 percent. The salaries tax was limited to income arising in or derived from Hong Kong.

Historically, the authorities set the standard tax on profits and salaries at a flat rate of 10 percent in 1947, increased it to 12.5 percent in

1951 in response to a budget deficit, and then raised it to 15 percent in 1966 in response to another deficit. A 10 percent surcharge was added to the corporate profits tax in the 1975–1976 fiscal year for a total rate of 16.5 percent. The financial secretary added two percentage points onto the tax rates in 1984 to reduce a string of deficits that erupted in 1983. Avoiding the cardinal sin of deficits won every struggle with the overriding tenet of low tax rates.

Personal allowances were extremely generous. In the 1982 tax year, for example, only 218,000 salaried taxpayers of a total population exceeding 5 million bore any direct income tax liability. Exactly 13,000 salaried taxpayers, about 6 percent of the total number in the salaried tax net, contributed over half the total yield from the salaries tax. In Hong Kong, the individual income tax was highly progressive, despite a statutory system of low rates.

Hong Kong imposed several taxes other than income taxes. In 1982, Hong Kong levied an interest tax of 10 percent (reduced from 15 percent in prior years) at the source on Hong Kong dollar deposits. This tax was abolished in 1983. The tax was repealed on foreign currency deposits to avoid losing business to such offshore financial centers as Singapore. A property tax was set at 17 percent of rateable value on investment property after an allowance was granted for repairs and maintenance; owner-occupants were exempt from the charge.

Apart from these four direct taxes, the government collected revenue from land and property sales, stamp and excise duties, entertainments tax on admission charges to movie theaters and race meetings, betting duty on horse racing and authorized cash sweeps, a hotel accommodation tax, and fees and charges from publicly supplied commercial services. The relative composition of revenue varied from year to year, with land sales contributing disproportionate shares during the boom years of the late 1970s and early 1980s. Overall, about two-thirds of revenue came from direct and indirect taxes, with one-third from fees and charges.[14] Hong Kong generated sufficient revenue from this tax system in normal political circumstances to pay its public bills and set funds aside for a rainy day, which arrived in 1982.

Public Expenditure

Despite a general commitment to the doctrine of nonintervention in the economy, the Hong Kong government undertook a surprising array of economic activities. The state was the ground landlord in Hong Kong and spent between 15 and 20 percent of the national income on roads, development of towns in the New Territories to relieve over-crowding on Hong Kong Island and in Kowloon, subsidized education through ninth grade, extensive medical and health services, subventions for numerous social welfare agencies, and public housing for about half the population.

Government spending and employment were closely monitored to prevent the growth rate of the public sector from getting out of line with that of the private sector. The government was watchful to prevent the public sector, which has a natural tendency to grow over time in most societies, from crowding out the private sector to the detriment of Hong Kong's external competitiveness. During the 1970s, the public sector grew from about 13 to 20 percent of the gross domestic product, but this figure contracted to just over 16 percent between 1982 and 1985 under belt-tightening measures, which included a freeze on civil service posts and reduced capital outlays.

MONETARY SYSTEM

Monetary policy was the most variable mosaic in Hong Kong's postwar economic environment.[15] Prior to 1935, Hong Kong, along with China, was on a silver standard. When China abandoned the silver standard in 1935 and instituted a managed currency, Hong Kong followed suit by adopting a pound sterling exchange standard. In 1972, Hong Kong again changed standards, this time switching from pounds sterling to U.S. dollars, but on November 26, 1974, Hong Kong gave up a fixed standard in favor of a floating exchange rate. Finally, in October 1983, the government refixed the Hong Kong currency to the U.S. dollar in order to stem a run on the local dollar.

Why did these changes occur? The answer to this question can be found in relation to the colony's trading arrangements and its economic, fiscal, and monetary policies. The cardinal goal of economic policy was to generate maximum output from the colony's resources of land, labor, and capital; efficient use of these resources in an externally dependent economy demands complete freedom of trade. Public spending was dictated by the self-imposed constraint of a balanced budget, weighted on the side of fiscal conservatism and the accumulation of fiscal surpluses. Finally, the goal of monetary policy was to inflate the domestic currency as little as possible to minimize distortions to the local cost/price structure. Before November 26, 1974, it was possible to realize all three of these goals under a fixed exchange rate regime. But with the advent of inflation in the 1970s, especially in Britain and the United States, it became difficult to maintain a fixed exchange rate and to avoid imported inflation through increases in the domestic money supply.

Until 1972, the Hong Kong money supply process rested on a direct or indirect commodity standard. On a commodity standard, money consists of a physical commodity, such as gold or silver, or rights to a certain number of ounces of that commodity. Prior to 1935, Hong Kong currency consisted of Spanish, Mexican, and other silver dollars (which were declared to be the colony's legal tender in 1842), British trade dollars minted in India from 1895 (equivalent to the Mexican coin), and locally issued bank notes of three commercial banks—the Hongkong and Shanghai Banking Corporation, the Chartered Bank, and the Mercantile Bank Limited. The latter ceased issuing notes in 1978. (Hong Kong never had a central bank.) These bank notes (liabilities of the three commercial banks) were backed almost completely by silver, bullion, or sterling securities held in bank vaults or with the Crown Agents; and by 1890 they had increasingly become the customary means of payment, although they were not legal tender. It was simply too inconvenient to deal with large amounts of silver.

When Hong Kong abandoned the silver standard in 1935, an ordinance established the Exchange Fund and required the note-issuing banks to surrender all silver previously held by them as backing for their note issues in exchange for certificates of indebtedness (CIs). The Fund, held by the government, in effect created money when it received payment in sterling from the note-issuing banks in exchange for CIs, which in turn authorized the three banks to issue Hong Kong dollar notes. These certificates were non-interest bearing and were issued and redeemed at the discretion of the financial secretary.

Under the pound sterling exchange standard, the exchange value of the Hong Kong dollar was initially set at 1*s*. 3*d*. sterling (or HK$16 = one pound). The relationship between the Hong Kong dollar with sterling was maintained by the operations of the Exchange Fund in conjunction with the note-issuing banks. The banks could increase their issue of currency notes by purchasing CIs from the Exchange Fund with their foreign currency assets. The banks paid 1*s*. 3*d*. to the Fund for the right to issue each dollar of Hong Kong currency notes. In turn, the Fund stood ready to buy back CIs from the banks at a rate of 1*s*. 2 7/8*d*. So long as the financial secretary did not call in outstanding certificates, the system was largely automatic. When the banks believed that the demand for currency was rising, they could purchase with sterling the necessary certificates and issue more bank notes. Conversely, if the banks felt their cash holdings were excessive, they could return some CIs to the Exchange Fund for sterling, which they could invest abroad. As the Exchange Fund kept its assets in pounds sterling, the domestic currency issue was fully backed by external assets. And as the Exchange Fund earned interest on its sterling assets, the government enjoyed a steady flow of revenue or seignorage from this source, although transfers to the government's fiscal accounts were not permitted under the Exchange Fund Ordinance unless the assets of the fund amounted to at least 105 percent of the fund's liabilities. For all intents and purposes, the Hong Kong dollar was a different denomination of pounds sterling, with the Exchange Fund reaping the interest earnings for the government's benefit.

Under this fixed sterling exchange rate system, the domestic money supply was jointly determined by the domestic credit-creation process and by the balance of payments (which includes the balance of merchandise trade, the sale of such invisibles as tourism, insurance, shipping, and financial services, and the movement of capital funds). Under this

Hong Kong version of the colonial currency board system, the banks and the government (through the Exchange Fund) passively accepted the net outcomes of all overseas transactions. If Hong Kong earned more foreign exchange than it spent, then either the banks or the Exchange Fund purchased the excess and thereby increased the Hong Kong dollar deposits held by the private sector by a proportionate amount. Conversely, if Hong Kong spent more foreign exchange than it earned, the reverse process led to a decrease in Hong Kong dollar deposits. Thus, under this type of fixed exchange rate system, any surplus in foreign exchange was almost automatically converted into Hong Kong dollars, leading to an increase in the domestic money supply. Any deficit in foreign exchange required the conversion of Hong Kong dollars into sterling to pay foreign bills, thereby causing a contraction of the domestic money supply. Banks in Hong Kong, as elsewhere, generate multiple credit creation on the basis of their liquid assets, and this factor could amplify or moderate the effect of the balance of payments, depending on the willingness of the banks to create new credit. Nevertheless, balance-of-payments surpluses tended to expand the money supply whereas deficits tended to shrink it. Hong Kong's internal cost/price structure adjusted to world prices through the balance of payments.

The exchange value of the Hong Kong dollar with sterling was not statutory, but it generally came to be regarded as fixed. As a dependent territory of the British Crown and a member of the sterling exchange control area, Hong Kong was required in practice to keep its money reserves, including the greater part of the reserves of the banking system, in the form of sterling securities.

The transition from a commodity standard based on silver to a pound sterling exchange standard gave way, in turn, to a U.S. dollar exchange standard. The link with sterling weakened when the pound was devalued by 14.3 percent against the U.S. dollar in November 1967. At that time the value of the Hong Kong dollar was set to a rate of HK$14.55 = one pound—a corresponding devaluation of only 5.7 percent relative to the U.S. dollar. When the pound was allowed to float downwards in June 1972 and the sterling area was largely disbanded, the Hong Kong government switched from sterling to U.S. dollars, set the exchange value of the Hong Kong dollar at US$1 = HK$5.65, and began to diversify the assets of the Exchange Fund away from sterling securities to a broader portfolio of currencies. When the U.S. dollar itself was devalued by 10 percent in February 1973, the Hong Kong dollar was revalued to HK$5.085 = US$1.

On November 26, 1974, the Hong Kong government announced that it would no longer use the assets of the Exchange Fund to keep the Hong Kong dollar at the official pegged rate and, under pressure of heavy selling of U.S. dollars, allowed the local currency to float upward from the official rate, until the rate reached HK$4.68 in 1978. Another, more subtle change in 1972 was that the Exchange Fund no longer required the banks to pay foreign currency for CIs or for the banks' right to issue Hong Kong dollar bank notes; instead, to purchase CIs, the note-issuing banks simply credited the Fund's account in Hong Kong dollars, and the Fund subsequently might have converted these funds to foreign currencies at its own discretion. In short, domestic money could be printed independent of the state of the balance of payments. From July 1972 to November 1974, the authorities remained willing to use the assets of the Exchange Fund to peg the currency at the official rate, but as exchange rate movements gradually became greater, the strain became increasingly burdensome.

In effect, the decision to float the Hong Kong dollar enabled the territory to insulate itself initially from inflation in overseas economies. In previous years, Hong Kong could maintain a balanced government budget, expedite foreign trade in a most efficient manner, and inflate its currency as little as possible. However, rising inflation in two of its major trading partners, the United States and Britain, threatened internal inflation inasmuch as a fixed exchange rate meant that monetary expansion in these countries was translated, through the balance of payments, into monetary expansion in Hong Kong. The decision to move to a floating rate system broke that chain of causation and thus offered the chance of greater price stability through an appreciating Hong Kong dollar.

The combination of the discretionary conversion of H.K. dollars into foreign assets (to back the currency) and the free floating of the currency after November 1974 marked a major turning point in Hong Kong's monetary history. Hong Kong switched to a *fiat* standard. Under a *fiat* standard, money consists solely of pieces of paper and rights to pieces of paper, without the backing of, or convertibility into, any physical commodity, such as gold or silver, or foreign assets. Because the Exchange Fund issued CIs (equivalent to banknotes) passively on demand, it had no control over the quantity of currency and, ultimately, credit.

Remember, under a fixed exchange rate system, the money supply could accelerate continuously only if the community as a whole had sufficient foreign currency to pay over to the Exchange Fund for new CIs (or new note issues), which would occur only if Hong Kong was running an overall balance of payments surplus. No such external constraint bound credit creation under a pure Hong Kong dollar *fiat* standard. Rather, rising local prices (internal inflation) or loss of confidence in the value of the currency would take the form of a depreciation in the exchange rate.

Between 1972 and 1977, the Hong Kong dollar was strong, appreciating in value against the U.S. dollar. During these years, the Fund used the Hong Kong dollar proceeds credited to its account by the note-issuing banks to purchase a variety of foreign currencies on the open market without unduly disturbing the foreign-exchange market. These newly acquired foreign assets served as *ex post* backing for the note issue. When the Hong Kong dollar weakened, problems arose. There was a tendency for the Fund not to convert proceeds from increases in the note issue into foreign exchange, and on occasion the Fund sold foreign currencies. At any moment, then, some proportion of the currency issue might not be backed by foreign exchange. Public knowledge of this condition, in turn, exerted further downward pressure on the Hong Kong dollar. A vicious circle was formed after 1997, and it became extremely violent in 1982–1983.[16]

Under the *fiat* standard, monetary control became essential.[17] However, Hong Kong's peculiar financial structure lacked any form of control. There was no central bank to regulate the growth of currency and credit. Money supply growth became extremely volatile, resulting in a boom/bust cycle during 1975–1982. During 1976–1981, fueled by rapid monetary expansion, Hong Kong's economy enjoyed double-digit real growth rates, the industrial world's best performance. This exaggerated boom gave way to a severe bust as money supply growth slowed.

In 1979–1981, Hong Kong experienced excess credit creation—domestic credit growth expressed in $HK\$M_3$ (the broadest definition of money supply) rose over 60 percent in 1981 alone—which was the major source of the booms in the property and stock markets, but since 1981 this was followed by a sharp contraction in the rate of growth of money and credit (falling by half in 1982 to 30 percent annual growth). This slowing led to a fall in property values, a crash on the stock market, and serious liquidity problems for many of the financial institutions that helped finance the boom.

Under the *fiat* currency arrangements, the authorities were powerless to prevent the persistent depreciation of the Hong Kong dollar since 1978. As the currency declined, the prices for imported food and fuel increased again and again. Complete loss of confidence in the value of the currency climaxed in a massive run on the Hong Kong dollar (which culminated on Black Saturday, September 24, 1983). Left unchecked, it threatened to bring down the entire structure of banking and credit in the colony.

A basic point of principle is also at stake. The role of government in enforcing the rule of law is to provide a framework within which individuals can conduct their personal affairs. A key element in that framework is to preserve the value of the medium of exchange, which requires a sensible monetary framework. It was highly desirable for the government to sustain a mechanism of monetary control that is compatible with a stable value of the currency and requires an absolute minimum of government intervention in the foreign-exchange market, which is consistent with Hong Kong's overall policies of noninterventionism and the absence of foreign-exchange controls.

During the 1974–1983 period, the authorities relied on several monetary instruments, all of which proved ineffective. These instruments included the specification of liquidity ratios for the banks, which were circumvented when banks accepted deposits from foreign banks and redeposited those funds in the same bank. The Hong Kong branch's deposit counted as a liquid asset, whereas the deposit from abroad was not subject to the liquidity requirement. In practice, the licensed banks maintained liquidity ratios exceeding 45 percent, as against the required ratio of 25 percent.

A second ineffective instrument of monetary control was the attempt to control interest rates. The government believed it could have a firm grip on interest rates and, hence, on bank credit creation. The government, in consultation with the licensed banks through the Hong Kong Association of Banks, set interest rates at weekly meetings, which the licensed banks were obliged to follow on customer deposits under HK$500,000 of less than 12 months maturity.

The weakness of the official interest rate agreement between the government and the banks surfaced during the growing skepticism over the possibility of a favorable outcome from the Sino-British talks. As holders of H.K. dollars bought U.S. dollars, the exchange rate fell. Neither the banks nor the authorities were willing to raise interest rates to a level that was sufficiently high to stem the financial panic. Indeed, it can be argued that there was no level in September 1983 to which short-term interest rates could have been increased that would have compensated for fears that holders of Hong Kong dollars would face drastically reduced rates of return on capital in Hong Kong. It was the change in Hong Kong people's perceptions about the declining expected long-term real rates of return on capital—especially businesses and properties in Hong Kong—that precipitated the currency crisis. As people lost confidence in the outcome of the talks, they sold buildings, businesses, and monetary assets in Hong Kong to acquire assets abroad. Given the fact that Hong Kong had a floating exchange rate and, under the existing monetary framework, no workable mechanism for supporting the exchange rate, the currency could have been driven down to the point where Hong Kong dollars were virtually valueless as residents attempted to export capital through the foreign-exchange market. It took a radical stabilization plan to restore confidence in the local currency in 1983.

In summary, Hong Kong went from a commodity standard to a foreign-exchange standard to a *fiat* standard (which failed), and returned to a foreign-exchange standard. Throughout its history, there were two pillars of a free and prosperous Hong Kong—the rule of law (property rights, minimum intervention, etc.) and a sound monetary system. Hong Kong's development through the postwar years owes much to the first, but the collapse of the monetary system in 1983 almost destroyed Hong Kong's prosperity for good.

HONG KONG IN TRANSITION: 1982-1985

Since 1949, Hong Kong constantly faced an uncertain future. Residents and investors alike knew that 1997 lay over the horizon. But from 1950 through 1982, Hong Kong enjoyed relatively stable relations with China.

China's views on Hong Kong's political status were consistently espoused by a succession of political leaders. They publicly claimed that the treaties ceding and leasing Hong Kong were "unequal," but that China alone would decide when this sole remaining foreign historical problem would be resolved. In 1972 China clearly stated for the United Nations Special Committee on Colonialism and Decolonization that the settlement of Hong Kong's political status was an internal Chinese matter, and that it would settle the matter "when the time is ripe for negotiations." In the meantime, investors were repeatedly assured "to keep their hearts at ease."

As the 1980s approached, the live-and-let-live arrangement between China and Hong Kong gave way to increasing anxiety among international and domestic investors concerned with the future of Hong Kong. Directly after British Prime Minister Margaret Thatcher's visit to China in late September 1982, the Chinese government declared its intention to assert its sovereign right to control the whole territory of Hong Kong no later than July 1, 1997. Diplomatic talks on the future of Hong Kong were held in Beijing from early October 1982 throughout 1984 against the backdrop of China's warning that it would impose a unilateral solution if a negotiated agreement was not reached by September 1984.

The Sino-British negotiators addressed a raft of issues that ranged across economic, political, legal, and social questions. Among the issues were changes in Hong Kong's free-market system of economic organization, any future administrative or constitutional link with Britain, the renewal of land leases, the independence and convertibility of the Hong Kong dollar, guarantees for civil rights, independence of the judiciary and the retention of the English common law system, immigration restrictions on travel to and from Hong Kong, pension guarantees for Hong Kong civil servants, the language of education in Hong Kong schools, the stationing of troops from the People's Liberation Army in Hong Kong, free elections within Hong Kong for local officials, and the right of pro-Taiwan organizations to operate freely, among others.

Although the worldwide recession hit Hong Kong's exporters earlier in 1982, reinforcing the economic slowdown produced by a monetary contraction, Beijing's summer announcement shattered political confidence in Hong Kong's economic future. Despite promises by Chinese authorities that Hong Kong's free-wheeling economy would not be integrated into China's socialistic, state-directed system, the stock, property, and foreign-exchange markets went into a virtual free-fall. Asset values on the stock exchanges fell by one-third within a few months, and land values in the choice sections of Hong Kong Island and Kowloon fell to as low as one-fifth of their pre-announcement 1982 prices. The Hong Kong dollar, free to float since 1974, fell from a rate of HK$6.20 = US$1 in mid-1982 to a low of HK$9.55 = US$1 on September 24, 1983, until the government linked the Hong Kong dollar to the U.S. dollar at a fixed rate of HK$7.80 = US$1, and required that new issue of Hong Kong bank notes be backed by equivalent U.S. dollar reserves.[18] The crisis also forced the government to depart from its traditional laissez-faire policy when it temporarily took over the Hang Lung Bank to ward off failure and further loss of confidence in the banking system.

The Hong Kong economy remained on shaky ground throughout the negotiations, which lasted until September 1984. The financial secretary presided over back-to-back budget deficits at or above HK$3 billion, raised the top corporate and individual tax rates 2 percent, entered the local credit markets for the first time to borrow HK$1 billion to reduce the deficit for the 1984–1985 fiscal year, and drew down a major chunk of Hong Kong's vaunted fiscal reserves. Land values stagnated. The stock exchanges did not recover until July 1984, when the outlines of an apparent agreement came into focus. Despite a strong recovery in export orders throughout 1983 and 1984, new investment in plant and equipment failed to materialize for the first time in Hong Kong's postwar history; in fact, real investment declined 8 percent in 1983 in an economy that has traditionally witnessed annual savings rates of 20 percent of GDP.[19] Investors lacked confidence in the prospect of Chinese rule.

One story that vividly illustrates investor anxiety appeared during the height of the talks on March 28, 1984. Jardine, Matheson and Company, Hong Kong's premier trading firm, which had played an integral part in Hong Kong's founding and history, announced that it was setting up a new holding company in Bermuda to be the parent of the company's international business interests—a sort of reverse takeover, including its Hong Kong operations.[20] Fearing that the colony's present British legal system might not survive, Jardine's *taipan*, Simon Keswick, wanted to ensure the firm's future operation under a British legal system. He bluntly explained that "when we are competing in the international marketplace, it is undoubtedly a disadvantage to have to deal with questions regarding the long-term future of Hong Kong."[21] Hong Kong share prices plummeted the day after, posting their biggest one-day slide since September 1983, closing at 1057.09 on the Hang Seng index, down 61.76 points.

The Sino-British joint declaration on Hong Kong that was initialed on September 26, 1984, approved in the British Parliament on December 19, 1984, and took effect on July 1, 1985, addressed virtually every major issue involving the colony's social, economic, legal, and political systems. But the political uncertainty surrounding the talks had already forced changes in economic, fiscal, and monetary policies on the part of the Hong Kong government. These changes, along with the terms of the joint declaration, altered the colony's economic climate. Economic and fiscal policies temporarily departed from traditional nonintervention and low tax rates, but the new monetary arrangements restored both stability and confidence in the currency.

ECONOMIC, FISCAL, AND MONETARY POLICY UNDER DURESS

Coming out of the 1974 oil crisis-induced recession, Hong Kong's economy underwent sustained expansion, recording the industrial world's highest growth rate between 1976 and 1981. Hong Kong uncharacteristically suffered a budget deficit of HK$380 million in the 1974–1975 fiscal year, only its third deficit since 1947, but surpluses became the order of the day as the economy boomed. The public finances were in the black by HK$487 million in 1975–1976, increasing in successive fiscal years to HK$903 million, HK$1.2 billion, and HK$2.9 billion. With a monetary system unhitched from the balance of payments, money supply growth exploded, sharply driving up land values; government auctions of new Crown land brought in a record 25 percent of receipts, generating surpluses of HK$6.7 billion and HK$6.5 billion in the two fiscal years encompassing 1980–1982. The public sector shared in the overall climate of prosperity.

Three factors shocked Hong Kong's public finances in 1982. Money supply growth (overall HKM_3$) slowed from 60 percent in 1981 to 30 percent in 1982, thus cooling the equity and land markets. Concurrently, the world recession hit Hong Kong's exporters hard, thereby slowing economic activity and taxable income. Finally, as the economy seemed poised to recover, China's 1982 announcement shattered political confidence. The bottom fell out of the values of land, equities, and the local currency.

An historical regime of surpluses was transformed into a string of deficits. In the 1982–1983 budget, for example, capital receipts from the sale of land declined from 25 percent to 6 percent of revenue. In one fell swoop, about one-fifth of receipts evaporated. Overnight, an HK$6 billion surplus became a projected unheard of HK$4 billion deficit, of which HK$3 billion materialized despite vigorous budget economies. Although the government scaled down some of its ambitious public works and other spending programs, it was not possible to cut billions of dollars from the budget so quickly. The largest chunk of spending pays the salaries of civil servants, whose numbers had grown by tens of thousands during the boom years of 1976–1981. The deficit turned out to be a no less upsetting HK$3 billion in 1983–1984 and HK$3.5 billion in 1984–1985. Although the original estimates for 1985–1986 projected a deficit of HK$1 billion, a small surplus of

HK$98 million materialized at year's end, and a surplus budget was planned for 1986–1987.

When Sir John Bremridge, former *taipan* of Swires, agreed to take the post of financial secretary for a term of five years, he must have wondered what he had gotten himself into. During his tenure, he had to manage three consecutive historically unprecedented deficits, raise tax rates (thus tampering with the colony's proven low tax structure), take over the operation of several private banks to prevent a loss of confidence in the banking system, and revamp the entire monetary system. Fortunately, his predecessors had accumulated massive reserves to tide him over during the fiscal storm.

The colony's financial secretaries have always administered stern medicine to eliminate fiscal deficits, and the post-1982 years were no different. In 1984, Bremridge raised the direct tax rate on businesses and individuals 2 percent to 18.5 percent on corporate profits and 17 percent maximum on salaries, floated a totally unprecedented domestic public loan of HK$1 billion (which counted as liquid assets under the banking ordinance), and drew down several billion dollars of Hong Kong's fiscal reserves. This condition was gradually corrected. An improving economy in 1984, along with a tightening of public expenditure since 1982, which declined from 19.4 percent of GDP in 1983–1984 to 18.3 percent in 1984–1985, the first fall in several years, gradually restored balance to the colony's public finances.

Monetary Reform

The Hong Kong dollar slowly depreciated since 1978 in response to rapid monetary expansion and the concomitant internal inflation. But when the Sino-British talks appeared on the point of collapse in late summer of 1983, panic set in, putting the currency and the colony's entire financial, banking, and credit systems in jeopardy. As the outcome of the talks began to appear increasingly unfavorable, people grew unwilling to hold Hong Kong physical and financial assets. Selling pressure on the Hong Kong dollar drove it steadily lower throughout 1983. In January the rate stood at HK$6.53 = US$1. In successive months, it declined in value to HK$6.61, HK$6.65, HK$6.80, HK$6.98, and HK$7.25. It turned up slightly in July to HK$7.18 in a bout of optimism over the talks, but August saw a rate of HK$7.43. As Hong Kong peoples' hopes about the future sagged in September, the Hong Kong dollar began to look like a banana republic currency.

Even rising interest rates failed to stem the run on the currency. By September 7, the U.S. dollar exchange rate fell to HK$7.74. A week later it reached HK$7.78, crashing the psychological HK$8.00 level on September 17. The 19th saw a rate of HK$8.40, which could not be sustained. Following the fourth round of Sino-British talks on September 22–23, 1983, the Hong Kong dollar suffered its sharpest fall to $8.83. Then came Black Saturday, September 24, 1983, when the rate dropped to another all-time low of HK$9.55 against the U.S. dollar.[22] Hoarding of rice and other staples started up in Hong Kong as consumers braced themselves for skyrocketing import prices. The colony's financial system was on the brink of collapse.

To stem the panic, the Hong Kong government issued a statement on September 25, 1983, that promised full convertibility of the currency, in effect guaranteeing holders of Hong Kong dollars that these notes could be exchanged into foreign currencies at fixed rates of exchange. The announcement hinted that the mechanics for issuing and redeeming of Certificates of Indebtedness, the legal backing for the Hong Kong dollar, would be changed. However, the acting financial secretary, Mr. Douglas Blye, did not spell out the details of the new arrangements.

The Hong Kong dollar recovered somewhat the next day to a range of HK$7.90–8.40 after the Hong Kong Association of Banks raised deposit interest rates by 3 percent. On September 27, 1983, the Legislative Council met in emergency session to pass a bill empowering the government to take over the Hang Lung Bank, which was the first time in history that the Exchange Fund had been mobilized to act as lender of last resort to a bank in the private sector.

During the following three weeks, while the details of the currency reform were being worked out, the Hong Kong dollar continued to trade between 8 and 9 against its U.S. counterpart. Despite extensive consultations with the British government—the governor and unofficials visited 10 Downing Street, and experts from the Bank of England and the treasury came out to Hong Kong to advise the financial secretary—politics dictated that the Hong Kong government had to be seen resolving the crisis without taking instructions from London. Partly for this reason, the U.S. dollar was ultimately selected as the currency against which to fix the Hong Kong currency. Finally, at noon on Saturday, October 15, 1983, Sir John Bremridge announced the stabilization scheme, which would be implemented from the opening of the foreign-exchange markets on October 17, 1983. The government would restore a fixed rate against the U.S. dollar for the issue and redemption of CIs at HK$7.80 per U.S. dollar.

The architect of the new system was John G. Greenwood, an economist with G.T. Management (Asia) Ltd. For several years he had warned of the potential danger in Hong Kong's free-floating currency arrangements. Under the new monetary arrangements, the Exchange Fund would issue and redeem CIs to the two note-issuing banks at the fixed rate of HK$7.80 = US$1. In turn, the two note-issuing banks would sell and repurchase local bank notes at this same rate with all other licensed banks, thus acting as agents for the Exchange Fund. An important point is that the government did not make the HK$7.80 conversion facility available to the general public, nor did it guarantee the foreign currency price of deposits or cash held by the public, these being free to trade at market rates.

The new mechanism was basically the same as an old-fashioned gold or silver standard, except that Hong Kong used the U.S. dollar as its monetary standard in place of a precious metal (or pounds sterling), and the public does not have direct access to convertibility at the official parity as under the classic gold standard.

Under this system, two main forces tend to produce market rates of exchange for the Hong Kong dollar close to the official 7.80 rate for CIs. First, licensed banks are free to arbitrage between the free-market rate for Hong Kong dollars or U.S. dollars and the Exchange Fund's rate for CIs, buying in the cheaper market and selling in the more expensive one. This process continues until the difference between the returns from holding deposits (making loans) and the returns from holding cash in either market is equal to the transaction costs of these operations. When the free-market rate for Hong Kong dollar bank notes is at a discount relative to the official rate (e.g., at 7.82, 7.83, etc.), banks will sell Hong Kong dollars to the Exchange Fund (because they can use the U.S. dollar proceeds to buy back Hong Kong dollars at 7.80, pocketing the two or three cents difference). Sales of Hong Kong bank notes in these circumstances will reduce the banks' cash-to-deposit ratio, causing them to restrict their Hong Kong dollar lending, tightening liquidity, and raising interest rates. A continued squeeze would reduce lending and slow money growth. As the Hong Kong dollar rate in the free market will be at a discount to the official parity only when the overall balance of payments is in deficit, or when political confidence is shaken, this type of bank-note arbitrage between the banks and the Exchange Fund will tend to bring the free market rate back toward the official parity.

When the free-market rate for the Hong Kong dollar is at a premium to the official parity for the U.S. dollar, this is generally the case because the overall balance of payments is favorable. At such times, interest rates in Hong Kong will tend to decline, thus encouraging banks to increase their lending, which in turn will lead to a monetary expansion. So long as the balance of payments remains favorable, banks will have the foreign-currency assets to obtain additional Hong Kong dollar bank notes such that the note issue can expand in step with credit and monetary expansion. In due course, the monetary expansion will lead to higher spending growth in Hong Kong, which, in turn, will induce balance-of-payments deficits that will ultimately eliminate the premium on the Hong Kong dollar.

The system is therefore a self-correcting mechanism that automatically adjusts the money supply, the price level, and hence other economic variables in Hong Kong to the constraints of the balance of payments.

A second factor keeping the free-market rate close to the official parity is competition among the banks. For example, because bank customers can convert their Hong Kong dollar deposits into cash at any time, they can shop around among the banks for the most favorable

HK$/US$ rate for their Hong Kong dollar bank notes. Banks offering unfavorable rates thus stand to lose business.[23]

Aside from stemming panic, the objective of the monetary reform was to install a monetary standard that would cost the economy a minimal amount of resources to produce and yet would perform the essential functions of money, acting both as an efficient medium of exchange and as a stable store of value. From a purely technical standpoint, the choice of currency and the choice of exchange rate were not particularly important. The real importance of the new-linked rate system is that it restored an automatic or nondiscretionary system, enabling the Hong Kong government to revert to an essentially non-interventionist role in monetary affairs. The mechanism depends solely on arbitrage by banks, firms, and individuals.

The selection of an official parity of HK$7.80 per U.S. dollar initially undervalued the Hong Kong dollar, thus helping generate an exceptionally strong trading performance by Hong Kong exporters in the last quarter of 1983 and throughout 1984 and, in the process, reliquifying the economy. Moreover, as the link has persisted, Hong Kong's inflation rate has gradually fallen; over time, in fact, it should move in tandem with the U.S. inflation rate. Since late 1983, the free-market rate generally remained within two cents of the official parity. Thus the linked rate system solved both the problem of the panic in September 1983 and the problem of underlying monetary control.

Throughout 1982–1984, while British and Chinese negotiators were hammering out an agreement, Hong Kong's economy turned in a subpar performance relative to its postwar historical standard. As the shadows of the agreement came into clearer focus in the summer of 1984, the stock market began to make a sharp recovery, property prices stabilized, and investment in capital goods picked up. However, capital outflows, which began in 1982, were not stemmed.

During late 1982 and through September 1983, a net capital outflow from Hong Kong residents almost certainly occurred.[24] After the linking of the Hong Kong dollar to the U.S. dollar, some residents repatriated funds held overseas partly because of a return of confidence and partly because of the high real interest rates available on Hong Kong dollars due to the linked-rate system. Once the agreement was announced and initialed, nonresident capital flowed in to Hong Kong.

Nonetheless, resident capital outflows exceeded nonresident inflows in 1984 and 1985. Greenwood estimates that capital outflows in 1984 might have run in the neighborhood of HK$12.5 billion, or about US$1.5 billion. This sum was equivalent to about 5 percent of gross incomes in Hong Kong. In 1985, Hong Kong residents accumulated an even larger US$3 billion worth of foreign assets.[25] Although the economy recovered in 1984 and 1985, Hong Kong investors used their restored prosperity to acquire foreign assets rather than increase domestic investments, indicating that political confidence remained fragile. In addition, the existence of a trade surplus in the first half of 1986 suggested that Hong Kong's residents continued to export capital.

If Hong Kong residents were exporting capital, China was trying to prop up confidence by quietly extending credit to various financial institutions in Hong Kong since 1983. Before 1982, China had consistently borrowed on a net basis from Hong Kong's financial institutions. Between 1982 and 1985, it lended to them on a net basis. By September 30, 1984, China's net claims reached US$1.76 billion.[26] One year later, China's net claims surpassed US$2.5 billion.[27] China was partially replacing financial assets that Hong Kong residents were placing abroad. A foreign-exchange squeeze in China in 1985 reversed this pattern, and China again became a net borrower from Hong Kong. Despite an agreement that appeared to ensure Hong Kong's autonomous economic future until 2047, local residents were buying the equivalent of offshore insurance.

Whether or not Hong Kong will continue to prosper in both the near and distant future depends on the actual implementation of the Sino-British Joint Declaration on the future of Hong Kong.[28] It is impossible either to evaluate the Hong Kong economy during 1982–1985 or to conjecture about its future performance without knowing the provisions in the agreement.

THE SINO-BRITISH JOINT DECLARATION ON THE FUTURE OF HONG KONG

On September 26, 1984, the British and Chinese governments initialed the draft agreement on the future of Hong Kong.[29] The agreement consisted of a "joint declaration" between the two parties, three annexes, and an exchange of memoranda. It provided for the transfer of sovereignty and administrative authority over Hong Kong from Britain to China on July 1, 1997, enumerated the basic policies that China would follow in Hong Kong, accorded Britain administrative responsibility through June 30, 1997, established a Sino-British Joint Liaison Group to facilitate the transfer of power, and stipulated an effective date of implementation before June 30, 1985.

Annex I was a detailed unilateral elaboration by the Chinese government (which the British presumably wrote) regarding its basic policies toward Hong Kong, intended to minimize ambiguities and uncertainties in their interpretation for the purpose of preserving confidence in the future. Annex II explained the operations of the Sino-British joint liaison group. Annex III resolved the sensitive issue of future land sales and land leases. The exchange of memoranda indicated the citizenship standing of Hong Kong residents after 1997.

Under the agreement, Hong Kong would be established as a Special Administrative Region of China in accordance with the provisions of Article 31 of the Constitution—as a region enjoying a high degree of autonomy, except in foreign affairs and defense. Hong Kong would retain its current laws and have a government composed of local inhabitants, "the chief executive [of which] will be appointed by the Central People's Government on the basis of the results of elections or consultations to be held locally." Hong Kong would retain its social and economic systems, including rights of person, free speech, press, assembly, association, travel, movement, correspondence, strike, choice of occupation, academic research, religion, and private ownership of property. Hong Kong would remain a free port and a separate customs territory; maintain its own independently backed, freely convertible currency; run independent finances (remitting no taxes to China); maintain external relations with other countries; issue its own travel documents; and operate its own police force. These policies would be stipulated in a Basic Law of Hong Kong (SAR) to be adopted by the National People's Congress (after consultation with Hong Kong persons) by 1990, and would remain unchanged for 50 years, thus implementing Deng Xiaoping's concept of "one country, two systems [socialism and capitalism]."

China elaborated its basic policies in Annex I of the agreement. The more important elements included constituting Hong Kong's legislature by elections after 1997, although no provision would be made for the mechanics of selecting the chief executive, who may be designated "by election or through consultations held locally and be appointed by the Central People's Government." English can be retained in government and the courts, but all symbols to colonialism must be removed from the flag, currency, oaths of office, and perhaps even street names. Annex I also established the supremacy of China's Basic Law, stating that any laws in force in Hong Kong (i.e., the common law, rules of equity, ordinances, subordinate legislation, and customary law) will remain valid, "save those that contravene the Basic Law," and subject to amendment by the Hong Kong SAR legislature.

The annex specifically prohibited expatriates from holding the position of heads in major departments and, in the cases of some departments including the police department, deputy heads; it also held that British and other expatriates may be retained as advisers and that qualified foreigners may be recruited in instances where need is demonstrated.

The annex provided as well for a separate shipping register and the right of Hong Kong to operate its own airline and maintain air service agreements with foreign countries (to protect the colony's flagship carrier, Cathay Pacific Airlines); it also spelled out the individual social and economic freedoms that Hong Kong residents will continue to enjoy after 1997.

Annex II set up a joint liaison group, to consist of five members from each side, that is empowered to conduct consultations on the implementation of the joint declaration. The group was "an organ for liaison and not an organ of power." It was to play no part in the administration of Hong Kong or the Hong Kong SAR. It was scheduled to meet in Beijing, Hong Kong, and London at least once each year up through June 30, 1988. Thereafter, its principal base will move to Hong Kong. During the second half of the group's scheduled life, it is to consider procedures to be adopted for the smooth transition in 1997 and to assist (after 1997 up to 2000) the Hong Kong SAR in maintaining and developing its relations with other nations and international organizations.

Annex III changed the conduct of public finances up to 1997. Evidently fearing that the British would rush to sell off all remaining valuable land in Hong Kong and export the proceeds to Britain, China severely restricted all future new land sales to a maximum of 123.5 acres a year and, after deducting the average cost of land production, required that the remaining receipts be evenly divided between the British Hong Kong government and the future Hong Kong SAR administration. It specified that the latter portion shall be deposited in banks incorporated in Hong Kong and shall not be spent without prior approval of a Land Commission, which shall be set up to monitor the terms of Annex III and consider British proposals for increasing the limit. The Land Commission will dissolve on June 30, 1997.

On the sensitive issue of land leases, the annex permits the British to grant new leases that extend 50 years beyond 1997, but provides for an annual rent to be charged from the date of extension after 1997 equivalent to 3 percent of rateable value. Current policy authorizes an annual rent on an extension, but the rent is fixed in nominal terms; the agreement maintains rents at 3 percent in real terms.

Finally, the Exchange of Memoranda designated all Chinese residents of Hong Kong as Chinese nationals, who will not be entitled to British consular protection in Hong Kong or elsewhere in China. This applies to current holders of "British Dependent Territories citizens" (BDTC) passports (although no mention is made of holders of British passports issued in London before 1971, who have the right of abode in Britain). However, China permits Chinese nationals in Hong Kong to continue to travel to other nations on British documents. Britain, for its part, guarantees overseas consular services and protection for those holding British travel documents, but such documents are transferable through descent for only one generation.

With final approval in the House of Lords on March 28, 1985, the British government passed the Hong Kong Bill to implement the terms of the Sino-British accord. On the issue of citizenship, the BDTC status was modified (inasmuch as Hong Kong will not be a dependent territory after 1997) to that of British National (Overseas), or BNO, which excludes any right of abode in Britain. Non-Chinese BDTCs would not automatically become Chinese nationals, although they could apply for naturalization. China views the prospect that some 30,000 to 50,000 non-Chinese residents (largely Indians, Pakistanis, Portuguese, and other Commonwealth subjects) will become stateless as Britain's problem.

Although these individuals may acquire British Overseas citizenship, it is neither transmissible by descent nor does it carry a right of abode anywhere.

China promised that it will draft and approve the Basic Law for the new Hong Kong SAR by 1990, consulting expert advice in Hong Kong in the process. Hong Kong's new basic law may take the form of an amendment to Article 31 of China's constitution. But the precise legal structure and contents of Hong Kong's "mini-constitution" are far less important than the extent to which domestic political forces in China operate to preserve the agreement. The Chinese concept of sovereignty is unlimited exercise of power. China can therefore override or disregard the terms of the agreement at will on sovereign grounds. More directly, it can amend its own constitution by a simple majority in the National People's Congress. As the British have no means of enforcing the joint declaration, the continuation of Hong Kong's economic system and policies depends wholly on China's good will.

ECONOMIC RESULTS

Until 1982, Hong Kong enjoyed a steady postwar pattern of remarkable economic growth under a regime of liberal economic policy and conservative fiscal policy. These policies remained largely intact during 1982–1985, but a sharp recession coupled with political uncertainty slowed the growth rate considerably during the latter years. With reference to the period through 1982, a former professor of economics at Hong Kong University compared Hong Kong's growth with neighboring China.

> This development, and these characteristics, mark Hong Kong off in a very different way from China. In the old days, before 1941, Hong Kong was not all that different from China. She was wealthier, certainly, but not enormously so; she relied on private enterprise, but there was almost as much private enterprise in Shanghai or Tianjin. For the past thirty years, however, Hong Kong and China have followed entirely different paths, and they now occupy very different economic positions.[30]

In 1948, per capita gross domestic product in Hong Kong stood at US$180. Hong Kong's postwar transformation was so dramatic that per capita income reached $5,800 by 1982, a sevenfold increase in real terms.[31] Per capita GDP declined to $5,383 in 1983, reflecting both an economic slowdown and the depreciation of the Hong Kong dollar from an annual average rate of HK$6.07 in 1982 to HK$7.27 in 1983. Despite further depreciation to HK$7.82 in 1978, economic recovery propelled per capita GDP to $5,935 in 1984 and $6,277 in 1985.[32] Living standards, in effect, stagnated for two years but then resumed their historical upward path.

From 1948 to 1960, real GDP grew about 7 percent per year, accelerating to an annual average of 9 percent between 1961 and 1981.

Productivity growth averaged 8 percent during the 1970s; the unemployment rate remained at less than 3 percent, absorbing the population inflows; and capital formation (savings as a share of GDP) exceeded 20 percent throughout the 1960s and 1970s. Hong Kong's economic transformation occurred without foreign aid or special concessions to overseas investors.

How did the common worker fare under this system? The limited evidence on postwar income distribution suggests that the 70 percent of the population in the third through the ninth deciles gained the greatest share of the increase in total national income.[33] Low-paid unskilled workers benefited most from the rapid increase in employment opportunities. The well-being of the poorest 20 percent dramatically improved: By 1976 their average household income had reached US$1,300, which surpassed the poverty index of all Asian countries. As low income households paid no income tax, rising incomes translated directly into a higher standard of living.

Living standards in China, compared with those in Hong Kong, are three decades behind. Deng Xiaoping's stated goal was to quadruple national income by the year 2,000. This goal requires an 8 percent average annual real growth and would uplift per capita income to $1,000. (Due to the sharp devaluation of China's currency, the Renminbi, in 1985 and 1986 after Deng's pronouncement, the figure of $1,000 now stands below $800, and would decline further on subsequent devaluations.) If the 8 percent growth figure is sustained, Chinese living standards would reach those enjoyed in Hong Kong in the late 1960s.[34] Even if Hong Kong's economy remained absolutely stagnant during the next decade and a half, its residents on average would enjoy an eightfold higher standard of living than their mainland counterparts.

Let us put the comparison more forcefully. In 1985, Hong Kong's 5 million residents owned more private automobiles than China had built since 1949. In 1983, for example, China produced only 5,600 passenger cars (which private Chinese citizens were forbidden to own until recently).[35] In 1981, there were over 190,000 licensed private cars, compared with just 9,000 in 1951. Telephones in usage increased from 27,000 in 1950, to 108,000 in 1960, to 580,000 in 1970, to 1.7 million in 1985; in other words, almost every household in Hong Kong now has its own private line. What's more, the phone system works splendidly in Hong Kong. Private phone lines in China virtually do not exist. Electricity consumption per capita in Hong Kong in 1982 averaged ten times that in China, which means that Hong Kong's 5 million people used as much electricity as 50 million mainland Chinese.[36] By every conceivable indicator—including the percentage of households served with electric lighting, gas, and piped water, the quantity and quality of daily caloric and protein intake, the percentage of school-age youths enrolled in educational institutions, ownership of such consumer durables as refrigerators, air conditioners, electric fans, washing machines, hi-fi stereo sets, and purchase of newspapers and magazines—Hong Kong's living standards dwarfed those of China.

The *World Development Report 1984* summarized the growth of both public and private consumption between 1960 and 1982. Separate figures were not available for public consumption in China—an indicator included in the country's overall figures for private consumption. Consumption in China increased at an average annual rate of 2.5 percent from 1960 to 1970, barely keeping pace with population growth, and rose to 5.1 percent between 1970 and 1982 (most of this increase occurred since 1978). In Hong Kong, public consumption increased at an average annual rate of 8.6 percent during 1960–1970, rising to 10.3 percent during 1970–1982. Private consumption increased by 8.6 percent between 1960 and 1970, accelerating to 10 percent since 1970.[37]

The implication of these numbers is this: Public consumption, the provision of public goods and services, increased two to three times more rapidly in Hong Kong's low-tax, free-market economy than in China's socialist, centrally planned system, thus explaining why Deng Xiaoping was so anxious to implement new pro-growth economic policies. Strong rates of economic growth over time make more resources available to both the public and the private sectors. Three decades of solid growth enabled the Hong Kong government to finance a considerable expansion in such public services as housing, education, health care, and income support programs, at the same time that the colony's individual residents increased their purchasing power as a result of steadily rising after-tax disposable incomes.

If China and Hong Kong enjoy similar rates of growth until 1997, when China recovers sovereignty and administrative authority over the British colony, living standards in Hong Kong will be more than twenty times higher than those in China. Under these conditions, Hong Kong's more than 5 million residents may have reason to be apprehensive.

NOTES

1. *Hong Kong 1986: A Review of 1985* (Hong Kong: Government Printer, 1985), p. 34.
2. Ibid., pp. 34–35. The financial sector fell from 19 percent in 1983 to 16 percent in 1984, reflecting a slump in the property market.
3. My treatment of economic policy is summarized from Alvin Rabushka, *Hong Kong: A Study in Economic Freedom* (Chicago: University of Chicago Press, 1979), pp. 44–51, 68–69, and 74–82.
4. *Hong Kong 1986*, pp. 36–37, and Appendix 6, p. 295.
5. Ibid., p. 45.
6. Ibid., pp. 57–59.
7. Ibid., pp. 143–146.
8. The Financial Secretary, *Hong Kong Hansard 1961*, p. 47.
9. Ibid., 1966, pp. 216, 218.
10. This treatment of budgetary policy draws from Alvin Rabushka, *Value for Money: The Hong Kong Budgetary Process* (Stanford, Calif.: Hoover Press, 1976), pp. 117–145.

11. *The 1984–85 Budget: Speech by the Financial Secretary, moving the Second Reading of the Appropriation Bill, 1984* (Hong Kong: Government Printer, 1984), p. 16, and Appendix, pp. 1–2.

12. The Financial Secretary, *Hong Kong Hansard 1960*, p. 62.

13. Ibid., 1964, p. 53.

14. *Hong Kong 1986*, pp. 43–45.

15. The first section on monetary policy is summarized from Alvin Rabushka, *Hong Kong: A Study in Economic Freedom*, pp. 56–61. For a history of money and banking in Hong Kong through the early 1970s, see Y.C. Jao, *Banking and Currency in Hong Kong: A Study of Post-war Financial Development* (London: Macmillan Press, 1974).

16. Y.C. Jao, "The 1997 Issue and Hong Kong's Financial Crisis," *Journal of Chinese Studies* 2, no. 1 (April 1985), pp. 115–116.

17. The architect of Hong Kong's refixed U.S. dollar exchange rate system is John G. Greenwood, an economist with G.T. Management (Asia) Ltd. in Hong Kong. Over the years he has published a series of articles describing the shortcomings in Hong Kong's floating exchange rate system and feasible reforms in the journal he edits, *Asian Monetary Monitor (AMM)*. The most important articles are "Hong Kong's Financial Crisis—History, Analysis, Prescription," *AMM* 6, no. 6 (November–December 1982), pp. 2–69; "How to Rescue the HK$: Three Practical Proposals," *AMM* 7, no. 5 (September–October 1983), pp. 11–39; "The Stabilisation of the Hong Kong Dollar," *AMM* 7, no. 6 (November–December 1983), pp. 9–37; "The Operation of the New Exchange Rate Mechanism," *AMM* 8, no. 1 (January–February 1984), pp. 2–12; "Why the HK$/US$ Linked Rate System Should not Be Changed," *AMM* 8, no. 6 (November–December 1984), pp. 2–17; and "Hong Kong: Adjusting to the Link," *AMM* 9, no. 4 (July–August 1985), pp. 2–12.

18. See Leo Goodstadt, "The Hong Kong dollar," *Asia Banking* (June 1983), pp. 62–67 and "Tugging the Currency off the Reefs," *Asia Banking* (November 1983), pp. 38–44. For a detailed treatment of this process by the architect of Hong Kong's linked rate, see John G. Greenwood, "The Stabilization of the Hong Kong Dollar," pp. 9–37.

19. *The 1984–85 Budget: Speech by the Financial Secretary Moving the Second Reading of the Appropriation Bill, 1984* (February 29, 1984), paragraph 13, p. 6.

20. *The Economist* (March 31, 1984), pp. 69–70; and *Wall Street Journal* (March 29, 1984), p. 30.

21. *Wall Street Journal* (March 29, 1984).

22. The day-to-day developments of Hong Kong's financial crisis are related by John G. Greenwood in "The Stabilization of the Hong Kong Dollar."

23. Hong Kong's new linked rate departs from John G. Greenwood's ideal plan, which includes full public access to convertibility at the official parity, the right of all banks to deal directly with the Exchange Fund instead of limiting Exchange Fund dealings to the two note-issuing banks, and the elimination of the Hong Kong Association of Bank's interest rate agreement, permitting full play to competition in deposit and lending rates. See "The Stabilization of the Hong Kong Dollar," pp. 24–25.

24. John G. Greenwood, "Hong Kong: Adjusting to the Link," p. 7.

25. *Far Eastern Economic Review* (February 13, 1986), p. 86.

26. Y.C. Jao, "The 1997 Issue and Hong Kong's Financial Crisis," pp. 141–142.

27. *Hong Kong Monthly Digest of Statistics* (November 1985), Tables 9.14 and 9.15, pp. 66, 68.

28. The future policies of Hong Kong during 1985–1997 and after the restoration of Chinese rule in 1997 are forecast in Bruce Bueno de Mesquita, David Newman, and Alvin Rabushka, *Forecasting Political Events: The Future of Hong Kong* (New Haven and London: Yale University Press, 1985).

29. This agreement was published under the title, "A Draft Agreement Between the Government of the United Kingdom and Northern Ireland and the Government of the People's Republic of China on the Future of Hong Kong." An official Chinese version in both languages was released in Hong Kong by New China News Agency on September 26, 1984. The official British version was presented to Parliament by the secretary of state for foreign and Commonwealth affairs as an official document, Miscellaneous No. 20 (1984) (London: Her Majesty's Stationery Office, 1984). The British version contained an introduction, which reviewed the history of the talks, the course of the negotiations, the views of the British government on the importance it attached to ratification of the agreement without changes, and a series of explanatory notes amplifying the contents of the agreement. Identical white paper versions in Chinese and English were simultaneously released in Hong Kong. In all, more than 3 million copies of the agreement were snatched up by an eager public.

30. A.J. Youngson, "Introduction," in A.J. Youngson, ed., *China and Hong Kong: The Economic Nexus* (Hong Kong: Oxford University Press, 1983), p. 7.

31. *Estimates of Gross Domestic Product 1966 to 1983,* Census and Statistics Department, Hong Kong (1984), Table 2, p. 8.

32. Derived from Census and Statistics Department, *Hong Kong in Figures, 1986 Edition* and *Hong Kong Monthly Digest of Statistics* (November 1985), Table 9.16, p. 70.

33. Steven C. Chow and Gustav F. Papanek, "Laissez-Faire, Growth and Equity—Hong Kong," *The Economic Journal* 91 (June 1981), pp. 466–485.

34. *Estimates of Gross Domestic Product 1966 to 1983,* Table 12, p. 62.

35. *Wall Street Journal* (August 20, 1984).

36. Selected indicators of Hong Kong consumption appear in *Hong Kong Monthly Digest of Statistics.*

37. *World Development Report 1984* (New York: Oxford University Press for the World Bank, 1984), Annex Table 4, pp. 224–225.

PART IV

THREE ECONOMIES

9

CONCLUSION AND
FUTURE PROSPECTS

The postwar developmental experiences of mainland China, Taiwan, and Hong Kong demonstrate that economic institutions matter more than cultural traits and natural resources in fostering growth and raising living standards. The Chinese, like people of other nationalities, respond to incentives. They flourish in an economic environment of free entry and competition, with property rights secured under the rule of law.

From its inception, Hong Kong practiced policies of economic liberalism and fiscal conservatism under British administration. In Hong Kong, the creation and distribution of wealth were left to the private sector. Economic growth was so spectacular that a war-devastated population in 1946 attained a per capita income in 1985 that rivalled Britain's own living standards. The colony successfully transformed itself from a poor, developing country into an advanced, industrial nation in one generation. Only downturns in the international business cycle and the occasional injection of political uncertainty into Hong Kong's solid climate of business confidence interrupted this pattern of sustained growth. Two political events in particular—the Red Guard riots in Hong Kong in 1966–1967, a spillover of the Cultural Revolution in China, and the September 1982 announcement that China would recapture Hong Kong in 1997—shocked the stock, property, and financial markets. In both cases, once the disturbances ceased, economic growth resumed its seemingly natural upward path. Hong Kong's prosperity from the mid-1980s into the next century depends on China's ability to maintain international confidence that Hong Kong's way of life and free economy will continue.

Taiwan, like Hong Kong, is overcrowded and resourceless. It differs from Hong Kong in two important respects. First, Taiwan is a country,

193

not a colony, and must look to its own resources for national security. This requirement has constantly posed a heavy burden of public spending and military service for national defense. Second, for 15 years after it occupied Taiwan, the Nationalist government depended heavily on U.S. military and economic assistance, during which it pursued an economic policy of import substitution.

Although external assistance financed infrastructure and some initial investment, these protectionist policies reduced economic efficiency and hampered exports of manufactured goods. Taiwan's costs were relatively high in the early 1950s due to an overvalued exchange rate, import controls on industrial inputs, and indirect business taxes. In the late-1950s, as U.S. aid wound down, Taiwan shifted economic policy from import substitution to export promotion. New policies included monetary reform and incentives for investment in export industries. Once Taiwan's internal cost/price structure made exporting profitable, external trade grew rapidly. Taiwan's industries achieved overnight success on international markets. Taiwan grew from a modest exporter of such traditional products as sugar and rice in the early 1950s to become one of the world's twenty largest industrial trading nations. At the end of 1986, its accumulated international reserves exceeded $40 billion, quadruple those of mainland China. The idea that "infant industries" require a period of protection for the domestic market prior to attempting to export was not readily confirmed by Taiwan's experience.[1]

At the other extreme of the economic spectrum, planners in mainland China pursued rigid collectivistic economic policies based on government ownership of the means of production until 1978. Government planners tried to control all enterprises, farms, and factories, set prices for all goods and services, assign production inputs, specify output targets, allocate labor, ration goods, determine individual incomes, and choose the mix between consumption and investment. Dissatisfied with the poor showing of these policies, Deng Xiaoping reversed course. He decollectivized agriculture in 1978 and injected a series of price, tax, credit, and monetary reforms into industry and commerce in subsequent years. Since the introduction of these liberal reforms in 1978, annual increases in output in agriculture more than doubled and light industry racked up large gains.

By the mid-1980s, economic policy makers in all three economies agreed on the merits of unregulated prices, free entry, competition, individual incentives, low levels of taxation, the rule of law, stable prices, realistic exchange rates, and participation in the international economy. These policies always prevailed in Hong Kong, took shape in Taiwan after 1958, and gradually emerged from successful experimentation in mainland China in 1978 despite sometimes vociferous disagreement among party officials. Whereas the Communist leaders in Beijing pursued collectivistic policies for 30 years before adopting market reforms in a frantic effort to stimulate economic growth, Taiwan's leaders abandoned the protectionist regime of import substitution in favor of promoting exports in ten short years. Both countries increased productivity and output with the introduction of market reforms.

Finally, it should be noted that market-oriented economic policies proved successful in three radically different political systems. These encompass colonial Hong Kong, the authoritarian Nationalist government of Taiwan, and the totalitarian Communist government on mainland China, where Western concepts of individual rights were rarely practiced.

FUTURE PROSPECTS

It is hazardous to forecast future economic developments. As 1997 draws near, continued prosperity in Hong Kong's market economy requires that China honor its agreement with Britain to let Hong Kong maintain its capitalistic system for 50 years and allow the full practice of all individual political, economic, legal, and social rights set forth in the Joint Declaration. Hong Kong's open economy is extremely sensitive to the slightest loss in international business confidence. Should China show any signs of reneging on the agreement, money and confidence in Hong Kong could dry up overnight, transforming a rich community into a poor appendage of Guangdong Province.

Until Deng Xiaoping passes from the scene, China is likely to be on its best behavior. Come 1990, internal developments within China, not Hong Kong, will dictate Hong Kong's future. China's record in Shanghai after 1949 provides little comfort to foreigners and Chinese residents in Hong Kong.

What about China's own development? Since the Communist party seized power in 1949, economic policy was marked by dramatic swings between extreme centralization and mild degrees of decollectivization. When Deng Xiaoping emerged as China's unchallenged leader, he mounted a sustained program of liberal reforms. Decollectivizing agriculture converted China from a food-short into a food-abundant nation. Decontrol of industry and commerce may be more tortuous. In early 1985, Deng, Party General Secretary Hu Yaobang, Premier Zhao Ziyang, and other officials publicly warned of "new unhealthy practices"—a reference to corruption, in that "some people were trying to make personal gains by taking advantage of reform."[2]

Party and government officials or their families set up companies to operate businesses that obtained unlawful supplies and facilities to make private profits; several government departments allegedly set up commercial fronts to generate illicit "staggering" profits. Other reported abuses include the diverting of imported machinery and foreign exchange to unauthorized uses, speculation in commodities, and distribution of illegal incentives in cash or kind. At a national conference held early in 1985, Deng felt compelled to announce that public ownership would remain the dominant feature of the economy. Did Deng's remarks signal a slight retreat from the idea that higher incomes are good in themselves and a movement toward the concept that higher growth should be for the common, rather than the individual's, good?

Chinese officials warned of copying "decadent capitalist ideas." In March 1985, Chinese leaders openly stated the need to slow the reckless growth of the economy, fearing rapid increases in retail commodity prices. Two years earlier, in 1983, a short-lived antispiritual pollution campaign, directed at the fear of political and cultural contamination from things foreign and capitalist, temporarily dampened enthusiasm for change and raised real fears about the permanence of the new liberal economic policies. The 1985 campaign to check the spread of official corruption had similar overtones and may retard the extension of further reforms, perhaps restoring tighter central controls.

Although China adopted some capitalist techniques in order to improve economic efficiency, it has resorted to tortuous Marxian arguments to justify liberal reforms as consonant with socialism. Marxism legitimizes the Communist Party's monopoly of political power and ownership of key industries.

Under Deng's conception of Marxism, China is a backward nation that must progress to communism through the commodity stage of capitalism. In the commodity stage of capitalism, goods and services are produced on the basis of market principles of supply and demand. The implication of Deng's view is that China cannot abolish or bypass the commodity economy through ultra-leftist transitions to communes or great leaps forward. As China must first pass through a capitalist economy en route to communism, during that passage the laws that govern capitalist development will apply to China as well. According to Deng, these circumstances will persist well into the next century, when the development of productive forces will have eliminated scarcity and created the preconditions for communism. According to this reasoning, Chinese planners can embrace market forces for the foreseeable future.

"Socialism with Chinese characteristics" showed signs of greater reliance on market forces—free movement of prices and increased competition—throughout 1986. New experiments encompassed the selling of bonds to private individuals (note the bond issued by the Beijing Industrial and Commercial Bank of $1.5 million at a rate of 9 percent for one year) rather than just to state-owned or collectively owned enterprises; the creation of joint-stock companies with freely tradeable shares; the signing of a memorandum of intent among the International Trade Research Institute, the Ministry of Foreign Economic Relations and Trade in Beijing, and the Chicago Board of Trade to have delegate exchanges regarding futures markets starting in 1986; the opening of a financial and stock market in Beijing to complement financial centers previously established in Shanghai and Shenyang; permitting a state-owned factory to declare bankruptcy in Shenyang, Shandong Province;

offering foreign investors improved incentives and conditions; and the adoption of a new form of labor contracts that permit employers to dismiss unproductive workers and workers to switch jobs to new employers at their own discretion.[3]

Reform was not unidirectional. In December 1986, China announced a new income tax beginning January 1987 that applied to anyone earning more than 400 yuan a month. A series of graduated rates, beginning at 20 percent on the first 100 yuan over 400 per month and rising to 60 percent over 800 yuan was the equivalent of a marginal tax rate of 60 percent for annual incomes over $2,580. The ostensible purpose of the tax was to narrow the income among Chinese people, especially by taxing those whose earnings rose steadily under economic reform. Yet it seems counterproductive to tax heavily the class of self-made entrepreneurs and skilled workers upon whose efforts China's modernization depends.[4]

More than any other country, China finds itself in the midst of a transition trap: How is it to unravel decades of state control and regulation in favor of the free play of market forces, while retaining the appearance if not the structure of a socialist economic system in which the state continues to own the assets of heavy industry? The literature on economic development has adequately described the successful development of the market economies of East and Southeast Asia, but it has little to offer in the way of guideposts to dismantle a centrally planned and controlled economy.

China's leaders and planners thus have to grope their way to efficiency, a process that sometimes requires a step backward after every two or three steps forward. A step backward (such as the spiritual pollution campaign) may lead some outside scholars to believe that China is likely to backtrack on or abort its reform policies. China's leading economists are aware of the economic achievements of Taiwan, Hong Kong, Korea, and Singapore, but have had little or no opportunity to observe these success stories firsthand.[5] Furthermore, they must continue to profess their commitment to socialism even as they deregulate the economy.

In a few short years, Deng Xiaoping and his colleagues transformed a collectivized agricultural economy into a private-enterprise system of leased, but tradeable, land rights. In the urban industrial sector, they built upon the policies of granting enterprises more autonomy and replacing the surrender of receipts with profits taxes by attempting to create both capital and labor markets in 1986. The central bank is using such macroeconomic techniques found in market economies as adjusting interest rates and the level of reserve deposits to control the money supply and the domestic price level. Urban land is still allocated by the state, but a dramatic extension of the experiments with capital and labor markets would free up two key factors of production to respond more efficiently to market forces. It is likely that party and state leaders will officially declare labor a commodity, like wheat and shoelaces, that will constitute a significant departure from strict Marxist treatment of labor.

If the reforms continue and expand, "socialism with Chinese characteristics" may in the near future see greater emphasis on Chinese characteristics and less on socialism. The point at which China's leaders no longer feel compelled to defend their right to govern in Marxist-Leninist terms remains to be seen.

Ninety miles across the South China Sea, the watchwords for the 1980s and 1990s are greater liberalization and internationalization of Taiwan's economy. Economic policy points to lower tariffs on imports, greater relaxation of travel and capital controls, financial deregulation, and improvement of its already attractive investment climate, without weakening national security. Unless external economic, political, or military shocks compel additional emphasis on defense, Taiwan's economy is likely to evolve in the direction of greater reliance on market forces.

Will Taiwan voluntarily rejoin the mainland? Its leaders and people doubt that the current themes in Communist economic policies will last, pointing to the radical shifts that characterized Chinese Communist politics since its earliest days. Nor do China's more than 1 billion people enjoy much in the way of civil or political rights. By contrast, Taiwan enjoyed stable development and gradually increasing political freedoms for its people. Finally, Taiwan has a well-equipped, half-million strong military with which to resist China's blandishments, whereas Hong Kong could have been brought to heel just by a shutting off of its supply of food and water.

The developmental experiences of all three economies reveals the benefits and costs of different degrees of competition and free entry, as well as different institutional arrangements. When the incentives and institutions of the market economy are combined with the Confucian traditions of thrift, hard work, and education, the nation and people prosper.

NOTES

1. Maurice Scott, "Foreign Trade," in Walter Galenson, ed., *Economic Growth and Structural Change in Taiwan: The Postwar Experience of the Republic of China* (Ithaca and London: Cornell University Press, 1979), pp. 379–381.
2. *Far Eastern Economic Review* (March 21, 1985), pp. 68–69.
3. These reforms were outlined in selected issues of the *Far Eastern Economic Review* throughout 1986 and *Wall Street Journal* (December 26, 1986).
4. *South China Morning Post* (December 14, 1986).
5. During a fact-finding tour of China sponsored by the World Media Association in August 1986 in which I participated, several leading economists of the Chinese Academy of Social Sciences expressed this view.

ECONOMIC STATISTICS

The availability and quality of economic statistics vary among mainland China, Taiwan, and Hong Kong, as well as over time. This appendix summarizes the main sources of economic statistics and the problems that must be taken into account in using them.

MAINLAND CHINA

An accurate assessment of the performance of the Chinese economy requires reliable data. Students of the U.S. economy enjoy ready access to census data, national income accounts, a wide variety of periodic surveys, tax return data, and so forth. In contrast, the problem of statistics has plagued students of the Chinese economy.

Between 1949 and 1960, the Chinese published economic statistics. But no statistics of any sort were published between 1960 and 1971, and those published after 1971 were sporadic.[1] The statistics that do exist, moreoever, are of questionable validity. It is widely acknowledged that overzealous cadres regularly inflated statistics to show that production targets were met or exceeded during such periods as the Great Leap Forward (1957–1958). Since 1978, Chinese economists and officials have admitted that substantial quantities of outputs and goods were of low or unusable quality, leading to acute shortages and the stockpiling of worthless inventory. Economists Liu Guoguang and Wang Ruisun reported that the commercial department of the city of Jinzhou contained an inventory of 1.41 million pocket knives, which would take at least 30 years to sell.[2] In the same volume, Li Chengrui and Zhang Zhuoyuan noted that published figures on revenues from state-owned enterprises yielded a false indication of income because output values embraced substandard goods and rejects purchased by state supply or commercial departments. Thus expenditure based on this false income was a latent deficit.[3]

The impact of the Cultural Revolution on the national statistical system was far reaching. The State Statistical Bureau was abolished in 1968. Its trained staff and professional manpower were assigned to other jobs or sent to the countryside for political education. Statistical work was put on a "care and maintenance basis." Data collection efforts that continued at the grass-roots level between 1966 and 1976 were uncoordinated and unsupervised. Recording carried out by unqualified staff produced suspect data, and local cadres routinely falsified data to exaggerate the achievements of their units or local cities. The abolition of county, provincial, and state statistical agencies precluded the aggregation of data.[4]

Ideally, a system of central economic planning requires detailed information about every aspect of the economy, down to the technical production capabilities of every industrial firm for each product and of every rural production team for each crop. The collapse of the state statistical system during the decade of the Cultural Revolution played havoc with the attempt to implement orderly planning. The inherent inefficiencies in central planning were compounded by the lack of economic data, not to mention the widespread breakdown of law and order that further disrupted production.

The Chinese have been trying to put their statistical house in order since 1978. With technical assistance from the United Nations in 1980, they conducted their first population census after a gap of 27 years. Since 1980, the State Statistical Bureau of the Chinese government has published its own estimates of Chinese national income in the *Almanac of China's Economy, 1981* and the *Statistical Yearbook of China, 1981.* Both are annually updated and contain hundreds of pages of tables on economic, social, and demographic trends. The State Statistical Bureau filled in missing data to the best of its ability. The State Statistical Bureau also began to publish a condensed compendium entitled *China: A Statistics Survey in 1985,* which has since become an annual issue. It should be noted that before 1984, China's national accounting system did not include services.[5]

Prior to 1980, analysts of China's economy developed private estimates of national income.[6] The Office of Economic Research at the Central Intelligence Agency, the U.S. Department of. Commerce, and such leading scholars as Alexander Eckstein, T.C. Liu and K.C. Yeh, Dwight H. Perkins, Subramanian Swamy, R.M. Field, and Nicholas Lardy have labored to fill in gaps and interpret trends.

Both Western and Chinese estimates of China's national income have suffered two serious problems. One has been the need to deflate output figures to take into account substandard and unusable goods and the stockpiling of worthless inventory. If there had been a free market in these goods, sellers could have lowered prices to clear inventories, thus placing a value on them. It makes dubious sense to include artificial values for worthless inventories in national income. There has been no systematic attempt to recalculate national output based solely on useful goods.

The second problem follows directly from the first. Under China's system of central planning, the state set all prices. Ideally, however, prices determined by competitive markets should be used to estimate the scarcity value of different outputs. As the value of national income is gross output multiplied by the price of each item, China's national income is an arbitrary figure that does not represent the true value of each good or service that would emerge from the bidding among competitive producers and consumers. In any economy where many prices are not determined by market forces, it is difficult to find appropriate prices with which to weigh the different products so as to form an estimate of national income. If political decisions change the ratio of industrial to agricultural prices over time, with no regard for the real value of the alternative use of inputs in one sector versus the other, it becomes difficult to estimate levels of national income or annual rates of real economic growth and to compare those estimates with income and growth rates of predominantly market economies such as Hong Kong and Taiwan.

It is equally problematic to compare living standards in the three economies. Both Hong Kong and Taiwan have generally maintained realistic exchange rates. Mainland China, in contrast, has often grossly overvalued its currency. Between 1984 and mid-1986, for example, the exchange rate between the U.S. dollar and the Renminbi declined from US$1 = 2.02 yuan to US$1 = 3.69 yuan, and some economists believe the free-trade exchange rate would be lower than US$1 = 5 yuan. Thus a paradox has emerged in which China scored significant gains in output and consumption during 1978–1985 but living standards expressed in U.S. dollar terms failed to increase between 1980 and 1985.

TAIWAN

In comparison with the dearth and incompleteness of economic statistics in the People's Republic of China, and the lack of comprehensive national income accounts for Hong Kong until 1971, economic statistics for Taiwan are abundant. In order to provide complete and systematic data, the Directorate-General of Budget, Accounting, and Statistics (DGBAS) in the Executive Branch has compiled statistics of national income since 1953. Each year the DGBAS publishes the *National Income of the Republic of China*, which includes the national accounts dating back to 1951. The DGBAS also publishes the *Statistical Yearbook of the Republic of China*, which uses the same format as that used in the annual *Statistical Yearbook* of the United Nations. The 1985 edition presents data from 1955 through 1984. Every three months the DGBAS releases *Quarterly National Economic Trends Taiwan Area, Republic of China*, which tracks the quarterly performance of the economy. As income distribution has been considered an important factor in policymaking circles, DGBAS conducts and publishes an annual survey entitled *Report on the Survey of Personal Income Distribution in Taiwan Area, Republic of China.*

Other valuable sources include the annual edition of the *Taiwan Statistical Data Book,* published by the Council for Economic Planning and Development; the *Annual Report* of the Central Bank of China; the *Geographical Survey of the Economy of Taiwan District, the Republic of China,* published by the Economic Research Department of the Central Bank of China; a graphical summary entitled *Economic Development, Taiwan, Republic of China,* published by the Ministry of Economic Affairs; and the *Annual Review of Government Administration, Republic of China,* released by the Research, Development, and Evaluation Commission, Executive Branch. The latter volume contains a comprehensive listing of sources of authoritative information, including the *China Yearbook, Monthly Statistics of the Republic of China, Yearbook of Labor Statistics, Republic of China,* annual reports on health, education, food, forestry, industrial production, communications, and tourism statistics, and annual reports on taxation, public finances, trade, and prices.

HONG KONG

Valuable descriptive material and statistics on Hong Kong are published in an annual report, of which the most recent edition used is *Hong Kong 1986: A Review of 1985* (Hong Kong: Government Printer, 1986).

Prior to 1947, there was no organization dealing specifically with statistical matters. Population censuses were generally carried out on an ad hoc basis. Other statistics collected by government departments were the by-products of everyday work and not part of any overall statistics program. The creation of a Department of Statistics in 1947 gave priority to cost-of-living surveys, which led to monthly publication of a retail price index.

The Department of Statistics was disbanded in 1952. In its place a statistical branch was set up in the Commerce and Industry Department, which routinely compiled trade statistics, the retail price index, and various statistical supplements.

A separate Census Department was set up in 1959 to prepare for the 1961 population census, the first to be taken in Hong Kong for 30 years. However, immediately following completion of the census, the department was disbanded and the work of preparing population projections was transferred to the statistical branch of the Commerce and Industry Department.

The present Department of Census and Statistics was established in 1967. It combined the functions of economic and social statistics. The establishment and growth of that department produced a marked improvement in the collection of such statistics.

The colony did not publish official estimates of national income until the printing of the *1973-74 Budget Estimates*, which contain an estimate of GDP for 1967–1971. Earlier data that exist on GDP or national income are limited to private scholarly estimates. Indeed, it was the deliberate policy of the then financial secretary (1961–1971), Sir John Cowperthwaite, to disdain the collection and publication of national income accounts lest the existence of official data foster a planning mentality. Sir John's successor, (now Sir) Charles Philip Haddon-Cave, installed the collection and publication of national accounts statistics.

In addition to the government's annual report, a wealth of information and statistics on the policies and performance of Hong Kong's economy appears in a series of periodic reports. These include the financial secretary's annual *Budget Address, Economic Background, Economic Prospects* for the coming year, *Estimates of Gross Domestic Product 1966-1983* (through the prior year), *Supporting Financial Statements and Statistical Appendices* for the proposed budget, *Quarterly Economic Reports*, and a *Half-Yearly Economic Report* for the current fiscal year. These exist in addition to the *Monthly Digest of Statistics*. Estimates of economic performance prior to 1966 are found in Edward Szczepanik, *The Economic Growth of Hong Kong* (London: Oxford University Press for the Royal Institute of International Affairs, 1958).

NOTES

1. *China: Socialist Economic Development* (Washington, D.C.: World Bank, 1983), pp. 223–227; and Christopher Howe, *China's Economy: A Basic Guide* (New York: Basic Books, Inc., 1978), pp. xiv–xv.
2. Liu Guoguang and Wang Ruisun, "Restructuring of the Economy," in Yu Guangyuan, ed., *China's Socialist Modernization* (Beijing: Foreign Languages Press, 1984), p. 96.
3. Li Chengrui and Zhang Zhuoyuan, "An Outline of Economic Development (1977–1980), in Yu Guangyuan, ed., *China's Socialist Modernization*, p. 7.
4. *China: Socialist Economic Development*, pp. 226–227.
5. Annex A in *China: Socialist Economic Development* describes the history of China's statistical development, the organization of the present statistical system, the methods and concepts in China's system of national accounts, and the way in which China's Soviet-style system of national income accounting is converted into conventional gross national product calculations for international comparisons.
6. Cited in Christopher Howe, *China's Economy*, p. xiv.

Table A1:   Main Indicators of Mainland China's Economy, 1952-1985

Item	Unit	1952	1957	1965	1978	1985
Population	million	574.8	646.5	725.4	962.6	1,045.3
Labor force	million	207.3	237.7	286.7	398.6	498.7
in industry	million	16.0	31.0	49.7	94.5	123.5
Index of gross output value of agriculture and industry (1952 = 100)	%	100.0	167.8	268.3	779.0	1,437.4
Index of national income (1952 = 100)	%	100.0	153.0	197.5	453.2	820.2
Accumulation rate	%	21.4	24.9	27.1	36.5	33.7
Index of gross agricultural output value (1952 = 100)	%	100.0	124.8	137.1	229.6	451.5
Output of major farm products						
Grain	million tons	163.9	195.1	194.5	304.8	379.1
Cotton	million tons	1.3	1.6	2.1	2.2	4.1
Oil-crops	million tons	4.2	4.2	3.6	5.2	15.8
Sugar cane	million tons	7.1	10.4	13.4	21.1	51.5
Tea	million tons	0.1	0.1	0.1	0.3	0.1
Fruits	million tons	2.4	3.2	3.2	6.6	11.6
Meat	million tons	3.4	4.0	5.5	8.6	17.6
Index of gross industrial output value (1952 = 100)	%	100.0	228.6	452.9	1601.6	3147.5
Light industry	%	100.0	183.2	344.7	970.6	2220.3
Heavy industry	%	100.0	310.7	651.0	2780.4	4808.8
Output of major industrial products						
Cloth	100 million meters	38.3	50.5	62.8	110.3	146.7
Paper	10 thousand tons	37	91	173	439	911
Bicycles	10 thousand	8.0	80.6	183.8	854.0	3227.7
Sewing machines	"	6.6	27.8	123.8	486.5	991.2
Wrist watches	"		.0	100.8	1351.1	5431.1
Coal	100 million tons	0.7	1.3	2.3	6.2	8.7
Crude oil	10 thousand tons	44	146	1,131	10,405	12,490
Electricity	100 million kwh	73	193	676	2,566	4,107
Steel	10 thousand tons	135	535	1,223	3,178	4,679
Cement	10 thousand tons	286	686	1,634	6,524	14,595

Table A1: Main Indicators of Mainland China's Economy (Continued)

Item	Unit	1952	1957	1965	1978	1985
Investments in state-owned units						
Total fixed assets	Rmb100 million	44	151	217	669	1,680
Total foreign trade	Rmb100 million	65	105	118	355	2,067
Exports	Rmb100 million	27	55	63	168	1,258
Imports	Rmb100 million	38	50	55	187	809
Price indexes						
Retail	%	100	109	120	122	156
Farm products	%	100	120	155	179	287
Staff and workers cost of living	%	100	110	120	125	168

Sources: Statistical Yearbook of China 1985, compiled by the State Statistical Bureau, PRC (Hong Kong: Economic Information and Agency, 1985), pp. 12-15; and Statistical Yearbook of China 1984, pp. 12-15. Figures for 1985 are taken from China: A Statistical Survey in 1986, compiled by the State Statistical Bureau, PRC (Hong Kong: Produced by the Longman Group for New World Press and China Statistical Information and Consultancy Service Center, 1986), pp. 4, 7, 8, 9, 38-40, 53-56, 96, and 101.

Table A2: National Income of Mainland China, 1949-1985

Year	National income (Rmb billion)	Per capita income (Rmb)	Per capita income (US$)
1949	35.8	66	
1950	42.6	77	
1951	49.7	88	
1952	58.9	104	
1953	70.9	122	
1954	74.8	126	
1955	78.8	129	
1956	88.2	142	
1957	90.8	142	58
1958	111.8	171	69
1959	122.2	183	74
1960	122.0	183	74
1961	99.6	151	61
1962	92.4	139	57
1963	100.0	147	60
1964	116.6	167	68
1965	138.7	194	79
1966	158.6	216	88
1967	148.7	198	80
1968	141.5	183	74
1969	161.7	203	83
1970	192.6	235	95
1971	207.7	247	100
1972	213.6	248	111
1973	231.8	263	130
1974	234.8	261	142
1975	250.3	273	139
1976	242.7	261	139
1977	264.4	280	162
1978	301.0	315	201
1979	335.0	346	231
1980	368.8	376	246
1981	394.0	396	226
1982	426.1	423	220
1983	473.0	464	233
1984	564.3	548	196
1985	682.2	650	204

Sources: _Statistical Yearbook of China 1985_, p. 33; and _China: A Statistical Survey in 1986_, pp. 7 and 98.

Note: The Renminbi/US$ exchange rate is taken from _International Financial Statistics, Supplement on Exchange Rates_, Supplement Series, No. 9, International Monetary Fund (1985), pp. 7-11, and from the Prices and Trends page in the _Far Eastern Economic Review_, which publishes weekly currency exchange rates.

Table A3:   Consumption and Accumulation in National Income in
            Mainland China, 1952-1985

Year	Consumption rate (%)	Accumulation rate (%)
1952	78.6	21.4
1953	76.9	23.1
1954	74.5	25.5
1955	77.1	22.9
1956	75.6	24.4
1957	75.1	24.9
1958	66.1	33.9
1959	56.2	43.8
1960	60.4	39.6
1961	80.8	19.2
1962	89.6	10.4
1963	82.5	17.5
1964	77.8	22.2
1965	72.9	27.1
1966	69.4	30.6
1967	78.8	21.3
1968	78.9	21.1
1969	76.8	23.2
1970	67.1	32.9
1971	65.9	34.1
1972	68.4	31.6
1973	67.1	32.9
1974	67.7	32.3
1975	66.1	33.9
1976	69.1	30.9
1977	67.7	32.3
1978	63.5	36.5
1979	65.4	34.6
1980	68.5	31.5
1981	71.7	28.3
1982	71.2	28.8
1983	70.3	29.7
1984	68.8	31.2
1985	66.3	33.7

Sources: Statistical Yearbook of China 1985, p. 36; and China:
A Statistical Survey in 1986, p. 7.

Table A4:   Gross Agriculture and Industrial Output Value in
            Mainland China, 1949-1985 (1952 = 100)

Year	Agriculture index	Industry index	Light industry	Heavy industry
1949	67.4	40.8	46.6	30.3
1950	79.3	55.7	60.6	46.7
1951	86.6	77.0	81.0	69.7
1952	100.0	100.0	100.0	100.0
1953	103.1	130.3	126.7	136.9
1954	106.6	151.6	144.8	163.9
1955	114.7	160.0	144.8	187.7
1956	120.5	204.9	173.3	262.3
1957	124.8	228.6	183.3	310.7
1958	127.8	353.9	245.1	555.5
1959	110.4	481.7	299.0	822.7
1960	96.4	535.7	269.7	1,035.8
1961	94.1	331.1	211.4	554.2
1962	99.9	276.1	193.6	429.0
1963	111.6	299.6	198.1	488.2
1964	126.7	358.3	233.4	590.7
1965	137.1	452.9	344.7	651.0
1966	149.0	547.6	394.7	830.0
1967	151.2	472.0	366.7	664.0
1968	147.5	448.4	348.7	630.1
1969	149.2	602.2	436.6	906.7
1970	166.3	787.1	515.6	1,290.3
1971	171.4	904.4	549.1	1,566.3
1972	171.1	964.1	583.1	1,675.9
1973	185.5	1,055.7	644.9	1,821.7
1974	193.2	1,058.9	662.3	1,792.6
1975	202.1	1,218.8	748.4	2,093.8
1976	207.1	1,234.6	766.4	2,104.3
1977	210.6	1,411.1	876.0	2,405.2
1978	229.6	1,601.6	970.6	2,780.4
1979	249.4	1,737.7	1,063.8	2,994.5
1980	259.1	1,888.9	1,259.5	3,036.4
1981	276.2	1,966.3	1,437.1	2,893.7
1982	306.8	2,111.7	1,519.0	3,177.3
1983	336.2	2,340.1	1,651.2	3,571.3
1984	393.7	2,667.7	1,880.7	4,078.4
1985	451.5	3,147.5	2,220.3	4,808.8

Sources: **Statistical Yearbook of China 1985**, p. 25; and **China:
A Statistical Survey in 1986**, p. 9.

Table A5:   Composition of Gross Output Value of Agriculture and
            Industry in Mainland China, 1949-1985

Year	Proportion of Agriculture and Industry (%)		Proportion of Industry (%)	
	Agriculture	Industry	Light Ind.	Heavy Ind.
1949	70.0	30.0	73.6	26.4
1950	66.8	33.2	70.7	29.3
1951	61.4	38.6	67.8	32.2
1952	56.9	43.1	64.5	35.5
1953	53.1	46.9	62.7	37.3
1954	50.9	49.1	61.6	38.4
1955	51.8	48.2	59.2	40.8
1956	48.7	51.3	57.6	42.4
1957	43.3	56.7	55.0	45.0
1958	34.3	65.7	46.5	53.5
1959	25.1	74.9	41.5	58.5
1960	21.8	78.2	33.4	66.6
1961	34.5	65.5	42.5	57.5
1962	38.8	61.2	47.2	52.8
1963	39.3	60.7	44.8	55.2
1964	38.2	61.8	44.3	55.7
1965	37.3	62.7	51.6	48.4
1966	35.9	64.1	49.0	51.0
1967	40.1	59.9	53.0	47.0
1968	41.9	58.1	53.7	46.3
1969	36.3	63.7	50.3	49.7
1970	33.7	66.3	46.2	53.8
1971	31.8	68.2	43.0	57.0
1972	30.9	69.1	42.9	57.1
1973	30.9	69.1	43.4	56.6
1974	31.9	68.1	44.4	55.6
1975	30.1	69.9	44.1	55.9
1976	30.4	69.6	44.2	55.8
1977	28.1	71.9	44.0	56.0
1978	27.8	72.2	43.1	56.9
1979	29.7	70.3	43.7	56.3
1980	30.8	69.2	47.2	52.8
1981	32.5	67.5	51.5	48.5
1982	33.6	66.4	50.2	49.8
1983	33.9	66.1	48.5	51.5
1984	34.8	65.2	47.4	52.6
1985	34.3	65.7	46.7	53.3

Sources: Statistical Yearbook of China 1985, p. 29; and China:
A Statistical Survey in 1986, p. 9.

Table A6:   Output of Major Farm Products in Mainland China,
1949-1985 (million tons)

Year	Grain	Cotton	Oil Crops	Sugar Cane	Beet Roots	Tea	Fruits
1949	113.2	0.4	2.6	2.6	0.2	0.04	1.2
1950	132.1	0.7	3.0	3.1	0.2	0.07	1.3
1951	143.7	1.0	3.6	4.6	0.4	0.08	1.6
1952	163.9	1.3	4.2	7.1	0.5	0.08	2.4
1953	166.8	1.2	3.9	7.2	0.5	0.09	3.0
1954	169.5	1.1	4.3	8.6	1.0	0.09	3.0
1955	183.9	1.6	4.8	8.1	1.6	0.11	2.6
1956	192.8	1.4	5.1	8.6	1.6	0.12	3.1
1957	195.1	1.6	4.2	10.4	1.5	0.11	3.2
1958	200.0	2.0	4.8	12.6	3.1	0.14	3.9
1959	170.0	1.7	4.1	9.0	3.2	0.15	4.3
1960	143.5	1.1	1.9	8.3	1.6	0.14	4.0
1961	147.5	0.8	1.8	4.3	0.8	0.08	2.8
1962	160.0	0.8	2.0	3.4	0.4	0.07	2.7
1963	170.0	1.2	2.5	7.8	0.5	0.08	2.9
1964	187.5	1.7	3.4	12.2	1.3	0.09	
1965	194.5	2.1	3.6	13.4	2.0	0.10	3.2
1966	214.0	2.3		11.4	2.6	0.11	
1967	217.8	2.4		12.6	2.6	0.11	
1968	209.1	2.4		10.3	2.2	0.12	
1969	211.0	2.1		10.5	2.4	0.12	
1970	240.0	2.2	3.8	13.5	2.1	0.14	3.7
1971	250.1	2.1	4.1	13.1	2.1	0.15	3.9
1972	240.5	2.0	4.1	16.4	2.3	0.17	4.4
1973	264.9	2.6	4.2	17.0	2.7	0.18	5.2
1974	275.3	2.5	4.4	16.4	2.3	0.20	5.2
1975	284.5	2.4	4.5	16.7	2.5	0.21	5.4
1976	286.3	2.1	4.0	16.6	2.9	0.23	5.4
1977	282.7	2.0	4.0	17.8	2.5	0.25	5.7
1978	304.8	2.2	5.2	21.1	2.7	0.27	6.6
1979	332.1	2.2	6.4	21.5	3.1	0.28	7.0
1980	320.6	2.8	7.7	22.8	6.3	0.30	6.8
1981	325.0	3.0	10.2	29.7	6.4	0.34	7.8
1982	354.5	3.6	11.8	36.9	6.7	0.40	7.7
1983	387.3	4.6	10.6	31.1	9.2	0.40	9.5
1984	407.3	6.3	11.9	39.5	8.3	0.41	9.8
1985	379.1	4.1	15.8	51.5	8.9	0.43	11.6

Sources: _Statistical Yearbook of China 1985_, pp. 255-256; and
China: A Statistical Survey in 1986, pp. 38-39.

Table A7:   Gross Industrial Output Value by Form of Ownership in
            Mainland China, 1949-1985 (in percentages)

Year	State ownership	Collective ownership	Joint state-private	Private ownership	Individual industry	Other forms
1949	26.2	0.5	1.6	48.7	23.0	
1950	32.7	0.8	2.1	38.1	26.3	
1951	34.5	1.3	3.0	38.4	22.8	
1952	41.5	3.3	4.0	30.6	20.6	
1953	43.0	3.9	4.5	29.3	19.3	
1954	47.1	5.3	9.8	19.9	17.9	
1955	51.3	7.6	13.1	13.2	14.8	
1956	54.5	17.1	27.2	0.04	1.2	
1957	53.8	19.0	26.3	0.1	0.8	
1965	90.1	9.9				
1975	83.2	16.8				
1979	81.0	19.0				
1980	78.7	20.7				0.6
1981	78.3	21.0				0.6
1982	77.8	21.4			0.1	0.7
1983	77.0	22.0			0.1	0.9
1984	73.6	25.0			0.2	1.2
1985	70.4	27.7			0.4	1.5

Sources: Statistical Yearbook of China 1985, p. 306; and China:
A Statistical Survey in 1986, p. 50.

Table A8:   Purchase Price of Farm and Sideline Products in Mainland China, 1978-1984

Item	1978	1981	1982	1983	1984
Proportion of total purchase value (percentages)					
(1) List price	84.7	58.2	57.5	48.0	33.9
(2) Subsidized prices for above-quota purchase	7.9	20.9	20.8	28.1	33.6
(3) Negotiated price	1.8	11.5	11.5	13.4	14.4
(4) Market price	5.6	9.4	10.2	10.5	18.1

Source: China: A Statistics Survey in 1985, compiled by State Statistical Bureau, PRC (Beijing: New World Press and China Statistical Information and Consultancy Service Center, 1985), p. 85. The 1985 data are omitted in China: A Statistical Survey in 1986.

Table A9:   Urban and Rural Market Fair Trade in Mainland China, 1979-1985

Item	1979	1980	1981	1982	1983	1984	1985
1. Number of market fairs	38,993	40,809	43,013	44,775	48,003	56,500	61,337
(a) Urban	2,226	2,919	3,298	3,591	4,488	6,144	8,013
(b) Rural	36,767	37,890	39,715	41,184	43,515	50,356	53,324
2. Volume of fair trade (RMB billion)	18.3	23.5	28.7	33.3	38.6	47.1	70.5
(a) Urban	1.2	2.4	3.4	4.5	5.6	8.0	18.1
(b) Rural	17.1	21.1	25.3	28.8	33.0	39.0	52.4

Source: China: A Statistical Survey in 1986, p. 93.

Table A10:   Total Value of Imports and Exports in Mainland China,
             1950-1985 (in US$ billion)

Year	Total	Exports	Imports
1950	1.13	0.55	0.58
1951	1.96	0.76	1.20
1952	1.94	0.82	1.12
1953	2.37	1.02	1.35
1954	2.44	1.15	1.29
1955	3.14	1.41	1.73
1956	3.21	1.65	1.56
1957	3.11	1.60	1.51
1958	3.87	1.98	1.89
1959	4.38	2.26	2.12
1960	3.81	1.86	1.95
1961	2.94	1.49	1.45
1962	2.66	1.49	1.17
1963	2.92	1.65	1.27
1964	3.47	1.92	1.55
1965	4.25	2.23	2.02
1966	4.62	2.37	2.25
1967	4.16	2.14	2.02
1968	4.05	2.10	1.95
1969	4.03	2.20	1.83
1970	4.59	2.26	2.33
1971	4.85	2.64	2.21
1972	6.30	3.44	2.86
1973	10.98	5.82	5.16
1974	14.57	6.95	7.62
1975	14.75	7.26	7.49
1976	13.41	6.86	6.58
1977	14.80	7.59	7.21
1978	20.61	9.75	10.89
1979	29.33	13.66	15.67
1980	38.14	18.12	20.02
1981	44.02	22.01	22.01
1982	41.63	22.35	19.28
1983	43.62	22.23	21.39
1984	53.55	26.14	27.41
1985	69.62	27.37	42.25

Sources: Statistical Yearbook of China 1985, p. 508; and China:
A Statistical Survey in 1986, p. 96.   The 1986 publication
substantially revised upward all figures after 1979 that appeared
in earlier editions.

Notes: (1) The trade figures are those reported by the Foreign
Trade Department.   The numbers based on customs statistics are
about 10 percent higher, but the trends are similar.   See
Statistical Yearbook of China 1985, p. 494.   (2) Foreign exchange
rates for conversion of RMB into U.S. dollars were issued by the
People's Bank of China for 1950-1978 and by the Bank of China for
1979-1985.

Table A11:   Total State Revenue and Expenditure in Mainland
              China, 1950-1985 (Rmb 100 million)

Year	Total Revenue	Total Expenditure	Balance
1950	65.2	68.1	- 2.9
1951	133.1	122.5	+ 10.6
1952	183.7	176.0	+ 7.7
1953	222.9	230.1	+ 2.8
1954	262.4	246.3	+ 16.1
1955	272.0	269.3	+ 2.7
1956	278.4	305.7	- 18.3
1957	310.2	304.2	+ 6.0
1958	387.6	409.4	- 21.8
1959	487.1	552.9	- 65.8
1960	572.3	654.1	- 81.8
1961	356.1	367.0	- 10.9
1962	313.6	305.3	+ 8.3
1963	342.3	339.6	+ 2.7
1964	399.5	399.0	+ 0.5
1965	473.3	466.3	+ 7.0
1966	558.7	541.6	+ 17.1
1967	419.4	441.9	- 22.5
1968	361.3	359.8	+ 1.5
1969	526.8	525.9	+ 0.9
1970	662.9	649.4	+ 13.5
1971	744.7	732.2	+ 12.5
1972	766.6	766.4	+ 0.2
1973	809.7	809.3	+ 0.4
1974	783.1	790.8	- 7.7
1975	815.6	820.9	- 5.3
1976	776.6	806.2	- 29.6
1977	874.5	843.5	+ 31.0
1978	1,121.1	1,111.0	+ 10.1
1979	1,103.3	1,273.9	-170.6
1980	1,085.2	1,212.7	-127.5
1981	1,089.5	1,115.0	- 25.5
1982	1,124.0	1,153.3	- 29.3
1983	1,249.0	1,292.5	- 43.3
1984	1,501.9	1,546.4	- 44.5
1985	1,854.2	1,825.9	+ 28.3

Sources: Statistical Yearbook of China 1985, p. 523; and China:
A Statistical Survey in 1986, p. 85.

Table A12:   Composition of State Revenue and Expenditure in
             Mainland China, Selected Years, 1952-1985
                                         (in percentages)

Item	1952	1957	1965	1978	1985
1. Total Revenue	100	100	100	100	100
Of which:					
(1) Income from enterprises	31.2	46.5	55.8	51.0	2.2
Of which: Industry	11.7	19.1	45.7	39.3	---
(2) Income from taxation	53.2	49.9	43.2	46.3	97.8
Of which: Industrial and Commercial Tax	33.5	36.5	35.0	40.3	53.8
Agricultural Tax	14.7	9.6	5.5	2.5	23.0
Income tax from state-owned enterprises	---	---	---	---	27.0
2. Total Expenditure	100	100	100	100	100
Of which:					
(1) Capital construction	26.5	40.7	34.0	40.7	31.2
(2) New enterprises	---	---	5.4	5.7	5.5
(3) Circulating funds for enterprises	10.6	6.8	5.9	6.0	0.8
(4) Culture, education, science, public health	7.7	9.1	6.2	5.9	17.4
(5) National defense	32.9	18.1	18.6	15.1	10.5
(6) Administration	8.3	7.1	5.4	4.4	7.3

Source: China: A Statistical Survey in 1986, pp. 84-85.

A13:   General Prices Indexes in Mainland China, 1951-1985

(1950 = 100)

Year	General retail price index	Urban cost of living	Purchasing prices of farm and sideline products
1951	112.2	112.5	119.6
1952	111.8	115.5	121.6
1953	115.6	121.4	132.5
1954	118.3	123.1	136.7
1955	119.5	123.5	135.1
1956	119.5	123.4	139.2
1957	121.3	126.6	146.2
1958	121.6	125.2	149.4
1959	122.7	125.6	152.1
1960	126.5	128.8	157.4
1961	147.0	149.6	201.4
1962	152.6	155.3	200.1
1963	143.6	146.1	194.4
1964	138.3	140.7	189.5
1965	134.6	139.0	187.9
1966	134.2	137.3	195.8
1967	133.2	136.4	195.5
1968	133.3	136.5	195.2
1969	131.8	137.8	194.9
1970	131.5	137.8	195.1
1971	130.5	137.7	198.3
1972	130.2	137.9	201.1
1973	131.0	138.0	202.8
1974	131.7	138.9	204.5
1975	131.9	139.5	208.7
1976	132.3	139.9	209.7
1977	135.0	143.7	209.2
1978	135.9	144.7	217.4
1979	138.6	147.4	265.5
1980	146.9	158.5	284.4
1981	150.4	162.5	301.2
1982	153.3	165.8	307.8
1983	155.6	169.1	321.3
1984	160.0	173.7	334.2
1985	174.1	194.4	362.9

Sources: Statistical Yearbook of China 1985, p. 530.   Figures for 1985 are derived from China: A Statistical Survey in 1986, p. 100.

Table B1:   Gross National Product of Taiwan, 1952-1985

Year	Amount (NT$ m)	Real growth rate (%)	Real growth index (1952=100)	Per capita GNP (US$)(a)	Real growth rate(b) (%)
1952	17,162	12.1	100	186	-
1953	22,859	9.3	109	159	5.8
1954	25,083	9.6	120	168	5.8
1955	29,835	8.1	130	192	4.1
1956	34,212	5.5	137	133	1.8
1957	39,881	7.3	147	149	4.0
1958	44,502	6.6	156	162	3.2
1959	51,369	7.7	168	122	4.3
1960	62,143	6.5	179	143	3.1
1961	69,594	6.8	191	151	3.5
1962	76,652	7.8	206	162	4.7
1963	86,710	9.4	226	178	6.2
1964	101,492	12.3	254	202	9.1
1965	111,895	11.0	281	216	7.9
1966	125,343	9.0	307	236	6.1
1967	144,839	10.6	339	266	7.9
1968	168,695	9.1	370	302	6.5
1969	195,693	9.0	403	343	6.6
1970	225,283	11.3	449	387	9.0
1971	262,125	12.9	507	441	10.6
1972	314,369	13.3	574	519	11.2
1973	407,419	12.8	648	695	10.7
1974	544,847	1.1	655	913	- 0.7
1975	581,150	4.3	683	956	2.4
1976	696,101	13.5	775	1,122	11.2
1977	815,349	10.1	853	1,288	7.9
1978	977,987	13.9	971	1,600	11.8
1979	1,180,952	8.5	1,054	1,895	6.4
1980	1,468,069	7.1	1,129	2,312	5.1
1981	1,739,794	5.7	1,193	2,548	3.8
1982	1,858,983	3.3	1,232	2,540	1.5
1983	2,044,090	7.9	1,330	2,748	6.1
1984	2,277,796	10.5	1,470	3,075	8.9
1985	2,394,837	4.7	1,539	3,295	3.4

Source: **Taiwan Statistical Data Book 1986** (Taipei: Council for Economic Planning and Development, 1986), pp. 24-29, 189.

Notes: (a)   Per capita GNP in US$ is computed at the exchange rate in effect at the end of the year.   The exchange rate was severely overvalued in the early 1950s.
(b)   Real per capita GNP growth is computed in NT$.

Table B2:   Industrial Origin of Net Domestic Product in Taiwan,
             1952-1985 (in percentages)

Year	Agriculture	Industry	Transportation and Communications	Commerce	Others
1952	35.9	18.0	3.9	18.8	23.4
1953	38.3	17.7	3.4	18.5	22.1
1954	31.7	22.2	3.7	17.6	24.8
1955	32.9	21.1	4.1	16.9	25.0
1956	31.6	22.4	3.9	17.1	25.0
1957	31.7	23.9	4.4	15.3	24.7
1958	31.0	23.9	4.1	15.7	25.3
1959	30.4	25.7	3.9	14.9	25.1
1960	32.8	24.9	4.1	14.5	23.7
1961	31.4	25.0	4.8	15.4	23.4
1962	29.2	25.7	4.6	15.9	24.6
1963	26.7	28.2	4.4	16.3	24.4
1964	28.2	28.9	4.5	15.3	23.1
1965	27.3	28.6	4.8	16.6	22.7
1966	26.2	28.8	5.4	15.2	24.4
1967	23.8	30.8	5.2	15.3	24.9
1968	22.0	32.5	5.7	15.3	24.5
1969	18.8	34.6	5.9	15.3	25.4
1970	17.9	34.7	5.9	15.5	26.0
1971	14.9	36.9	6.1	16.4	25.7
1972	14.1	40.4	6.1	15.1	24.3
1973	14.1	43.8	6.0	13.3	22.8
1974	14.5	41.2	5.7	15.2	23.4
1975	14.9	39.2	5.9	14.5	25.5
1976	13.4	42.7	5.9	13.8	24.3
1977	12.5	43.5	5.9	13.7	24.4
1978	11.2	45.1	5.9	13.5	24.3
1979	10.3	45.3	6.0	13.8	24.6
1980	9.2	45.0	6.2	14.8	24.8
1981	8.7	44.6	5.7	15.3	25.7
1982	9.2	43.0	5.7	15.3	26.8
1983	8.8	43.7	5.7	14.9	26.9
1984	7.6	45.4	5.8	14.9	26.3
1985	7.0	44.8	5.7	15.2	27.3

Source: _Taiwan Statistical Data Book 1986_ (Taipei: Council for Economic Planning and Development, 1986), p. 39.

Table B3:   Distribution of Industrial Production by Ownership in
            Taiwan, 1952-1985 (in percentages)

Year	Private	Public
1952	43.4	56.6
1953	44.1	55.9
1954	47.3	52.7
1955	48.9	51.1
1956	49.0	51.0
1957	48.7	51.3
1958	50.0	50.0
1959	51.3	48.7
1960	52.1	47.9
1961	51.8	48.2
1962	53.8	46.2
1963	55.2	44.8
1964	56.3	43.7
1965	58.7	41.3
1966	61.8	38.2
1967	65.3	34.7
1968	68.9	31.1
1969	70.6	29.4
1970	72.3	27.7
1971	79.5	20.5
1972	80.9	19.1
1973	81.1	18.9
1974	80.4	19.6
1975	81.2	18.8
1976	79.8	20.2
1977	79.5	20.5
1978	80.7	19.3
1979	81.0	19.0
1980	81.3	18.7
1981	82.1	17.9
1982	82.0	18.0
1983	82.6	17.4
1984	83.6	16.4
1985	83.9	16.1

Source: Taiwan Statistical Data Book 1986 (Taipei: Council for
Economic Planning and Development, 1986), p. 87.

Table B4:   Price Indices in Taiwan, 1953-1985   (1952 = 100)

Year	Wholesale Prices	Urban Consumer Prices
1953	108.77	118.79
1954	111.33	120.77
1955	127.02	132.74
1956	143.16	146.69
1957	153.50	157.73
1958	155.63	159.73
1959	171.62	176.62
1960	195.90	209.22
1961	202.24	225.56
1962	208.38	230.86
1963	221.83	235.99
1964	227.34	235.54
1965	216.79	235.35
1966	219.97	240.10
1967	225.55	248.14
1968	232.25	267.77
1969	231.65	281.29
1970	237.96	291.33
1971	238.02	299.55
1972	248.57	308.51
1973	305.44	333.72
1974	429.40	492.17
1975	407.63	517.91
1976	418.85	530.86
1977	430.46	568.23
1978	445.65	601.02
1979	507.28	659.68
1980	616.55	785.09
1981	663.53	913.30
1982	662.34	944.17
1983	654.52	961.54
1984	657.66	963.46
1985	640.63	951.31
1953-62 Average	7.6	8.7
1963-72 Average	1.8	2.9
1973-85 Average	7.6	9.0

Source: Taiwan Statistical Data Book 1986 (Taipei: Council for Economic Planning and Development, 1986), p. 175.

Table B5:   Revenues and Expenditures of all Levels of Government
            in Taiwan, 1954-1985   (NT$ million)

Year	Revenue	Expenditure	Balance
1954	5,302	5,356	− 54
1955	6,689	6,534	+ 155
1956	7,368	7,551	− 183
1957	9,096	8,906	+ 190
1958	10,833	10,670	+ 163
1960	12,111	12,193	− 82
1961	14,026	14,068	− 42
1962	15,040	15,414	− 374
1963	15,841	16,457	− 616
1964	19,094	18,486	+ 568
1965	23,384	22,391	+ 993
1966	25,192	23,836	+ 1,356
1967	31,639	30,727	+ 912
1968	35,235	33,002	+ 2,233
1969	45,046	41,869	+ 3,177
1970	51,215	49,153	+ 2,062
1971	57,345	54,829	+ 2,156
1972	66,368	63,668	+ 2,700
1973	89,637	79,856	+ 9,781
1974	115,832	89,934	+25,898
1975	134,034	126,436	+ 7,598
1976	166,103	149,994	+16,109
1977	193,828	192,493	+ 1,335
1978	233,644	226,900	+ 6,744
1979	287,420	254,711	+32,709
1980	366,589	345,396	+21,193
1981	437,707	433,221	+ 4,486
1982	491,069	493,741	− 2,672
1983	503,024	498,159	+ 4,865
1984	525,630	519,049	+ 6,581
1985	574,538	563,729	+10,809

Source: _Taiwan Statistical Data Book 1986_ (Taipei: Council for
Economic Planning and Development, 1986), p. 161.

Note: Fiscal years 1954-1958 covered July 1 of the designated
year through June 30 of the ensuing year.   Since 1960 the fiscal
year was changed to begin July 1 of the preceding year and to end
on June 30 of the designated year.

222

Table B6:   Foreign Trade of Taiwan, 1952-1985   (US$ million)

Year	Total	Exports	Imports	Balance
1952	303	116	187	- 71
1953	320	128	192	- 64
1954	304	93	211	- 118
1955	324	123	201	- 78
1956	312	118	194	- 76
1957	360	148	212	- 64
1958	382	156	226	- 70
1959	388	157	231	- 74
1960	461	164	297	- 133
1961	517	195	322	- 127
1962	522	218	304	- 86
1963	694	332	362	- 30
1964	861	433	428	+ 5
1965	1,006	450	556	- 106
1966	1,158	536	622	- 86
1967	1,447	641	806	- 165
1968	1,692	789	903	- 114
1969	2,262	1,049	1,213	- 164
1970	3,005	1,481	1,524	- 43
1971	3,904	2,060	1,844	+ 216
1972	5,502	2,988	2,514	+ 474
1973	8,275	4,483	3,792	+ 691
1974	12,605	5,639	6,966	- 1,327
1975	11,261	5,309	5,952	- 643
1976	15,765	8,166	7,599	+ 567
1977	17,872	9,361	8,511	+ 850
1978	23,714	12,687	11,027	+ 1,660
1979	30,877	16,103	14,774	+ 1,329
1980	39,544	19,811	19,733	+ 78
1981	43,811	22,611	21,200	+ 1,411
1982	41,092	22,204	18,888	+ 3,316
1983	45,410	25,123	20,287	+ 4,836
1984	52,415	30,456	21,959	+ 8,497
1985	50,825	30,723	20,102	+10,621

Source: *Taiwan Statistical Data Book 1986* (Taipei: Council for Economic Planning and Development, 1986), p. 202.

Table B7:   Output of Principal Industrial Products in Taiwan,
             Selected Years, 1952-1985

Item	1952	1959	1965	1971	1977	1985
Electric power (million kwh)	1,420	3,213	6,455	15,171	29,724	52,553
Coal (1,000 m.t.)	2,286	3,563	5,054	4,097	2,956	1,858
Cotton yarn (10 m.t.)	1,358	3,072	5,442	11,034	14,221	19,186
Cotton fabric (10,000 m)	8,764	15,610	26,802	62,468	84,020	61,846
Man-made fibers (10 m.t.)	-	174	550	10,310	42,347	102,869
Polyvinyl chloride (10 m.t.)	-	234	2,530	12,715	29,710	63,203
Paper (10 m.t.)	2,591	7,427	13,341	23,366	34,511	53,022
Pig iron (10 m.t.)	992	3,310	7,204	10,845	27,503	22,573
Steel bars (100 m.t.)	178	1,589	2,661	7,222	19,767	55,132
Machine tools (100 units)	-	-	87	131	2,167	9,711
Sewing machines (100 units)	250	667	794	7,879	15,466	23,154
TV sets (1,000 units)	-	-	50	1,892	4,926	3,641
Automobiles (10 units)	-	-	326	1,959	4,427	15,964
Motorcycles (10 units)	-	-	5,605	16,587	41,358	68,179
Electronic calculators (1,000 units)	-	-	-	-	4,445	48,194
Shipbuilding (10 gross tons)	57	3,607	1,606	27,971	70,229	51,671

Source: _Taiwan Statistical Data Book 1986_ (Taipei: Council for
Economic Planning and Development, 1984), pp. 90-92.

Table B8:   Gross Savings as Percentage of Gross National Product
            in Taiwan, 1952-1980

Year	Percentage
1952	9.2
1953	8.9
1954	7.7
1955	9.0
1956	9.2
1957	10.2
1958	9.9
1959	10.3
1960	12.7
1961	12.8
1962	12.4
1963	17.1
1964	19.6
1965	19.6
1966	21.5
1967	22.5
1968	22.1
1969	23.8
1970	25.5
1971	28.8
1972	32.1
1973	34.6
1974	31.7
1975	26.9
1976	32.5
1977	32.9
1978	34.9
1979	34.5
1980	33.0
1981	32.0
1982	30.4
1983	32.1
1984	33.7
1985	32.1

Source: Taiwan Statistical Data Book 1986 (Taipei: Council for
Economic Planning and Development, 1986), p. 54.

Table B9:   Population Growth in Taiwan, 1952-1985

Year	Number (1,000 persons)	Growth rate (%)
1952	8,128	3.3
1953	8,438	3.8
1954	8,749	3.7
1955	9,078	3.8
1956	9,390	3.4
1957	9,690	3.2
1958	10,039	3.6
1959	10,431	3.9
1960	10,792	3.5
1961	11,149	3.3
1962	11,512	3.3
1963	11,884	3.2
1964	12,257	3.1
1965	12,628	3.0
1966	12,993	2.9
1967	13,297	2.3
1968	13,650	2.7
1969	14,335 (a)	5.0
1970	14,676	2.4
1971	14,995	2.2
1972	15,289	2.0
1973	15,565	1.8
1974	15,852	1.8
1975	16,150	1.9
1976	16,508	2.2
1977	16,813	1.8
1978	17,136	1.9
1979	17,479	2.0
1980	17,805	1.9
1981	18,136	1.9
1982	18,458	1.8
1983	18,733	1.5
1984	19,012	1.5
1985	19,258	1.3

Source: <u>Taiwan Statistical Data Book 1986</u> (Taipei: Council for Economic Planning and Development, 1986), p. 4.

Note: (a)   Since 1969, including servicemen.

Table Cl: Gross Domestic Product in Hong Kong, 1966-1985

Year	Amount (HK$ billion)	Real growth rate (%)	Per capita GDP (HK$)	Real growth rate (%)	Per capita GDP (US$)
1966	13.6		3,758		658
1967	14.7	1.9	3,955	- 0.6	652
1968	15.7	3.2	4.118	1.0	680
1969	18.4	11.8	4,757	10.0	785
1970	21.9	9.4	5,526	6.8	912
1971	25.2	7.3	6,224	5.0	1,115
1972	30.4	11.0	7,382	9.1	1,307
1973	39.1	12.7	9,282	10.1	1,827
1974	44.6	2.2	10,320	- 0.3	2,098
1975	46.5	0.2	10,570	- 1.5	2,097
1976	59.3	17.1	13,353	15.8	2,859
1977	68.9	12.5	15,279	10.9	3,307
1978	81.2	9.5	17,656	7.4	3,671
1979	107.0	11.7	21,942	5.2	4,423
1980	137.2	11.0	27,232	7.4	5,308
1981	165.3	9.4	32,080	7.0	5,649
1982	186.9	1.1	35,229	- 0.4	5,420
1983	207.9	5.9	39,138	4.3	5,031
1984	249.0	9.4	46,418	8.5	5,936
1985	265.5	0.8	48,964	-0.3	6,277

Sources: The GDP figures are taken from Census and Statistics Department, Estimates of Gross Domestic Product 1966 to 1983 (Hong Kong, 1984), Table 12, p. 62, and Table 1, p. 7; Census and Statistics Department, "Hong Kong in Figures, 1986 Edition"; Third Quarter Economic Report 1985 (Hong Kong: Government Printer, November 1985), p. 58. Exchange rate information is taken from Hong Kong 1986: A Review of 1985 (Hong Kong: Government Printer, 1986), Appendix 3, p. 292; and Hong Kong Monthly Digest of Statistics, selected issues, Table 9.17; and Economic Background (attached to each budget), 1974-1978, Ch. 3.

Table C2:   Value of Merchandise Trade in Hong Kong, 1947-1985
(HK$ millions)

Year	Imports	Exports	Re-exports	Total trade	Balance
1947	1,550	1,217		2,767	− 333
1948	2,077	1,583		3,660	− 494
1949	2,750	2,319		5,069	− 431
1950	3,788	3,715		7,503	− 73
1951	4,879	4,433	Included	9,303	− 437
1952	3,779	2,899		6,678	− 880
1953	3,872	2,734	in	6,606	− 1,138
1954	3,435	2,417		5,852	− 1,018
1955	3,719	2,534	exports	6,253	− 1,185
1956	4,566	3,210		7,776	− 1,356
1957	5,150	3,016		8,166	− 2,134
1958	4,594	2,989		7,583	− 1,605
1959	4,949	2,282	996	8,227	− 1,671
1960	5,864	2,867	1,070	9,801	− 1,927
1961	5,970	2,939	991	9,900	− 2,040
1962	6,657	3,318	1,070	11,045	− 2,269
1963	7,412	3,831	1,160	12,403	− 2,421
1964	8,550	4,428	1,356	14,334	− 2,776
1965	8,965	5,027	1,502	15,494	− 2,436
1966	10,097	5,730	1,833	17,660	− 2,534
1967	10,449	6,700	2,081	19,230	− 1,668
1968	12,472	8,428	2,142	23,042	− 1,902
1969	14,893	10,518	2,679	28,090	− 1,696
1970	17,607	12,346	2,892	32,845	− 2,369
1971	20,256	13,749	3,414	37,420	− 3,093
1972	21,764	15,245	4,154	41,163	− 2,365
1973	29,005	19,474	6,525	55,004	− 3,006
1974	34,120	22,911	7,124	64,115	− 4,085
1975	33,472	22,859	6,973	63,304	− 3,640
1976	43,293	32,629	8,928	84,850	− 1,736
1977	48,701	35,004	9,829	93,524	− 3,868
1978	63,056	40,711	13,197	116,964	− 9,148
1979	85,837	55,912	20,022	161,771	− 9,903
1980	111,651	68,171	30,072	209,894	− 13,408
1981	138,375	80,423	41,739	260,537	− 16,212
1982	142,893	83,032	44,353	270,278	− 15,508
1983	175,442	104,415	56,294	336,151	− 14,743
1984	223,370	137,936	85,504	446,810	− 1,929
1985	231,420	129,882	105,270	466,572	+ 3,733

Sources: Hong Kong Statistics, 1947-1967, Table 6.1, p. 88; and
Hong Kong Monthly Digest of Statistics (June 1986), Table 3.1,
p. 19.

Table C3:   Revenue and Expenditure of the Hong Kong Government,
            1947-1985   (HK$ million)

Financial Year	Revenue	Expenditure	Surplus (+) Deficit (-)
1947-48	164.3	127.7	+36.6
1948-49	194.9	160.0	+35.0
1949-50	264.3	182.1	+82.1
1950-51	291.7	251.7	+40.0
1951-52	308.6	275.9	+32.7
1952-53	384.6	311.7	+72.8
1953-54	396.9	355.4	+41.5
1954-55	434.5	373.3	+61.1
1955-56	454.7	402.5	+52.3
1956-57	509.7	469.5	+40.1
1957-58	584.2	532.7	+51.5
1958-59	629.3	590.0	+39.4
1959-60	664.6	710.0	-45.3
1960-61	859.2	845.3	+13.9
1961-62	1,030.4	953.2	+77.2
1962-63	1,253.1	1,113.3	+139.8
1963-64	1,393.9	1,295.4	+98.5
1964-65	1,518.3	1,440.5	+77.8
1965-66	1,631.7	1,769.1	-137.4
1966-67	1,817.8	1,806.1	+11.7
1967-68	1,899.5	1,766.0	+133.5
1968-69	2,081.1	1,873.0	+208.1
1969-70	2,480.7	2,032.2	+448.5
1970-71	3,070.9	2,452.2	+618.7
1971-72	3,541.0	2,901.0	+640.0
1972-73	4,936.0	4,300.0	+636.0
1973-74	5,240.8	5,169.2	+71.6
1974-75	5,875.3	6,255.2	-379.9
1975-76(b)	6,255.0	6,023.0	+232.0
1976-77	7,494.0	6,577.0	+917.0
1977-78	9,383.0	8,158.0	+1,225.0
1978-79	12,442.0	10,956.0	+1,486.0
1979-80	16,796.0	13,821.0	+2,975.0
1980-81	30,187.0	19,675.0	+10,512.0
1981-82	33,494.0	26,795.0	+6,699.0
1982-83	31,097.6	34,597.8	-3,500.2
1983-84	30,400.0	33,393.0	-2,993.0
1984-85	36,342.5	39,901.7	-3,559.2
1985-86	39,911.0	38,813.0	+98.0

Sources: Hong Kong Statistics, 1947-1967, Table 9.11, p. 158;
Supporting Financial Statements and Statistical Appendices from
the Estimates of Revenue and Expenditure for the Year Ending 31st
March 1984, Appendix I (Hong Kong: Government Printer, 1984);
The 1986-87 Budget; and Hong Kong 1986, pp. 296-298.

Note: From 1975 on, the figures incorporate adjustments in
several budgetary categories.

Table C4: Contribution of Economic Sectors to Hong Kong GDP, 1982

Sector	Percentage	HK$ million
Agriculture and fishing	0.7	1,229
Mining and quarrying	0.2	296
Manufacturing	21.8	37,890
Electricity, gas, and water	1.4	2,405
Construction	7.3	12,611
Wholesale and retail, import/export trades, restaurants and hotels	19.5	33,878
Transport, storage, and communication	8.0	13,850
Financing, insurance, real estate, and business services	22.1	38,369
Community, social, and personal services	14.9	25,921
Ownership of premises	10.9	19,038

Source: Estimates of Gross Domestic Product 1966 to 1983, Table 10, p. 22.

Notes: (1) The total adds to 106.8 percent, which reflects an imputed service charge equal to net interest receipts for the banking sector. Hence, to reach 100 percent, 6.8 percent must be subtracted as a nominal account to which is debited the total imputed banking charge. This sector may thus be described as a provision for the adjustment for financial services. (2) At the end of 1982, the exchange rate was US$1 = HK$6.52.

Table C5:   Population Growth in Hong Kong, 1947-1985

Year	Mid-year
1947	1,750,000
1948	1,800,000
1949	1,857,000
1950	2,237,000
1951	2,015,300
1952	2,125,300
1953	2,242,200
1954	2,364,900
1955	2,490,400
1956	2,614,600
1957	2,736,300
1958	2,854,100
1959	2,967,400
1960	3,075,300
1961	3,174,700
1962	3,346,600
1963	3,503,700
1964	3,594,200
1965	3,692,300
1966	3,732,400
1967	3,834,000
1968	3,802,700
1969	3,863,900
1970	3,959,000
1971	4,045,300
1972	4,078,400
1973	4,159,900
1974	4,248,700
1975	4,395,800
1976	4,443,800
1977	4,513,900
1978	4,606,300
1979	4,900,000
1980	5,038,500
1981	5,154,100
1982	5,232,900
1983	5,313,200
1984	5,364,000
1985	5,422,800

Sources: Hong Kong Statistics 1947-1967, Table 2.2, p. 14; and
Monthly Digest of Statistics (annual August issue), Table 15.3.

Table C6:   Exchange Rate of the Hong Kong Dollar, 1946-1985

Year	US$1 = HK$
12/18/1946 - 9/18/1949	3.97
9/18/1949 - 11/20/1967	5.71
11/20/1967 - 11/23/1967	6.67
11/23/1967 - 12/18/1971	6.06
12/18/1971 - 7/6/1972	5.58
7/6/1972 - 2/14/1973	5.65
1974 (a)	4.92
1975	5.04
1976	4.67
1977	4.62
1978	4.81
1979	4.96
1980	5.14
1981	5.68
1982	6.50
1983	7.78
1984	7.82
1985	7.80

Sources: Hong Kong 1986, Appendix 3, p. 292; and Monthly Digest of Statistics, selected issues.

Note: (a)   As of December 31st.

232

Table C7: Gross Domestic Fixed Capital Formation in Hong Kong,
           1966-1985   (in percentage of GDP)

Year	Percentage
1966	33.9
1967	21.3
1968	17.7
1969	17.3
1970	21.7
1971	26.1
1972	25.1
1973	23.2
1974	23.9
1975	22.7
1976	21.8
1977	25.5
1978	27.5
1979	31.0
1980	33.2
1981	33.5
1982	31.2
1983	26.5
1984	25.9
1985	20.4

Source: **Estimates of Gross Domestic Product 1966 to 1983**, Table
3, p. 10, Table 14, p. 64; and "Hong Kong in Figures, 1986
Edition."

BIBLIOGRAPHY

MAINLAND CHINA

Ashton, Basil, Kenneth Hill, Alan Piazza, and Robin Zeitz. "Famine in China, 1958–61." *Population and Development Review* 10, no. 4 (December 1984), pp. 613–645.

Barber, Noel. *The Fall of Shanghai*. New York: Coward, McCann & Geoghegan, 1979.

Barker, Randolph, Radha Sinha, and Beth Rose, eds. *The Chinese Agricultural Economy*. Boulder, Colo.: Westview Press, 1982.

Barnett, A. Doak. *China's Economy in Global Perspective*. Washington, D.C.: Brookings Institution, 1981.

Baum, Richard, ed. *China's Four Modernizations: The New Technological Revolution*. Boulder, Colo.: Westview Press, 1980.

Bonavia, David. *The Chinese*. New York: Lippincott and Crowell, 1980.

Butterfield, Fox. *China: Alive in the Bitter Sea*. New York: New York Times Books, 1982.

Byrd, William. *China's Financial System: The Changing Role of Banks*. Boulder, Colo.: Westview Press, 1982.

Byrd, William, "Recent Chinese Economic Reforms: Studies of Two Industrial Enterprises." World Bank Staff Working Papers; No. 652. Washington, D.C.: The World Bank, 1984.

Chao, Kang. *Agricultural Production in Communist China, 1949–1965*. Madison: University of Wisconsin Press, 1971.

_____. *The Rate and Pattern of Industrial Growth in Communist China*. Ann Arbor: University of Michigan Press, 1965.

Cheng, Chu-yuan. *China's Economic Development: Growth and Structural Change*. Boulder, Colo.: Westview Press, 1982.

Chou, Shun-hsin. *The Chinese Inflation 1937–1949*. New York: Columbia University Press, 1963.

Chow, Gregory C. *The Chinese Economy*. New York: Harper & Row, 1985.

233

Constitution of the People's Republic of China. Adopted on December 4, 1982 by the 5th National People's Congress of the People's Republic of China at its Fifth Session. Beijing: Foreign Languages Press, 1983.

"Decision of the Central Committee of the Communist Party of China on Reform of the Economic Structure." Adopted by the 12th Central Committee of the Communist Party of China at its Third Plenary Session on October 20, 1984. *Beijing Review* 27, no. 44 (October 29, 1984), pp. i–xvi.

Deleyne, Jan. *The Chinese Economy.* New York: Harper Torch books, 1973.

Dernberger, Robert F., ed. *China's Developmental Experience in Comparative Perspective.* Cambridge: Harvard University Press, 1980.

Dittmer, Lowell. "Ideology and Organization in Post-Mao China." *Asian Survey* 24, no. 3 (March 1984), pp. 349–369.

_____. "The 12th Congress of the Communist Party of China." *The China Quarterly,* no. 93 (March 1983), pp. 108–124.

Donnithorne, Audrey. "The Chinese Economy Today." *Journal of Northeast Asian Studies* 2, no. 3 (September 1983), pp. 3–21.

_____. *China's Economic System.* New York: Praeger Publishers, 1967.

Eckstein, Alexander. *China's Economic Development.* Ann Arbor: University of Michigan Press, 1975.

_____. *China's Economic Revolution.* Cambridge: Cambridge University Press, 1977.

_____. *The National Income of Communist China.* Glencoe, Ill.: Free Press, 1961.

Eckstein, Alexander, ed. *Quantitative Measures of China's Economic Output.* Ann Arbor: University of Michigan Press, 1979.

Field, Robert Michael. "Changes in Chinese Industry Since 1978." *The China Quarterly,* no. 100 (December 1984), pp. 742–761.

_____. "Slow Growth of Labor Productivity in Chinese Industry, 1952–81." *The China Quarterly,* no. 96 (December 1983), pp. 641–664.

Fitting, George. "Export Processing Zones in Taiwan and the People's Republic of China." *Asian Survey* 22, no. 8 (August 1982), pp. 732–744.

Gold, Thomas B. "Just in Time! China Battles Spiritual Pollution on the Eve of 1984." *Asian Survey* 24, no. 9 (September 1984), pp. 947–974.

Goodstadt, Leo. *China's Search for Plenty: The Economics of Mao Tse-tung.* New York: Weatherhill, 1972.

Greenwood, John G. "People's Republic of China: Problems of Monetary Control." *Asian Monetary Monitor* 9, no. 4 (July–August 1985), pp. 13–21.

Hamrin, Carol Lee. "Competing 'Policy Packages' in Post-Mao China." *Asian Survey* 24, no. 5 (May 1984), pp. 487–518.

Harding, Harry. "Reform in China: A Mid-course Assessment." *Journal of Northeast Asian Studies* 3, no. 2 (Summer 1984), pp. 3–26.

Howe, Christopher. *China's Economy: A Basic Guide.* New York: Basic Books, 1978.

_____. *Wage Patterns and the Wage Policy in Modern China 1919–1972.* New York: Cambridge University Press, 1974.

_____. *Employment and Economic Growth in Urban China 1949–1957.* New York: Cambridge University Press, 1973.

Howe, Christopher, ed. *Shanghai: Revolution and Development in an Asian Metropolis.* Cambridge: Cambridge University Press, 1981.

Hsiao, Katharine H.Y. *Money and Banking in the Chinese Mainland.* Mainland China Economic Series No. 1. Taipei: Chung-Hua Institution for Economic Research, June 1984.

_____. *Money and Monetary Policy in Communist China.* New York: Columbia University Press, 1971.

Hsin Chang. "The 1982–83 Overinvestment Crisis in China." *Asian Survey* 24, no. 12 (December 1984), pp. 1275–1301.

Hsu, Robert C. "Grain Procurement and Distribution in China's Rural Areas." *Asian Survey* 24, no. 12 (December 1984), pp. 1229–1246.

_____. "Agricultural Financial Policies in China, 1949–1980." *Asian Survey* 22, no. 4 (April 1982), pp. 638–658.

International Monetary Fund. *International Financial Statistics: Supplement on Exchange Rates.* Supplement Series; No. 9 (1985).

Ishikawa, Shigeru. "China's Economic Growth Since 1949—An Assessment." *The China Quarterly*, no. 94 (June 1982), pp. 242–281.

Johnson, Constance A. "The 1982 Constitution of the PRC: One Small Step for Legal Development." *Journal of Chinese Studies* 2, no. 1 (April 1985), pp. 87–93.

Johnson, D. Gale. *Progress of Economic Reform in the People's Republic of China.* Washington, D.C.: American Enterprise Institute, 1982.

Johnson, Graham E. "The Production Responsibility System in Chinese Agriculture: Some Examples from Guangdong." *Pacific Affairs* 55, no. 3 (Fall 1982), pp. 430–451.

Kallgren, Joyce. "China in 1983: The Turmoil of Modernization." *Asian Survey* 24, no. 1 (January 1984), pp. 60–80.

King, Frank H.H. *A Concise Economic History of Modern China, 1840–1961.* New York: Praeger Publishers, 1970.

Klatt, W. "The Staff of Life: Living Standards in China." *The China Quarterly*, no. 93 (March 1983), pp. 17–50.

Koziara, Edward Clifford, and Chiou-shuang Yan. "The Distribution System for Producers' Goods in China." *The China Quarterly*, no. 96 (December 1983), pp. 689–702.

Kueh, Y.Y. "Economic Reform in China at the *Xian* Level." *The China Quarterly*, no. 96 (December 1983), pp. 665–688.

Kueh, Y.Y., and Christopher Howe. "China's International Trade: Policy and Organizational Change and Their Place in the 'Economic Readjustment.'" *The China Quarterly*, no. 100 (December 1984), pp. 813–848.

Lardy, Nicholas R. "Consumption and Living Standards in China, 1978–83." *The China Quarterly*, no. 100 (December 1984), pp. 849–865.

_____. *Agriculture in China's Economic Development.* Cambridge: Cambridge University Press, 1983.

_____. "Agricultural Prices in China." World Bank Staff Working Paper No. 606. Washington, D.C.: The World Bank, 1983.

_____. *Economic Growth and Distribution in China.* New York: Cambridge University Press, 1978.

Lardy, Nicholas R., and Kenneth Lieberthal, eds. and introduction. *Ch'en Yun's Strategy for China's Development: A Non-Maoist Alternative.* Armonk, N.Y.: Sharpe, 1982.

Lee, Hong-yung. "Deng Xiaoping's Reform of the Chinese Bureaucracy." *Journal of Northeast Asian Studies* 1, no. 2 (June 1982), pp. 21–35.

Legge, James, trans. *Confucius: Confucian Analects, The Great Learning and the Doctrine of the Mean.* New York: Dover Publications, 1971. Replication of second revised edition. Oxford: Clarendon Press, 1893.

Lethbridge, Henry James, intro. *All About Shanghai: A Standard Guidebook.* Hong Kong: Oxford University Press, 1983. Reprint of 1934–1935 edition. Shanghai: The University Press, 1934.

Li Choh-ming. *The Economic Development of Communist China.* Berkeley: University of California Press, 1959.

Liu, Jung-Chao. "Wages and Profits of Selected Industries in China." *Economic Development and Cultural Change* 26, no. 4 (July 1978), pp. 747–761.

Ma Hong. *New Strategy for China's Economy.* Beijing: New World Press, 1983.

Mosher, Steven W. *Journey to the Forbidden China.* New York: Free Press, 1985.

_____ . *Broken Earth: The Rural Chinese.* New York: Free Press, 1983.

Murphey, Rhoads. *Shanghai: Key to Modern China.* Cambridge: Harvard University Press, 1953.

Myers, Ramon H. "How Well Did American Economists Understand China's Economy?" *Issues and Studies* 20, no. 11 (November 1984), pp. 33–49.

_____ . "Can Communist China's New Price System Work?" *Issues and Studies* 19, no. 10 (October 1983), pp. 33–48.

_____ . *The Chinese Economy: Past and Present.* Belmont, Calif.: Wadsworth, 1980.

Peebles, Gavin. "Inflation in the People's Republic of China, 1950–1982." *Three Banks Review*, no. 142 (June 1984), pp. 37–57.

_____ . "Money and Prices in the People's Republic of China, 1950–1982." Mimeo, n.d.

Perkins, Dwight H. "China's Economic Policy and Performance During the Cultural Revolution and its Aftermath." Development Discussion Paper No. 161. Cambridge: Harvard Institute for International Development, January 1984.

_____ . "Research on the Economy of the People's Republic of China." *Journal of Asian Studies* 42, no. 2 (February 1983), pp. 345–372.

_____ . *Agricultural Development in China 1368–1968.* Chicago: Aldine, 1969.

_____ . *Market Control and Planning in Communist Countries.* Cambridge: Harvard University Press, 1966.

Perkins, Dwight H. and Shahid Yusuf. *Rural Development in China.* Baltimore and London: The Johns Hopkins University Press for the World Bank, 1984.

Perkins, Dwight H., ed. *China's Modern Economy in Historical Perspective.* Stanford: Stanford University Press, 1975.

Piazza, Alan. "Trends in Food and Nutrient Availability in China, 1950–81." World Bank Staff Working Papers. No. 607. Washington, D.C.: World Bank, 1983.

Prybyla, Jan S. "Economic Problems of Communism: A Case Study of China." *Asian Survey* 22, no. 12 (December 1982), pp. 1206–1237.

_____ . "Where Is China's Economy Headed? A Systems Analysis." *Journal of Northeast Asian Studies* 1, no. 4 (December 1982), pp. 3–24.

_____ . "Key Issues in the Chinese Economy." *Asian Survey* 21, no. 9 (September 1981), pp. 925–946.

_____ . "Changes in the Chinese Economy: An Interpretation." *Asian Survey* 19, no. 5 (May 1979), pp. 409–435.

_____ . *The Chinese Economy: Problems and Policies.* Columbia: University of South Carolina Press, 1978.

Rawski, Thomas G. *Economic Growth and Employment in China.* New York: Oxford University Press for the World Bank, 1979.

Reynolds, Paul D. *China's International Banking and Financial System.* New York: Praeger Publishers, 1982.

Schram, Stuart R. " 'Economics in Command?' Ideology and Policy Since the Third Plenum, 1978-84." *The China Quarterly,* no. 99 (September 1984), pp. 417-461.

Sigurdson, Jon. *Rural Industrialization in China.* Cambridge: Harvard University Press, 1977.

Solinger, Dorothy J. *Chinese Business Under Socialism: The Politics of Domestic Commerce, 1949-1980.* Berkeley, Los Angeles, and London: University of California Press, 1984.

_____. "The Fifth National People's Congress and the Process of Policy Making: Reform, Readjustment, and the Opposition." *Asian Survey* 22, no. 12 (December 1982), pp. 1238-1275.

_____. "Economic Reform via Reformation in China: Where do Rightist Ideas come from?" *Asian Survey* 21, no. 9 (September 1981), pp. 947-960.

State Statistical Bureau, People's Republic of China. *China: A Statistical Survey in 1986.* Hong Kong: Produced by the Longman Group for New World Press and China Statistical Information and Consultancy Service Center, 1986.

_____. *Statistical Yearbook of China 1985.* Hong Kong: Economic Information and Agency, 1985.

Stoltenberg, Clyde D. "China's Special Economic Zones: Their Development and Prospects." *Asian Survey* 24, no. 6 (June 1984), pp. 637-654.

Travers, Lee. "Post-1978 Rural Economic Policy and Peasant Income in China." *The China Quarterly,* no. 98 (June 1984), pp. 241-259.

Trescott, Paul B. "Incentives Versus Equality: What Does China's Recent Experience Show?" *World Development* 13, no. 2 (1985), pp. 205-217.

United States Congress Joint Economic Committee, ed. *China's Economy Looks Toward the Year 2000.* Washington, D.C.: Government Printing Office, 1986.

_____. *China Under the Four Modernizations.* Washington, D.C.: Government Printing Office, 1982.

_____. *Chinese Economy Post-Mao.* Washington, D.C.: Government Printing Office, 1978.

_____. *China: A Reassessment of the Economy.* Washington, D.C.: Government Printing Office, 1975.

Vogel, Ezra. *Canton Under Communism.* Cambridge: Harvard University Press, 1969.

Walker, Kenneth R. "Chinese Agriculture During the Period of the Readjustment, 1978-83." *The China Quarterly,* no. 100 (December 1984), pp. 783-812.

Wang, Tong-eng. *Economic Policies and Price Stability in China.* Berkeley: University of California Press, Center for Chinese Studies, Chinese Research Monograph No. 16, 1980.

Weng, Byron. "Some Key Aspects of the 1982 Draft Constitution of the People's Republic of China." *The China Quarterly,* no. 91 (September 1982), pp. 492-506.

World Bank. *China: Long-Term Development Issues and Options.* A World Bank Country Economic Report. Baltimore and London: Johns Hopkins University Press for the World Bank, 1985.

———. *China: Socialist Economic Development.* Vol. I. The Economy, Statistical System, and Basic Data. Washington, D.C., 1983.

Wortzel, Larry M. "Incentive Mechanisms and Policies of the Eleventh Central Committee." *Asian Survey* 21, no. 9 (September 1981), pp. 961–976.

Wu, Yuan-li. *The Economy of Communist China.* New York: Praeger Publishers, 1965.

Wu, Yuan-li, and Chun-hsi Wu, *Economic Development in Southeast Asia: The Chinese Dimension.* Stanford: Hoover Press, 1980.

Xu Dixin et al. *China's Search for Economic Growth: The Chinese Economy Since 1949.* Beijing: New World Press, 1982.

Xue Muqiao. *China's Socialist Economy.* Beijing: Foreign Language Press, 1981.

Yu Guangyuan, ed. *China's Socialist Modernization.* Beijing: Foreign Languages Press, 1984.

Zagoria, Donald S. "China's Quiet Revolution." *Foreign Affairs* (Spring 1984), pp. 879–904.

Zweig, David. "Opposition to Change in Rural China: The System of Responsibility and People's Communes." *Asian Survey* 23, no. 7 (July 1983), pp. 879–900.

TAIWAN

Belassa, Bela. *The Newly Industrializing Countries in the World Economy.* London: Pergamon Press, 1981.

Belassa, Bela, ed. *Development Strategies in Semi-Industrial Countries.* Baltimore: Johns Hopkins Press, 1981.

Central Bank of China. *Annual Report.*

Central Bank of China, Economics Research Department. *Financial Statistics Monthly, Taiwan District, the Republic of China.*

———. *Geographical Survey of the Economy of Taiwan District, the Republic of China.* June 1985.

Conference on Experiences and Lessons of Economic Development in Taiwan. December 18–20, 1981. The Institute of Economics, Academia Sinica. Taipei, Taiwan, Republic of China.

Constitution, Republic of China. Taipei: Government Information Office, 1984.

Council for Economic Planning and Development, Executive Yuan. *Taiwan Statistical Data Book 1986.*

Directorate-General of Budget, Accounting, and Statistics, Executive Yuan. *National Income of the Republic of China.*

———. *Quarterly National Economic Trends, Taiwan Area, the Republic of China.*

———. *Statistical Yearbook of the Republic of China.*

———. *Report on the Survey of Personal Income Distribution in Taiwan Area, Republic of China.*

Fei, John C.H., Gustav Ranis, and Shirley W.Y. Kuo. *Growth with Equity: The Taiwan Case.* London: Oxford University Press, 1979.

Galenson, Walter, ed. *Economic Growth and Structural Change in Taiwan: The Postwar Experience of the Republic of China.* Ithaca, N.Y.: Cornell University Press, 1979.

Ho, Samuel P.S. *Economic Development in Taiwan: 1860–1970.* New Haven and London: Yale University Press, 1978.

Jacoby, Neil H. *U.S. Aid to Taiwan: A Study of Foreign Aid, Self-Help, and Development*. New York: Praeger Publishers, 1966.

Koo, A.Y.C. *The Role of Land Reform in Economic Development—A Case Study of Taiwan*. New York: Praeger Publishers, 1968.

Kuo, Shirley W.Y. *The Taiwan Economy in Transition*. Boulder, Colo.: Westview Press, 1983.

Kuo, Shirley W.Y., Gustav Ranis, and John C.H. Fei. *The Taiwan Success Story: Rapid Growth with Improved Distribution in the Republic of China, 1952-1979*. Boulder, Colo.: Westview Press, 1981.

Li, K.T. *The Experience of Dynamic Economic Growth on Taiwan*. Taipei: Mei Ya, 1976.

Lin, C.Y. *Industrialization in Taiwan, 1946-1972*. New York: Praeger Publishers, 1973.

Lu, Alexander Ya-li. "Future Domestic Developments in the Republic of China on Taiwan." *Asian Survey* 25, no. 11 (November 1985), pp. 1075-1095.

McKinnon, Ronald I. *Money and Capital in Economic Development*. Washington, D.C.: Brookings Institution, 1973.

Ministry of Economic Affairs. *Economic Development, Taiwan, Republic of China*. April 1984.

Ministry of Finance, Department of Statistics. *Monthly Statistics of Exports and Imports, The Republic of China*.

———. *Yearbook of Financial Statistics of the Republic of China*.

Myers, Ramon H. "The Economic Transformation of the Republic of China on Taiwan." *The China Quarterly*, no. 99 (September 1984), pp. 500-528.

Research, Development, and Evaluation Commission, Executive Yuan. *Annual Review of Government Administration, Republic of China 1981-1982*.

Sih, Paul K.T., ed. *Taiwan in Modern Times*. New York: St. John's University Press, 1973.

Werner, Roy A. "Taiwan's Trade Flows: The Underpinning of Political Legitimacy?" *Asian Survey* 25, no. 11 (November 1985), pp. 1096-1114.

World Bank. *World Development Report*. Annual issue.

Wu, Yuan-li. *Becoming an Industrialized Nation: ROC's Development on Taiwan*. New York: Praeger Publishers, 1985.

HONG KONG

"A Draft Agreement Between the Government of the United Kingdom and Northern Ireland and the Government of the People's Republic of China on the Future of Hong Kong." Miscellaneous No. 20 (1984). London: Her Majesty's Stationery Office, 1984.

Beazer, William F. *The Commercial Future of Hong Kong*. New York: Praeger Publishers, 1978.

Blakely, Brian L. *The Colonial Office, 1868-1892*. Durham, N.C.: Duke University Press, 1972.

Bonavia, David. *Hong Kong 1997*. Hong Kong: South China Morning Post, 1983.

Budget Economic Background. Hong Kong: Government Printer, various years.

Bueno de Mesquita, Bruce, David Newman, and Alvin Rabushka. *Forecasting Political Events: The Future of Hong Kong*. New Haven and London: Yale University Press, 1986.

Chang, E.R. *Report on the National Income Survey of Hong Kong.* Hong Kong: Government Printer, 1969.

Cheng, Joseph Y.S. *Hong Kong: In Search of a Future.* Hong Kong: Oxford University Press, 1984.

Cheng, T.Y. *The Economy of Hong Kong.* Hong Kong: Far East Publications, 1977.

Chou, K.R. *The Hong Kong Economy.* Hong Kong: Academic Publications, 1966.

Chow, Steven C., and Gustav F. Papanek. "Laissez-Faire, Growth and Equity—Hong Kong." *The Economic Journal* 91 (June 1981), pp. 466–485.

Endacott, G.B. *A History of Hong Kong.* Hong Kong: Oxford University Press, 1964.

England, Joe, and John Rear. *Chinese Labor Under British Rule.* Hong Kong: Oxford University Press, 1975.

Estimates of Gross Domestic Product 1966 to 1983. Hong Kong: Government Printer, 1984.

Financial Secretary. *Annual Budget Speeches.* Hong Kong: Government Printer, various years.

First Quarter Economic Report. Hong Kong: Government Printer, various years.

Geiger, Theodore. *Tales of Two City-States: The Developmental Progress of Hong Kong and Singapore.* Washington, D.C.: National Planning Association, 1973.

Greenwood, John G. "Hong Kong: Adjusting to the Link." *Asian Monetary Monitor* 9, no. 4 (July–August 1985), pp. 2–12.

———. "Why the HK$/US$ Linked Rate System Should Not Be Changed." *Asian Monetary Monitor* 8, no. 6 (November–December 1984), pp. 2–17.

———. "The Operation of the New Exchange Rate Mechanism." *Asian Monetary Monitor* 8, no. 1 (January–February 1984), pp. 2–12.

———. "The Stabilization of the Hong Kong Dollar." *Asian Monetary Monitor* 7, no. 6 (November–December 1983), pp. 9–37.

———. "How to Rescue the HK$: Three Practical Proposals." *Asian Monetary Monitor* 7, no. 5 (September–October 1983), pp. 11–39.

———. "Hong Kong's Financial Crisis: History, Analysis, Prescription." *Asian Monetary Monitor* 6, no. 6 (November–December, 1982), pp. 2–69.

Half-yearly Economic Report. Hong Kong: Government Printer, various years.

Ho, H.C.Y. *The Fiscal System of Hong Kong.* London: Croom Helm, 1979.

Hong Kong 1986: A Review of 1985. Hong Kong: Government Printer, 1986 (and various other years).

Hong Kong Hansard (proceedings of the Legislative Council).

Hong Kong Monthly Digest of Statistics. Census and Statistics Department, Hong Kong.

Hong Kong Statistics 1947–1967. Census and Statistics Department, Hong Kong, 1969.

Hopkins, Keith, ed. *Hong Kong: The Industrial Colony.* Hong Kong: Oxford University Press, 1971.

Hsia, Ronald, and Laurence Chau. *Industrialization, Employment and Income Distribution: A Case Study of Hong Kong.* London: Croom Helm, 1978.

Hughes, Richard. *Hong Kong: Borrowed Place—Borrowed Time.* London: Andre Deutsch, 1968.

Jao, Y.C. "The 1997 Issue and Hong Kong's Financial Crisis." *Journal of Chinese Studies* 2, no. 1 (April 1985), pp. 113–153.

———. *Banking and Currency in Hong Kong: A Study of Postwar Financial Development.* London: Macmillan, 1974.

Jao, Y.C., and Leung Chi-keung, Peter Wesley-Smith, and Wong Siu-lin, eds. *Hong Kong and 1997: Strategies for the Future.* Hong Kong: Center of Asian Studies, University of Hong Kong, 1985.

Jeffries, Sir Charles. *The Colonial Office.* London: George Allen & Unwin, 1956.

Johnson, Chalmers. "The Mousetrapping of Hong Kong." *Asian Survey* 24, no. 9 (September 1984), pp. 887–909.

Lethbridge, David, ed. *The Business Environment in Hong Kong.* Hong Kong: Oxford University Press, 1980.

Letters Patent and Royal Instructions to the Governor of Hong Kong. Hong Kong: Government Printer, 1972.

Miners, Norman. *The Government and Politics of Hong Kong,* 3rd ed. Hong Kong: Oxford University Press, 1981.

Newton, E. *Hong Kong Taxation—A Taxpayer's Guide.* Hong Kong: Chinese University Press of Hong Kong, 1977.

Overholt, William H. "Hong Kong and the Crisis of Sovereignty." *Asian Survey* 24, no. 4 (April 1984), pp. 471–484.

Rabushka, Alvin. *Hong Kong: A Study in Economic Freedom.* Chicago: University of Chicago Press for the Graduate School of Business, 1979.

———. *Value for Money: The Hong Kong Budgetary Process.* Stanford, Calif.: Hoover Press, 1976.

———. *The Changing Face of Hong Kong: New Departures in Public Policy.* Washington, D.C.: American Enterprise Institute, 1973.

Riedel, James. *The Industrialization of Hong Kong.* Tubingen: Institut for Welwirt shaft an der Universitat Kiel, 1974.

Rules and Regulations for Her Majesty's Colonial Service. London: Her Majesty's Stationery Office, 1843.

Smith, H. *John Stuart Mill's Other Island: A Study of the Economic Development of Hong Kong.* London: Institute of Economic Affairs, 1966.

Supporting Financial Statements and Statistical Appendices from the Estimates of Revenue and Expenditure. Hong Kong: Government Printer, various years.

Szczepanik, Edward F. *The Economic Growth of Hong Kong.* London: Oxford University Press, 1958.

Third Quarter Economic Report. Hong Kong: Government Report, various years.

"White Paper: The Further Development of Representative Government in Hong Kong." Hong Kong, November 1984.

Willoughby, Peter G. *Hong Kong Taxation—A Miscellany.* Hong Kong: South China Morning Post, 1977.

World Development Report 1984. New York: Oxford University Press for the World Bank, 1984.

Youngson, A.J., ed. *China and Hong Kong: The Economic Nexus.* Hong Kong: Oxford University Press, 1983.

———. *Hong Kong: Economic Growth and Policy.* Hong Kong: Oxford University Press, 1982.

ENGLISH-LANGUAGE SERIALS

Asiabanking (Hong Kong)

Asiaweek (Hong Kong)
Atlantic
Beijing Review (Beijing)
Business Week
Economist
Euromoney
Far Eastern Economic Review (Hong Kong)
Forbes
Fortune
Hongkong Standard (Hong Kong)
Hong Kong Economic Papers (Hong Kong)
Industry of Free China (Taipei)
New York Times
Newsweek
South China Morning Post (Hong Kong)
Time
Wall Street Journal

INDEX

ABOUT THE BOOK
AND AUTHOR

In a thoroughly researched and clearly written account of the development experiences of mainland China, Taiwan, and Hong Kong, Alvin Rabushka examines three societies with similar populations but very different political and economic institutions. Rejecting one-dimensional explanations of successful development, Rabushka looks at the way in which the incentives and institutions of the market economy have combined with the Confucian traditions of thrift, hard work, and education to produce prosperity for Hong Kong and Taiwan.

Following a different strategy, the Chinese Communists first adopted the Soviet model of central economic planning, with disappointing results. But since 1978 Deng Xiaoping has deemphasized central planning in favor of greater reliance upon market forces. Rabushka documents this change and looks at how productivity has increased on the mainland as a result.

Rabushka's discussion is a model of balanced analysis of the factors behind economic growth: people, resources, politics, and economics. The reader will come away not only with a grasp of the fundamentals of development strategy, but also with a solid background in the recent political and economic history of what will surely be three enormously important economic forces in the next century. Rabushka's conclusion thoughtfully surveys the future prospects of each. Useful for the scholar and accessible to the layman, this book is essential reading for any citizen concerned with East Asia today.

Alvin Rabushka, currently a Senior Fellow at the Hoover Institution of Stanford University, received his B.A. in Far Eastern studies and his M.A. and Ph.D. in political science from Washington University.

253

He served as assistant professor, associate professor, and professor of political science at the University of Rochester from 1968 to 1976. He has lectured at universities in the Far East, including the Fudan University in Shanghai. Dr. Rabushka is the author of numerous books and monographs, including four books on Hong Kong—*The Changing Face of Hong Kong: New Departures in Public Policy; Forecasting Political Events: The Future of Hong Kong; Hong Kong—A Study in Economic Freedom;* and *Value for Money; The Hong Kong Budgetary Process* as well as three books on tax reform—*The Flat Tax; Low Tax, Simple Tax, Flat Tax;* and *The Tax Revolt.* He is also a frequent contributor to the *Wall Street Journal.*

PACIFIC RESEARCH INSTITUTE
FOR PUBLIC POLICY

The Pacific Research Institute for Public Policy is an independent, tax-exempt research and educational organization. The Institute's program is designed to broaden public understanding of the nature and effects of market processes and government policy.

With the bureaucratization and politicization of modern society, scholars, business and civic leaders, the media, policymakers, and the general public have too often been isolated from meaningful solutions to critical public issues. To facilitate a more active and enlightened discussion of such issues, the Pacific Research Institute sponsors in-depth studies into the nature of and possible solutions to major social, economic, and environmental problems. Undertaken regardless of the sanctity of any particular government program, or the customs, prejudices, or temper of the times, the Institute's studies aim to ensure that alternative approaches to currently problematic policy areas are fully evaluated, the best remedies discovered, and these findings made widely available. The results of this work are published as books and monographs, and form the basis for numerous conference and media programs.

Through this program of research and commentary, the Institute seeks to evaluate the premises and consequences of government policy, and provide the foundations necessary for constructive policy reform.

PACIFIC STUDIES IN PUBLIC POLICY

FORESTLANDS
Public and Private
Edited by Robert T. Deacon and M. Bruce Johnson
Foreword by B. Delworth Gardner

URBAN TRANSIT
The Private Challenge to Public Transportation
Edited by Charles A. Lave
Foreword by John Meyer

POLITICS, PRICES, AND PETROLEUM
The Political Economy of Energy
By David Glasner
Foreword by Paul W. MacAvoy

RIGHTS AND REGULATION
Ethical, Political, and Economic Issues
Edited by Tibor M. Machan and M. Bruce Johnson
Foreword by Aaron Wildavsky

FUGITIVE INDUSTRY
The Economics and Politics of Deindustrialization
By Richard B. McKenzie
Foreword by Finis Welch

MONEY IN CRISIS
The Federal Reserve, the Economy, and Monetary Reform
Edited by Barry N. Siegel
Foreword by Leland B. Yeager

NATURAL RECOURCES
Bureaucratic Myths and Environmental Management
By Richard Stroup and John Baden
Foreword by William Niskanen

FIREARMS AND VIOLENCE
Issues of Public Policy
Edited by Don B. Kates, Jr.
Foreword by John Kaplan

WATER RIGHTS
Scarce Resource Allocation, Bureaucracy, and the Environment
Edited by Terry L. Anderson
Foreword by Jack Hirshleifer

LOCKING UP THE RANGE
Federal Land Controls and Grazing
By Gary D. Libecap
Foreword by Jonathan R. T. Hughes

THE PUBLIC SCHOOL MONOPOLY
A Critical Analysis of Education and the State in American Society
Edited by Robert B. Everhart
Foreword by Clarence J. Karier

RESOLVING THE HOUSING CRISIS
Government Policy, Decontrol, and the Public Interest
Edited with an Introduction by M. Bruce Johnson

OFFSHORE LANDS
Oil and Gas Leasing and Conservation on the Outer Continental Shelf
By Walter J. Mead, et al.
Foreword by Stephen L. McDonald

ELECTRIC POWER
Deregulation and the Public Interest
Edited by John C. Moorhouse
Foreword by Harold Demsetz

TAXATION AND THE DEFICIT ECONOMY
Fiscal Policy and Capital Formation in the United States
Edited by Dwight R. Lee
Foreword by Michael J. Boskin

THE AMERICAN FAMILY AND THE STATE
Edited by Joseph R. Peden and Fred R. Glahe
Foreword by Robert Nisbet

DEALING WITH DRUGS
Consequences of Government Control
Edited by Ronald Hamowy
Foreword by Dr. Alfred Freedman

CRISIS AND LEVIATHAN
Critical Episodes in the Growth of American Government
By Robert Higgs
Foreword by Arthur A. Ekirch, Jr.

THE NEW CHINA
Comparative Economic Development in Mainland China, Taiwan, and Hong Kong
By Dr. Alvin Rabushka

FORTHCOMING

ADVERTISING AND THE MARKET PROCESS
The Emerging View

THE HEALTH CARE IN AMERICA
Political Economy of Hospitals and Health Insurance

For futher information on the Pacific Research Institute's program and a catalog of publications, please contact:

PACIFIC RESEARCH INSTITUTE FOR PUBLIC POLICY
177 Post Street
San Francisco, California 94108
(415) 989-0833

Manufactured by Amazon.ca
Acheson, AB